C-166   CAREER EXAMINATION SERIES

This is your
PASSBOOK for...

Correction Lieutenant

Test Preparation Study Guide
Questions & Answers

COPYRIGHT NOTICE

This book is SOLELY intended for, is sold ONLY to, and its use is RESTRICTED to individual, bona fide applicants or candidates who qualify by virtue of having seriously filed applications for appropriate license, certificate, professional and/or promotional advancement, higher school matriculation, scholarship, or other legitimate requirements of education and/or governmental authorities.

This book is NOT intended for use, class instruction, tutoring, training, duplication, copying, reprinting, excerption, or adaptation, etc., by:

1) Other publishers
2) Proprietors and/or Instructors of "Coaching" and/or Preparatory Courses
3) Personnel and/or Training Divisions of commercial, industrial, and governmental organizations
4) Schools, colleges, or universities and/or their departments and staffs, including teachers and other personnel
5) Testing Agencies or Bureaus
6) Study groups which seek by the purchase of a single volume to copy and/or duplicate and/or adapt this material for use by the group as a whole without having purchased individual volumes for each of the members of the group
7) Et al.

Such persons would be in violation of appropriate Federal and State statutes.

PROVISION OF LICENSING AGREEMENTS – Recognized educational, commercial, industrial, and governmental institutions and organizations, and others legitimately engaged in educational pursuits, including training, testing, and measurement activities, may address request for a licensing agreement to the copyright owners, who will determine whether, and under what conditions, including fees and charges, the materials in this book may be used them. In other words, a licensing facility exists for the legitimate use of the material in this book on other than an individual basis. However, it is asseverated and affirmed here that the material in this book CANNOT be used without the receipt of the express permission of such a licensing agreement from the Publishers. Inquiries re licensing should be addressed to the company, attention rights and permissions department.

All rights reserved, including the right of reproduction in whole or in part, in any form or by any means, electronic or mechanical, including photocopying, recording, or by any information storage and retrieval system, without permission in writing from the Publisher.

Copyright © 2025 by
National Learning Corporation

212 Michael Drive, Syosset, NY 11791
(516) 921-8888 • www.passbooks.com
E-mail: info@passbooks.com

PASSBOOK® SERIES

THE *PASSBOOK® SERIES* has been created to prepare applicants and candidates for the ultimate academic battlefield – the examination room.

At some time in our lives, each and every one of us may be required to take an examination – for validation, matriculation, admission, qualification, registration, certification, or licensure.

Based on the assumption that every applicant or candidate has met the basic formal educational standards, has taken the required number of courses, and read the necessary texts, the *PASSBOOK® SERIES* furnishes the one special preparation which may assure passing with confidence, instead of failing with insecurity. Examination questions – together with answers – are furnished as the basic vehicle for study so that the mysteries of the examination and its compounding difficulties may be eliminated or diminished by a sure method.

This book is meant to help you pass your examination provided that you qualify and are serious in your objective.

The entire field is reviewed through the huge store of content information which is succinctly presented through a provocative and challenging approach – the question-and-answer method.

A climate of success is established by furnishing the correct answers at the end of each test.

You soon learn to recognize types of questions, forms of questions, and patterns of questioning. You may even begin to anticipate expected outcomes.

You perceive that many questions are repeated or adapted so that you can gain acute insights, which may enable you to score many sure points.

You learn how to confront new questions, or types of questions, and to attack them confidently and work out the correct answers.

You note objectives and emphases, and recognize pitfalls and dangers, so that you may make positive educational adjustments.

Moreover, you are kept fully informed in relation to new concepts, methods, practices, and directions in the field.

You discover that you are actually taking the examination all the time: you are preparing for the examination by "taking" an examination, not by reading extraneous and/or supererogatory textbooks.

In short, this PASSBOOK®, used directedly, should be an important factor in helping you to pass your test.

CORRECTION LIEUTENANT

DUTIES:
Under the general supervision of a Correction Captain, an employee in this class supervises the activities of sergeants and lower-level officers on an assigned shift. During night shifts, evening shifts and on weekends, the incumbent is completely responsible for the management of the jail or honor farm. Correction Lieutenants are designated by State law as peace officers and may be required to carry firearms in the performance of their duties. Does related work as required.

SCOPE OF THE EXAMINATION:
The written test will cover knowledge, skills, and/or abilities in such areas as:

1. Administrative supervision;
2. State correction laws, rules, regulations and minimum standards governing local correctional facilities and jails;
3. Coordinating appropriate responses to emergencies, disturbances and other unusual situations;
4. Custody, security and building maintenance procedures in correctional facilities; and
5. Preparing written material.

HOW TO TAKE A TEST

I. YOU MUST PASS AN EXAMINATION

A. WHAT EVERY CANDIDATE SHOULD KNOW

Examination applicants often ask us for help in preparing for the written test. What can I study in advance? What kinds of questions will be asked? How will the test be given? How will the papers be graded?

As an applicant for a civil service examination, you may be wondering about some of these things. Our purpose here is to suggest effective methods of advance study and to describe civil service examinations.

Your chances for success on this examination can be increased if you know how to prepare. Those "pre-examination jitters" can be reduced if you know what to expect. You can even experience an adventure in good citizenship if you know why civil service exams are given.

B. WHY ARE CIVIL SERVICE EXAMINATIONS GIVEN?

Civil service examinations are important to you in two ways. As a citizen, you want public jobs filled by employees who know how to do their work. As a job seeker, you want a fair chance to compete for that job on an equal footing with other candidates. The best-known means of accomplishing this two-fold goal is the competitive examination.

Exams are widely publicized throughout the nation. They may be administered for jobs in federal, state, city, municipal, town or village governments or agencies.

Any citizen may apply, with some limitations, such as the age or residence of applicants. Your experience and education may be reviewed to see whether you meet the requirements for the particular examination. When these requirements exist, they are reasonable and applied consistently to all applicants. Thus, a competitive examination may cause you some uneasiness now, but it is your privilege and safeguard.

C. HOW ARE CIVIL SERVICE EXAMS DEVELOPED?

Examinations are carefully written by trained technicians who are specialists in the field known as "psychological measurement," in consultation with recognized authorities in the field of work that the test will cover. These experts recommend the subject matter areas or skills to be tested; only those knowledges or skills important to your success on the job are included. The most reliable books and source materials available are used as references. Together, the experts and technicians judge the difficulty level of the questions.

Test technicians know how to phrase questions so that the problem is clearly stated. Their ethics do not permit "trick" or "catch" questions. Questions may have been tried out on sample groups, or subjected to statistical analysis, to determine their usefulness.

Written tests are often used in combination with performance tests, ratings of training and experience, and oral interviews. All of these measures combine to form the best-known means of finding the right person for the right job.

II. HOW TO PASS THE WRITTEN TEST

A. NATURE OF THE EXAMINATION

To prepare intelligently for civil service examinations, you should know how they differ from school examinations you have taken. In school you were assigned certain definite pages to read or subjects to cover. The examination questions were quite detailed and usually emphasized memory. Civil service exams, on the other hand, try to discover your present ability to perform the duties of a position, plus your potentiality to learn these duties. In other words, a civil service exam attempts to predict how successful you will be. Questions cover such a broad area that they cannot be as minute and detailed as school exam questions.

In the public service similar kinds of work, or positions, are grouped together in one "class." This process is known as *position-classification*. All the positions in a class are paid according to the salary range for that class. One class title covers all of these positions, and they are all tested by the same examination.

B. FOUR BASIC STEPS

1) Study the announcement

How, then, can you know what subjects to study? Our best answer is: "Learn as much as possible about the class of positions for which you've applied." The exam will test the knowledge, skills and abilities needed to do the work.

Your most valuable source of information about the position you want is the official exam announcement. This announcement lists the training and experience qualifications. Check these standards and apply only if you come reasonably close to meeting them.

The brief description of the position in the examination announcement offers some clues to the subjects which will be tested. Think about the job itself. Review the duties in your mind. Can you perform them, or are there some in which you are rusty? Fill in the blank spots in your preparation.

Many jurisdictions preview the written test in the exam announcement by including a section called "Knowledge and Abilities Required," "Scope of the Examination," or some similar heading. Here you will find out specifically what fields will be tested.

2) Review your own background

Once you learn in general what the position is all about, and what you need to know to do the work, ask yourself which subjects you already know fairly well and which need improvement. You may wonder whether to concentrate on improving your strong areas or on building some background in your fields of weakness. When the announcement has specified "some knowledge" or "considerable knowledge," or has used adjectives like "beginning principles of…" or "advanced … methods," you can get a clue as to the number and difficulty of questions to be asked in any given field. More questions, and hence broader coverage, would be included for those subjects which are more important in the work. Now weigh your strengths and weaknesses against the job requirements and prepare accordingly.

3) Determine the level of the position

Another way to tell how intensively you should prepare is to understand the level of the job for which you are applying. Is it the entering level? In other words, is this the position in which beginners in a field of work are hired? Or is it an intermediate or advanced level? Sometimes this is indicated by such words as "Junior" or "Senior" in the class title. Other jurisdictions use Roman numerals to designate the level – Clerk I, Clerk II, for example. The word "Supervisor" sometimes appears in the title. If the level is not indicated by the title, check the description of duties. Will you be working under very close supervision, or will you have responsibility for independent decisions in this work?

4) Choose appropriate study materials

Now that you know the subjects to be examined and the relative amount of each subject to be covered, you can choose suitable study materials. For beginning level jobs, or even advanced ones, if you have a pronounced weakness in some aspect of your training, read a modern, standard textbook in that field. Be sure it is up to date and has general coverage. Such books are normally available at your library, and the librarian will be glad to help you locate one. For entry-level positions, questions of appropriate difficulty are chosen – neither highly advanced questions, nor those too simple. Such questions require careful thought but not advanced training.

If the position for which you are applying is technical or advanced, you will read more advanced, specialized material. If you are already familiar with the basic principles of your field, elementary textbooks would waste your time. Concentrate on advanced textbooks and technical periodicals. Think through the concepts and review difficult problems in your field.

These are all general sources. You can get more ideas on your own initiative, following these leads. For example, training manuals and publications of the government agency which employs workers in your field can be useful, particularly for technical and professional positions. A letter or visit to the government department involved may result in more specific study suggestions, and certainly will provide you with a more definite idea of the exact nature of the position you are seeking.

III. KINDS OF TESTS

Tests are used for purposes other than measuring knowledge and ability to perform specified duties. For some positions, it is equally important to test ability to make adjustments to new situations or to profit from training. In others, basic mental abilities not dependent on information are essential. Questions which test these things may not appear as pertinent to the duties of the position as those which test for knowledge and information. Yet they are often highly important parts of a fair examination. For very general questions, it is almost impossible to help you direct your study efforts. What we can do is to point out some of the more common of these general abilities needed in public service positions and describe some typical questions.

1) General information

Broad, general information has been found useful for predicting job success in some kinds of work. This is tested in a variety of ways, from vocabulary lists to questions about current events. Basic background in some field of work, such as sociology or economics, may be sampled in a group of questions. Often these are principles which have become familiar to most persons through exposure rather than through formal training. It is difficult to advise you how to study for these questions; being alert to the world around you is our best suggestion.

2) Verbal ability

An example of an ability needed in many positions is verbal or language ability. Verbal ability is, in brief, the ability to use and understand words. Vocabulary and grammar tests are typical measures of this ability. Reading comprehension or paragraph interpretation questions are common in many kinds of civil service tests. You are given a paragraph of written material and asked to find its central meaning.

3) Numerical ability

Number skills can be tested by the familiar arithmetic problem, by checking paired lists of numbers to see which are alike and which are different, or by interpreting charts and graphs. In the latter test, a graph may be printed in the test booklet which you are asked to use as the basis for answering questions.

4) Observation

A popular test for law-enforcement positions is the observation test. A picture is shown to you for several minutes, then taken away. Questions about the picture test your ability to observe both details and larger elements.

5) Following directions

In many positions in the public service, the employee must be able to carry out written instructions dependably and accurately. You may be given a chart with several columns, each column listing a variety of information. The questions require you to carry out directions involving the information given in the chart.

6) Skills and aptitudes

Performance tests effectively measure some manual skills and aptitudes. When the skill is one in which you are trained, such as typing or shorthand, you can practice. These tests are often very much like those given in business school or high school courses. For many of the other skills and aptitudes, however, no short-time preparation can be made. Skills and abilities natural to you or that you have developed throughout your lifetime are being tested.

Many of the general questions just described provide all the data needed to answer the questions and ask you to use your reasoning ability to find the answers. Your best preparation for these tests, as well as for tests of facts and ideas, is to be at your physical and mental best. You, no doubt, have your own methods of getting into an exam-taking mood and keeping "in shape." The next section lists some ideas on this subject.

IV. KINDS OF QUESTIONS

Only rarely is the "essay" question, which you answer in narrative form, used in civil service tests. Civil service tests are usually of the short-answer type. Full instructions for answering these questions will be given to you at the examination. But in case this is your first experience with short-answer questions and separate answer sheets, here is what you need to know:

1) Multiple-choice Questions

Most popular of the short-answer questions is the "multiple choice" or "best answer" question. It can be used, for example, to test for factual knowledge, ability to solve problems or judgment in meeting situations found at work.

A multiple-choice question is normally one of three types—
- It can begin with an incomplete statement followed by several possible endings. You are to find the one ending which *best* completes the statement, although some of the others may not be entirely wrong.
- It can also be a complete statement in the form of a question which is answered by choosing one of the statements listed.

- It can be in the form of a problem – again you select the best answer.

Here is an example of a multiple-choice question with a discussion which should give you some clues as to the method for choosing the right answer:

When an employee has a complaint about his assignment, the action which will *best* help him overcome his difficulty is to
   A. discuss his difficulty with his coworkers
   B. take the problem to the head of the organization
   C. take the problem to the person who gave him the assignment
   D. say nothing to anyone about his complaint

In answering this question, you should study each of the choices to find which is best. Consider choice "A" – Certainly an employee may discuss his complaint with fellow employees, but no change or improvement can result, and the complaint remains unresolved. Choice "B" is a poor choice since the head of the organization probably does not know what assignment you have been given, and taking your problem to him is known as "going over the head" of the supervisor. The supervisor, or person who made the assignment, is the person who can clarify it or correct any injustice. Choice "C" is, therefore, correct. To say nothing, as in choice "D," is unwise. Supervisors have and interest in knowing the problems employees are facing, and the employee is seeking a solution to his problem.

2) True/False Questions

The "true/false" or "right/wrong" form of question is sometimes used. Here a complete statement is given. Your job is to decide whether the statement is right or wrong.

SAMPLE: A roaming cell-phone call to a nearby city costs less than a non-roaming call to a distant city.

This statement is wrong, or false, since roaming calls are more expensive.

This is not a complete list of all possible question forms, although most of the others are variations of these common types. You will always get complete directions for answering questions. Be sure you understand *how* to mark your answers – ask questions until you do.

V. RECORDING YOUR ANSWERS

Computer terminals are used more and more today for many different kinds of exams.
For an examination with very few applicants, you may be told to record your answers in the test booklet itself. Separate answer sheets are much more common. If this separate answer sheet is to be scored by machine – and this is often the case – it is highly important that you mark your answers correctly in order to get credit.
An electronic scoring machine is often used in civil service offices because of the speed with which papers can be scored. Machine-scored answer sheets must be marked with a pencil, which will be given to you. This pencil has a high graphite content which responds to the electronic scoring machine. As a matter of fact, stray dots may register as answers, so do not let your pencil rest on the answer sheet while you are pondering the correct answer. Also, if your pencil lead breaks or is otherwise defective, ask for another.

Since the answer sheet will be dropped in a slot in the scoring machine, be careful not to bend the corners or get the paper crumpled.

The answer sheet normally has five vertical columns of numbers, with 30 numbers to a column. These numbers correspond to the question numbers in your test booklet. After each number, going across the page are four or five pairs of dotted lines. These short dotted lines have small letters or numbers above them. The first two pairs may also have a "T" or "F" above the letters. This indicates that the first two pairs only are to be used if the questions are of the true-false type. If the questions are multiple choice, disregard the "T" and "F" and pay attention only to the small letters or numbers.

Answer your questions in the manner of the sample that follows:

32. The largest city in the United States is
    A. Washington, D.C.
    B. New York City
    C. Chicago
    D. Detroit
    E. San Francisco

1) Choose the answer you think is best. (New York City is the largest, so "B" is correct.)
2) Find the row of dotted lines numbered the same as the question you are answering. (Find row number 32)
3) Find the pair of dotted lines corresponding to the answer. (Find the pair of lines under the mark "B.")
4) Make a solid black mark between the dotted lines.

VI. BEFORE THE TEST

Common sense will help you find procedures to follow to get ready for an examination. Too many of us, however, overlook these sensible measures. Indeed, nervousness and fatigue have been found to be the most serious reasons why applicants fail to do their best on civil service tests. Here is a list of reminders:

- Begin your preparation early – Don't wait until the last minute to go scurrying around for books and materials or to find out what the position is all about.
- Prepare continuously – An hour a night for a week is better than an all-night cram session. This has been definitely established. What is more, a night a week for a month will return better dividends than crowding your study into a shorter period of time.
- Locate the place of the exam – You have been sent a notice telling you when and where to report for the examination. If the location is in a different town or otherwise unfamiliar to you, it would be well to inquire the best route and learn something about the building.
- Relax the night before the test – Allow your mind to rest. Do not study at all that night. Plan some mild recreation or diversion; then go to bed early and get a good night's sleep.
- Get up early enough to make a leisurely trip to the place for the test – This way unforeseen events, traffic snarls, unfamiliar buildings, etc. will not upset you.
- Dress comfortably – A written test is not a fashion show. You will be known by number and not by name, so wear something comfortable.

- Leave excess paraphernalia at home – Shopping bags and odd bundles will get in your way. You need bring only the items mentioned in the official notice you received; usually everything you need is provided. Do not bring reference books to the exam. They will only confuse those last minutes and be taken away from you when in the test room.
- Arrive somewhat ahead of time – If because of transportation schedules you must get there very early, bring a newspaper or magazine to take your mind off yourself while waiting.
- Locate the examination room – When you have found the proper room, you will be directed to the seat or part of the room where you will sit. Sometimes you are given a sheet of instructions to read while you are waiting. Do not fill out any forms until you are told to do so; just read them and be prepared.
- Relax and prepare to listen to the instructions
- If you have any physical problem that may keep you from doing your best, be sure to tell the test administrator. If you are sick or in poor health, you really cannot do your best on the exam. You can come back and take the test some other time.

VII. AT THE TEST

The day of the test is here and you have the test booklet in your hand. The temptation to get going is very strong. Caution! There is more to success than knowing the right answers. You must know how to identify your papers and understand variations in the type of short-answer question used in this particular examination. Follow these suggestions for maximum results from your efforts:

1) Cooperate with the monitor
The test administrator has a duty to create a situation in which you can be as much at ease as possible. He will give instructions, tell you when to begin, check to see that you are marking your answer sheet correctly, and so on. He is not there to guard you, although he will see that your competitors do not take unfair advantage. He wants to help you do your best.

2) Listen to all instructions
Don't jump the gun! Wait until you understand all directions. In most civil service tests you get more time than you need to answer the questions. So don't be in a hurry. Read each word of instructions until you clearly understand the meaning. Study the examples, listen to all announcements and follow directions. Ask questions if you do not understand what to do.

3) Identify your papers
Civil service exams are usually identified by number only. You will be assigned a number; you must not put your name on your test papers. Be sure to copy your number correctly. Since more than one exam may be given, copy your exact examination title.

4) Plan your time
Unless you are told that a test is a "speed" or "rate of work" test, speed itself is usually not important. Time enough to answer all the questions will be provided, but this does not mean that you have all day. An overall time limit has been set. Divide the total time (in minutes) by the number of questions to determine the approximate time you have for each question.

5) Do not linger over difficult questions

If you come across a difficult question, mark it with a paper clip (useful to have along) and come back to it when you have been through the booklet. One caution if you do this – be sure to skip a number on your answer sheet as well. Check often to be sure that you have not lost your place and that you are marking in the row numbered the same as the question you are answering.

6) Read the questions

Be sure you know what the question asks! Many capable people are unsuccessful because they failed to *read* the questions correctly.

7) Answer all questions

Unless you have been instructed that a penalty will be deducted for incorrect answers, it is better to guess than to omit a question.

8) Speed tests

It is often better NOT to guess on speed tests. It has been found that on timed tests people are tempted to spend the last few seconds before time is called in marking answers at random – without even reading them – in the hope of picking up a few extra points. To discourage this practice, the instructions may warn you that your score will be "corrected" for guessing. That is, a penalty will be applied. The incorrect answers will be deducted from the correct ones, or some other penalty formula will be used.

9) Review your answers

If you finish before time is called, go back to the questions you guessed or omitted to give them further thought. Review other answers if you have time.

10) Return your test materials

If you are ready to leave before others have finished or time is called, take ALL your materials to the monitor and leave quietly. Never take any test material with you. The monitor can discover whose papers are not complete, and taking a test booklet may be grounds for disqualification.

VIII. EXAMINATION TECHNIQUES

1) Read the general instructions carefully. These are usually printed on the first page of the exam booklet. As a rule, these instructions refer to the timing of the examination; the fact that you should not start work until the signal and must stop work at a signal, etc. If there are any *special* instructions, such as a choice of questions to be answered, make sure that you note this instruction carefully.

2) When you are ready to start work on the examination, that is as soon as the signal has been given, read the instructions to each question booklet, underline any key words or phrases, such as *least, best, outline, describe* and the like. In this way you will tend to answer as requested rather than discover on reviewing your paper that you *listed without describing*, that you selected the *worst* choice rather than the *best* choice, etc.

3) If the examination is of the objective or multiple-choice type – that is, each question will also give a series of possible answers: A, B, C or D, and you are called upon to select the best answer and write the letter next to that answer on your answer paper – it is advisable to start answering each question in turn. There may be anywhere from 50 to 100 such questions in the three or four hours allotted and you can see how much time would be taken if you read through all the questions before beginning to answer any. Furthermore, if you come across a question or group of questions which you know would be difficult to answer, it would undoubtedly affect your handling of all the other questions.

4) If the examination is of the essay type and contains but a few questions, it is a moot point as to whether you should read all the questions before starting to answer any one. Of course, if you are given a choice – say five out of seven and the like – then it is essential to read all the questions so you can eliminate the two that are most difficult. If, however, you are asked to answer all the questions, there may be danger in trying to answer the easiest one first because you may find that you will spend too much time on it. The best technique is to answer the first question, then proceed to the second, etc.

5) Time your answers. Before the exam begins, write down the time it started, then add the time allowed for the examination and write down the time it must be completed, then divide the time available somewhat as follows:
    - If 3-1/2 hours are allowed, that would be 210 minutes. If you have 80 objective-type questions, that would be an average of 2-1/2 minutes per question. Allow yourself no more than 2 minutes per question, or a total of 160 minutes, which will permit about 50 minutes to review.
    - If for the time allotment of 210 minutes there are 7 essay questions to answer, that would average about 30 minutes a question. Give yourself only 25 minutes per question so that you have about 35 minutes to review.

6) The most important instruction is to *read each question* and make sure you know what is wanted. The second most important instruction is to *time yourself properly* so that you answer every question. The third most important instruction is to *answer every question*. Guess if you have to but include something for each question. Remember that you will receive no credit for a blank and will probably receive some credit if you write something in answer to an essay question. If you guess a letter – say "B" for a multiple-choice question – you may have guessed right. If you leave a blank as an answer to a multiple-choice question, the examiners may respect your feelings but it will not add a point to your score. Some exams may penalize you for wrong answers, so in such cases *only*, you may not want to guess unless you have some basis for your answer.

7) Suggestions
    a. Objective-type questions
        1. Examine the question booklet for proper sequence of pages and questions
        2. Read all instructions carefully
        3. Skip any question which seems too difficult; return to it after all other questions have been answered
        4. Apportion your time properly; do not spend too much time on any single question or group of questions

5. Note and underline key words – *all, most, fewest, least, best, worst, same, opposite,* etc.
6. Pay particular attention to negatives
7. Note unusual option, e.g., unduly long, short, complex, different or similar in content to the body of the question
8. Observe the use of "hedging" words – *probably, may, most likely,* etc.
9. Make sure that your answer is put next to the same number as the question
10. Do not second-guess unless you have good reason to believe the second answer is definitely more correct
11. Cross out original answer if you decide another answer is more accurate; do not erase until you are ready to hand your paper in
12. Answer all questions; guess unless instructed otherwise
13. Leave time for review

  b. Essay questions
   1. Read each question carefully
   2. Determine exactly what is wanted. Underline key words or phrases.
   3. Decide on outline or paragraph answer
   4. Include many different points and elements unless asked to develop any one or two points or elements
   5. Show impartiality by giving pros and cons unless directed to select one side only
   6. Make and write down any assumptions you find necessary to answer the questions
   7. Watch your English, grammar, punctuation and choice of words
   8. Time your answers; don't crowd material

8) Answering the essay question

Most essay questions can be answered by framing the specific response around several key words or ideas. Here are a few such key words or ideas:

M's: manpower, materials, methods, money, management
P's: purpose, program, policy, plan, procedure, practice, problems, pitfalls, personnel, public relations

  a. Six basic steps in handling problems:
   1. Preliminary plan and background development
   2. Collect information, data and facts
   3. Analyze and interpret information, data and facts
   4. Analyze and develop solutions as well as make recommendations
   5. Prepare report and sell recommendations
   6. Install recommendations and follow up effectiveness

  b. Pitfalls to avoid
   1. *Taking things for granted* – A statement of the situation does not necessarily imply that each of the elements is necessarily true; for example, a complaint may be invalid and biased so that all that can be taken for granted is that a complaint has been registered

2. *Considering only one side of a situation* – Wherever possible, indicate several alternatives and then point out the reasons you selected the best one
3. *Failing to indicate follow up* – Whenever your answer indicates action on your part, make certain that you will take proper follow-up action to see how successful your recommendations, procedures or actions turn out to be
4. *Taking too long in answering any single question* – Remember to time your answers properly

IX. AFTER THE TEST

Scoring procedures differ in detail among civil service jurisdictions although the general principles are the same. Whether the papers are hand-scored or graded by machine we have described, they are nearly always graded by number. That is, the person who marks the paper knows only the number – never the name – of the applicant. Not until all the papers have been graded will they be matched with names. If other tests, such as training and experience or oral interview ratings have been given, scores will be combined. Different parts of the examination usually have different weights. For example, the written test might count 60 percent of the final grade, and a rating of training and experience 40 percent. In many jurisdictions, veterans will have a certain number of points added to their grades.

After the final grade has been determined, the names are placed in grade order and an eligible list is established. There are various methods for resolving ties between those who get the same final grade – probably the most common is to place first the name of the person whose application was received first. Job offers are made from the eligible list in the order the names appear on it. You will be notified of your grade and your rank as soon as all these computations have been made. This will be done as rapidly as possible.

People who are found to meet the requirements in the announcement are called "eligibles." Their names are put on a list of eligible candidates. An eligible's chances of getting a job depend on how high he stands on this list and how fast agencies are filling jobs from the list.

When a job is to be filled from a list of eligibles, the agency asks for the names of people on the list of eligibles for that job. When the civil service commission receives this request, it sends to the agency the names of the three people highest on this list. Or, if the job to be filled has specialized requirements, the office sends the agency the names of the top three persons who meet these requirements from the general list.

The appointing officer makes a choice from among the three people whose names were sent to him. If the selected person accepts the appointment, the names of the others are put back on the list to be considered for future openings.

That is the rule in hiring from all kinds of eligible lists, whether they are for typist, carpenter, chemist, or something else. For every vacancy, the appointing officer has his choice of any one of the top three eligibles on the list. This explains why the person whose name is on top of the list sometimes does not get an appointment when some of the persons lower on the list do. If the appointing officer chooses the second or third eligible, the No. 1 eligible does not get a job at once, but stays on the list until he is appointed or the list is terminated.

X. HOW TO PASS THE INTERVIEW TEST

The examination for which you applied requires an oral interview test. You have already taken the written test and you are now being called for the interview test – the final part of the formal examination.

You may think that it is not possible to prepare for an interview test and that there are no procedures to follow during an interview. Our purpose is to point out some things you can do in advance that will help you and some good rules to follow and pitfalls to avoid while you are being interviewed.

What is an interview supposed to test?

The written examination is designed to test the technical knowledge and competence of the candidate; the oral is designed to evaluate intangible qualities, not readily measured otherwise, and to establish a list showing the relative fitness of each candidate – as measured against his competitors – for the position sought. Scoring is not on the basis of "right" and "wrong," but on a sliding scale of values ranging from "not passable" to "outstanding." As a matter of fact, it is possible to achieve a relatively low score without a single "incorrect" answer because of evident weakness in the qualities being measured.

Occasionally, an examination may consist entirely of an oral test – either an individual or a group oral. In such cases, information is sought concerning the technical knowledges and abilities of the candidate, since there has been no written examination for this purpose. More commonly, however, an oral test is used to supplement a written examination.

Who conducts interviews?

The composition of oral boards varies among different jurisdictions. In nearly all, a representative of the personnel department serves as chairman. One of the members of the board may be a representative of the department in which the candidate would work. In some cases, "outside experts" are used, and, frequently, a businessman or some other representative of the general public is asked to serve. Labor and management or other special groups may be represented. The aim is to secure the services of experts in the appropriate field.

However the board is composed, it is a good idea (and not at all improper or unethical) to ascertain in advance of the interview who the members are and what groups they represent. When you are introduced to them, you will have some idea of their backgrounds and interests, and at least you will not stutter and stammer over their names.

What should be done before the interview?

While knowledge about the board members is useful and takes some of the surprise element out of the interview, there is other preparation which is more substantive. It *is* possible to prepare for an oral interview – in several ways:

1) Keep a copy of your application and review it carefully before the interview

This may be the only document before the oral board, and the starting point of the interview. Know what education and experience you have listed there, and the sequence and dates of all of it. Sometimes the board will ask you to review the highlights of your experience for them; you should not have to hem and haw doing it.

2) Study the class specification and the examination announcement

Usually, the oral board has one or both of these to guide them. The qualities, characteristics or knowledges required by the position sought are stated in these documents. They offer valuable clues as to the nature of the oral interview. For example, if the job involves supervisory responsibilities, the announcement will usually indicate that knowledge of modern supervisory methods and the qualifications of the candidate as a supervisor will be tested. If so, you can expect such questions, frequently in the form of a hypothetical situation which you are expected to solve. NEVER go into an oral without knowledge of the duties and responsibilities of the job you seek.

3) Think through each qualification required

Try to visualize the kind of questions you would ask if you were a board member. How well could you answer them? Try especially to appraise your own knowledge and background in each area, *measured against the job sought*, and identify any areas in which you are weak. Be critical and realistic – do not flatter yourself.

4) Do some general reading in areas in which you feel you may be weak

For example, if the job involves supervision and your past experience has NOT, some general reading in supervisory methods and practices, particularly in the field of human relations, might be useful. Do NOT study agency procedures or detailed manuals. The oral board will be testing your understanding and capacity, not your memory.

5) Get a good night's sleep and watch your general health and mental attitude

You will want a clear head at the interview. Take care of a cold or any other minor ailment, and of course, no hangovers.

What should be done on the day of the interview?

Now comes the day of the interview itself. Give yourself plenty of time to get there. Plan to arrive somewhat ahead of the scheduled time, particularly if your appointment is in the fore part of the day. If a previous candidate fails to appear, the board might be ready for you a bit early. By early afternoon an oral board is almost invariably behind schedule if there are many candidates, and you may have to wait. Take along a book or magazine to read, or your application to review, but leave any extraneous material in the waiting room when you go in for your interview. In any event, relax and compose yourself.

The matter of dress is important. The board is forming impressions about you – from your experience, your manners, your attitude, and your appearance. Give your personal appearance careful attention. Dress your best, but not your flashiest. Choose conservative, appropriate clothing, and be sure it is immaculate. This is a business interview, and your appearance should indicate that you regard it as such. Besides, being well groomed and properly dressed will help boost your confidence.

Sooner or later, someone will call your name and escort you into the interview room. *This is it.* From here on you are on your own. It is too late for any more preparation. But remember, you asked for this opportunity to prove your fitness, and you are here because your request was granted.

What happens when you go in?

The usual sequence of events will be as follows: The clerk (who is often the board stenographer) will introduce you to the chairman of the oral board, who will introduce you to the other members of the board. Acknowledge the introductions before you sit down. Do not be surprised if you find a microphone facing you or a stenotypist sitting by. Oral interviews are usually recorded in the event of an appeal or other review.

Usually the chairman of the board will open the interview by reviewing the highlights of your education and work experience from your application – primarily for the benefit of the other members of the board, as well as to get the material into the record. Do not interrupt or comment unless there is an error or significant misinterpretation; if that is the case, do not hesitate. But do not quibble about insignificant matters. Also, he will usually ask you some question about your education, experience or your present job – partly to get you to start talking and to establish the interviewing "rapport." He may start the actual questioning, or turn it over to one of the other members. Frequently, each member undertakes the questioning on a particular area, one in which he is perhaps most competent, so you can expect each member to participate in the examination. Because time is limited, you may also expect some rather abrupt switches in the direction the questioning takes, so do not be upset by it. Normally, a board member will not pursue a single line of questioning unless he discovers a particular strength or weakness.

After each member has participated, the chairman will usually ask whether any member has any further questions, then will ask you if you have anything you wish to add. Unless you are expecting this question, it may floor you. Worse, it may start you off on an extended, extemporaneous speech. The board is not usually seeking more information. The question is principally to offer you a last opportunity to present further qualifications or to indicate that you have nothing to add. So, if you feel that a significant qualification or characteristic has been overlooked, it is proper to point it out in a sentence or so. Do not compliment the board on the thoroughness of their examination – they have been sketchy, and you know it. If you wish, merely say, "No thank you, I have nothing further to add." This is a point where you can "talk yourself out" of a good impression or fail to present an important bit of information. Remember, *you close the interview yourself*.

The chairman will then say, "That is all, Mr. _____, thank you." Do not be startled; the interview is over, and quicker than you think. Thank him, gather your belongings and take your leave. Save your sigh of relief for the other side of the door.

How to put your best foot forward

Throughout this entire process, you may feel that the board individually and collectively is trying to pierce your defenses, seek out your hidden weaknesses and embarrass and confuse you. Actually, this is not true. They are obliged to make an appraisal of your qualifications for the job you are seeking, and they want to see you in your best light. Remember, they must interview all candidates and a non-cooperative candidate may become a failure in spite of their best efforts to bring out his qualifications. Here are 15 suggestions that will help you:

1) Be natural – Keep your attitude confident, not cocky

If you are not confident that you can do the job, do not expect the board to be. Do not apologize for your weaknesses, try to bring out your strong points. The board is interested in a positive, not negative, presentation. Cockiness will antagonize any board member and make him wonder if you are covering up a weakness by a false show of strength.

2) Get comfortable, but don't lounge or sprawl

Sit erectly but not stiffly. A careless posture may lead the board to conclude that you are careless in other things, or at least that you are not impressed by the importance of the occasion. Either conclusion is natural, even if incorrect. Do not fuss with your clothing, a pencil or an ashtray. Your hands may occasionally be useful to emphasize a point; do not let them become a point of distraction.

3) Do not wisecrack or make small talk

This is a serious situation, and your attitude should show that you consider it as such. Further, the time of the board is limited – they do not want to waste it, and neither should you.

4) Do not exaggerate your experience or abilities
In the first place, from information in the application or other interviews and sources, the board may know more about you than you think. Secondly, you probably will not get away with it. An experienced board is rather adept at spotting such a situation, so do not take the chance.

5) If you know a board member, do not make a point of it, yet do not hide it
Certainly you are not fooling him, and probably not the other members of the board. Do not try to take advantage of your acquaintanceship – it will probably do you little good.

6) Do not dominate the interview
Let the board do that. They will give you the clues – do not assume that you have to do all the talking. Realize that the board has a number of questions to ask you, and do not try to take up all the interview time by showing off your extensive knowledge of the answer to the first one.

7) Be attentive
You only have 20 minutes or so, and you should keep your attention at its sharpest throughout. When a member is addressing a problem or question to you, give him your undivided attention. Address your reply principally to him, but do not exclude the other board members.

8) Do not interrupt
A board member may be stating a problem for you to analyze. He will ask you a question when the time comes. Let him state the problem, and wait for the question.

9) Make sure you understand the question
Do not try to answer until you are sure what the question is. If it is not clear, restate it in your own words or ask the board member to clarify it for you. However, do not haggle about minor elements.

10) Reply promptly but not hastily
A common entry on oral board rating sheets is "candidate responded readily," or "candidate hesitated in replies." Respond as promptly and quickly as you can, but do not jump to a hasty, ill-considered answer.

11) Do not be peremptory in your answers
A brief answer is proper – but do not fire your answer back. That is a losing game from your point of view. The board member can probably ask questions much faster than you can answer them.

12) Do not try to create the answer you think the board member wants
He is interested in what kind of mind you have and how it works – not in playing games. Furthermore, he can usually spot this practice and will actually grade you down on it.

13) Do not switch sides in your reply merely to agree with a board member
Frequently, a member will take a contrary position merely to draw you out and to see if you are willing and able to defend your point of view. Do not start a debate, yet do not surrender a good position. If a position is worth taking, it is worth defending.

14) Do not be afraid to admit an error in judgment if you are shown to be wrong

The board knows that you are forced to reply without any opportunity for careful consideration. Your answer may be demonstrably wrong. If so, admit it and get on with the interview.

15) Do not dwell at length on your present job

The opening question may relate to your present assignment. Answer the question but do not go into an extended discussion. You are being examined for a *new* job, not your present one. As a matter of fact, try to phrase ALL your answers in terms of the job for which you are being examined.

Basis of Rating

Probably you will forget most of these "do's" and "don'ts" when you walk into the oral interview room. Even remembering them all will not ensure you a passing grade. Perhaps you did not have the qualifications in the first place. But remembering them will help you to put your best foot forward, without treading on the toes of the board members.

Rumor and popular opinion to the contrary notwithstanding, an oral board wants you to make the best appearance possible. They know you are under pressure – but they also want to see how you respond to it as a guide to what your reaction would be under the pressures of the job you seek. They will be influenced by the degree of poise you display, the personal traits you show and the manner in which you respond.

ABOUT THIS BOOK

This book contains tests divided into Examination Sections. Go through each test, answering every question in the margin. We have also attached a sample answer sheet at the back of the book that can be removed and used. At the end of each test look at the answer key and check your answers. On the ones you got wrong, look at the right answer choice and learn. Do not fill in the answers first. Do not memorize the questions and answers, but understand the answer and principles involved. On your test, the questions will likely be different from the samples. Questions are changed and new ones added. If you understand these past questions you should have success with any changes that arise. Tests may consist of several types of questions. We have additional books on each subject should more study be advisable or necessary for you. Finally, the more you study, the better prepared you will be. This book is intended to be the last thing you study before you walk into the examination room. Prior study of relevant texts is also recommended. NLC publishes some of these in our Fundamental Series. Knowledge and good sense are important factors in passing your exam. Good luck also helps. So now study this Passbook, absorb the material contained within and take that knowledge into the examination. Then do your best to pass that exam.

EXAMINATION SECTION

EXAMINATION SECTION
TEST 1

DIRECTIONS: Each question or incomplete statement is followed by several suggested answers or completions. Select the one that BEST answers the question or completes the statement. *PRINT THE LETTER OF THE CORRECT ANSWER IN THE SPACE AT THE RIGHT.*

1. In a uniformed correction force, the limits of authority and responsibility of each position should be clearly defined.
   Of the following, the MAIN reason for this is to

   A. avoid overlapping authority and possible conflicts
   B. facilitate an exchange of viewpoints at parallel levels of authority
   C. improve the training and therefore the competence of personnel
   D. provide well-defined promotional levels for personnel

   1.____

2. When some correction officers complained about a new department order, a superior officer remarked, *I agree with you but you can't fight the central office.*
   Such a remark is *unwise* CHIEFLY because

   A. correction officers may assume that the superior officer will back them when they do not enforce the order
   B. correction officers will be motivated to have doubts about all other orders
   C. the superior officer cannot know all the reasons for the promulgation of the order
   D. the superior officer is undermining discipline by his criticism of department policies

   2.____

3. Correction Officer A is asked a question by Correction Officer B concerning a matter which is primarily B's responsibility. Although Correction Officer A is not sure of the correct answer, he gives one to the best of his knowledge, not giving any indication of his uncertainty.
   A's action in this instance was

   A. *acceptable;* B has the basic responsibility in this matter and is most likely seeking only A's informal opinion
   B. *not acceptable;* A should not have answered B's question since the matter is B's responsibility
   C. *acceptable;* the search for absolute certainty prior to making a decision leads to undesirable delay
   D. *not acceptable;* B may act on the basis of the uncertain answer given by A

   3.____

4. Since a correction superior officer expects subordinates to carry out commands to the letter, it is MOST important for the superior officer to

   A. check on the execution of all commands immediately
   B. issue commands clearly and make sure they are understood
   C. issue only commands that seem obviously reasonable to anyone
   D. make only one officer responsible for the execution of any command

   4.____

5. A new correction officer under your supervision lacks confidence in his (her) ability to perform the duties of the position.
Of the following, it would be BEST for you to

   A. assign simple and routine tasks to this officer for a few months
   B. recommend that the officer be dropped at the end of probation if no improvement is shown
   C. assign this officer to work along with and under the guidance of an experienced officer for a while
   D. recommend to your superior that this officer be returned to the academy for extended and intensive classroom training

6. In evaluating the capability of a correction officer to use independent judgment, the one of the following to which the superior officer should usually give GREATEST consideration is the

   A. ability of the officer to establish good relationships with prople
   B. number of times the officer speaks to the superior officer
   C. officer's record of emotional stability
   D. decisions made by the officer in previous work situations

7. If a superior officer is to be an effective leader of the correction officers he commands, the superior officer must

   A. assign to each officer an equal amount of responsibility and authority
   B. develop the individual capabilities of each officer and motivate them all to work for the good of the institution as a whole
   C. give them close and strict supervision at all times
   D. permit them to follow their own initiative whenever they strongly disagree with established procedures

8. A superior officer notices that one correction officer does not get along too well with the other officers.
Of the following, the BEST thing for the superior officer to do in such a situation is to

   A. make an effort to learn the reasons for the difficulty in an effort to resolve the problem
   B. overlook the matter since the work will probably be unaffected
   C. prepare a report of the situation to a superior officer and be guided by the latter's decision
   D. tell all the officers they must work together harmoniously or risk disciplinary action

9. You observe that a correction officer under your command is not carrying out a specific assignment in accordance with the instructions you gave.
Of the following, the MOST important reason why you should have this officer repeat the instructions you gave is that

   A. instructions can be misunderstood even by excellent correction officers
   B. it will indicate that incorrect instructions were given
   C. inefficiency usually has serious consequences
   D. oral instructions should be repeated when issued as a safeguard that they are understood

10. It is generally considered that the use of a police training program for the purpose of training correction personnel would be *undesirable* MAINLY because   10.____

    A. those attracted to correctional work would for the most part not be interested in police work
    B. the two uniformed forces should be kept distinct, the one from the other
    C. emphasis in police work is on the apprehension of law violators
    D. correction training facilities do not measure up to those available to police forces

11. When correction officers ask a certain superior officer's advice about handling specific work problems, the superior officer now and then responds to the request by first asking the correction officer what the latter thinks should be done.
    This practice by the superior officer is GENERALLY   11.____

    A. *bad,* since subordinates will not ask questions in the future
    B. *good,* since it motivates subordinates to think about possible solutions
    C. *bad,* since correction officers will question the motives of the superior officer
    D. *good,* since poorly thought out action can lead to undesirable results

12. If a correction officer comes to a superior officer with a minor grievance that seems of great importance to the officer, it would be BEST for the superior officer to   12.____

    A. explain that supervisory personnel should not be involved in petty grievances
    B. explain why the grievance is of no importance
    C. listen attentively and give the grievance serious consideration
    D. re-direct the officer's attention to a major department problem

13. When delivering a training talk to new correction officers, a superior officer who uses technical terms which may not be familiar to the rookies acts CORRECTLY *provided* that (s)he   13.____

    A. explains such terms as soon as (s)he uses them
    B. invites the rookies to ask questions about anything they do not understand
    C. questions the rookies at the end of the lecture to evaluate their grasp of the material
    D. tells the rookies the names of standard correctional works in which they are to look up the terms

14. The superior officer whose subordinates never have any complaints about anything should probably re-appraise his role as a supervisor.
    Upon such a re-appraisal, the superior officer is MOST likely to discover that   14.____

    A. supervision is too strict
    B. the officers are afraid
    C. the officers are well satisfied with everything
    D. communication is poor

15. It is *generally* bad for subordinate employees to become aware of pending or contemplated changes in policy via the *grapevine* MAINLY because   15.____

    A. subordinates may feel that the administration thinks the staff cannot be trusted with the information
    B. subordinates may feel that the administration lacks the courage to make an unpopular announcement

C. information circulated by this method is seldom completely accurate and often spreads needless apprehension among the staff
D. evidence that a responsible official has proven to be secretive will undermine confidence

16. The one of the following training methods likely to be MOST effective in developing in correction officers a specific skill, such as taking inmate counts, is

    A. meticulously planned lectures
    B. repeated and supervised practice
    C. selected and comprehensive readings
    D. well designed demonstrations using visual aids

17. For a superior officer to give equally close supervision to all correction officers would be

    A. *desirable,* all correction officers can benefit from the superior officer's guidance
    B. *undesirable,* the degree of supervision needed varies with the capabilities of each officer
    C. *desirable,* all subordinates would be assured of fair and equal treatment
    D. *undesirable,* the demands on the superior officer's time would be too great

18. Of the following, the BEST technique for a superior officer to use in training correction officers is to

    A. encourage them to ask questions at all times
    B. change their assignments frequently
    C. teach them how to analyze important facts in order to make their own decisions
    D. teach them how to evaluate inmate morale

19. A superior officer should not permit correction officers who have just been appointed to learn institutional procedures entirely on the basis of their own experience MAINLY because they will

    A. learn more quickly under correct guidance
    B. learn quickest when left to their own resources
    C. remember best what they learn first
    D. lose too much time worrying about whether they are learning the proper things in the proper manner

20. Superior officers may find that some correction officers who have been on the job a long time require more supervision than correction officers with less experience.
    Of the following, the CHIEF implication of this statement for the superior officer as a supervisor is that

    A. correction officers with years of experience generally break more minor regulations than do the newer correction officers
    B. the ability of correction officers does not increase with years of experience
    C. the newer correction officers are usually better acquainted with the detailed rules and regulations of the department
    D. the number of years of experience a correction officer has may not be a reliable index of the amount of supervision needed

21. When instructing correction officers under his (her) supervision, a superior officer should realize that

    A. after the age of 20, a person's ability to learn decreases progressively at a slow rate
    B. learning should be uniform if instruction is uniform
    C. learning should be uniform if there is active participation by each learner
    D. persons of the same age differ in the amount they can learn in a given time

22. A superior officer must be strict in enforcing discipline, but at the same time should also show sympathy and understanding toward subordinates.
    The superior officer who BEST illustrates this is the one who

    A. gives orders that are precise and unambiguous
    B. overlooks minor infractions
    C. seeks to discover the reasons behind an officer's misconduct
    D. shows no favoritism toward anyone

23. Which one of the following is the LEAST desirable supervisory practice for a superior officer to follow?

    A. Discuss with correction officers theoretical situations which they may conceivably encounter in their work and their possible solutions
    B. Observe for a few days the mistakes a correction officer makes and then discuss these mistakes with the officer
    C. Praise a correction officer for good work in the presence of other correction officers
    D. Question correction officers from time to time on provisions of the rules and regulations relating to their work

24. When a superior officer must often take disciplinary action against subordinates, the superior officer SHOULD realize that

    A. this is normal practice if officers are to be well disciplined
    B. (s)he was probably assigned to this troublesome group because (s)he had the ability to handle it
    C. it would be best to ask for a new assignment for the good of the department
    D. (her) his methods of supervision need self-review to determine whether they are faulty

25. A superior officer just before instructing a correction officer in the correct method of searching a cell for contraband, explained to the officer why it was important to follow the correct procedure.
    The superior officer's action was

    A. *good,* a procedure is less likely to be forgotten if its purpose is understood
    B. *poor,* since the importance of searching for contraband is obvious, the explanation is a waste of time
    C. *good,* repetition is an effective aid in learning an operation
    D. *poor,* such an explanation will distract the correction officer from the main points in the instruction

26. The use of positive discipline by a superior officer will enhance the morale of the institution.
    Of the following, the BEST example of positive discipline is

    A. assigning unpleasant duties purely as an educational device
    B. reprimanding in private and very soon after the negligent act
    C. suggesting methods of work improvement when reviewing work that is poorly done
    D. adjusting the severity of the punishment to the severity of the offense

27. If a correction officer wants to talk to his superior about a personal problem, the superior should

    A. be willing to discuss the matter with the officer
    B. refer the officer to his deputy so as to keep the superior officer-correction officer relationship impersonal
    C. tell the officer to discuss the matter with another correction officer with whom (s)he is friendly
    D. tell the officer that personal problems should not be discussed on the job

28. Assume you are a correction superior officer. Another superior officer has been newly assigned to your institution.
    For you to tell this new superior officer the strengths and weaknesses of some of the individual correction officers (s)he will supervise, would be

    A. *bad,* bias will be introduced unknowingly into the work situation
    B. *good,* the new captain will be able to make various assignments of officers more intelligently
    C. *bad,* it will delay the new captain's adjustment to new responsibilities
    D. *good,* the abilities of a correction officer change from day to day due to various factors

29. Of the following, the BEST way to help to assure that procedures on a particular post will be carried out uniformly is to

    A. assign officers of approximately the same ability to the post
    B. assign the same officers to this post as much as possible
    C. have the same captain instruct any personnel assigned to this post for the first time
    D. require that every officer assigned to the post read and know the procedural orders and job analysis of the post

30. A superior officer who is asked for information about the department by a visiting member of the public should

    A. advise the individual that information about the department is restricted
    B. give the individual the information requested unless it is restricted
    C. refer the individual to the office of the Commissioner
    D. refer the individual to the office of the Director of Operations

KEY (CORRECT ANSWERS)

1.	A	16.	B
2.	D	17.	B
3.	D	18.	C
4.	B	19.	A
5.	C	20.	D
6.	D	21.	D
7.	B	22.	C
8.	A	23.	B
9.	A	24.	D
10.	C	25.	A
11.	B	26.	B
12.	C	27.	A
13.	A	28.	B
14.	D	29.	D
15.	C	30.	B

TEST 2

DIRECTIONS: Each question or incomplete statement is followed by several suggested answers or completions. Select the one that BEST answers the question or completes the statement. *PRINT THE LETTER OF THE CORRECT ANSWER IN THE SPACE AT THE RIGHT.*

1. A superior officer on patrol of a cell block at night sees an inmate writhing on the floor in apparent pain.
   In this situation, the superior officer should

   A. bear in mind that the inmate may be feigning and take necessary precautions
   B. enter the cell immediately to get the inmate back on the bed and give first aid
   C. notify the officer in command of the tour right away
   D. summon a doctor immediately and wait for him to arrive

   1.____

2. Of the following, the BEST method of counting inmates in an open area is to have

   A. the most capable officer make two successive counts
   B. two officers make the count simultaneously
   C. one officer make the count with a second officer watching for any movement of inmates
   D. one officer make one count and then immediately after have another officer make an independent count

   2.____

3. Strict limitation and control of telephone calls by inmates of a correctional institution is

   A. *desirable,* it is a necessary security precaution
   B. *undesirable,* it causes a loss of incentive for good behavior
   C. *desirable,* the number of available telephone instruments is limited
   D. *undesirable,* it is destructive of morale

   3.____

4. Of the following prisoners, which one is LEAST likely to attempt to escape?
   One

   A. about to complete his sentence
   B. afraid of being assaulted by other prisoners
   C. just denied parole
   D. with no family ties

   4.____

5. Of the following, the MAIN purpose of the tool shadow board is to

   A. enable employees to locate needed tools quickly
   B. indicate when a tool is missing
   C. provide a central place for the storage of tools
   D. reduce accidents by storing tools in a safe place

   5.____

6. Which one of the following is a problem of LEAST immediate concern at the time of admission of a new inmate to a correctional institution?

   A. Exclusion of contraband
   B. Safeguarding the inmate's money and valuables
   C. Proper work assignment
   D. Safeguarding the institution from vermin and disease

   6.____

7. Assume a riot of prison inmates is in progress.
Of the following, it would be LEAST desirable for the prison authorities to

   A. separate the apparent ringleaders from the rest of the inmates as soon as practicable
   B. keep a reserve group of officers away from the riot area until the situation has been assessed
   C. follow a pre-established emergency plan for riots
   D. bargain with the rioting inmates if their complaints seem legitimate

8. A correction officer in a court pen searches police cases delivered to the pen for temporary detention before (s)he assumes custody of these prisoners. The prisoners are later taken before the judge.
For the correction officer to search the prisoners *again* when they are returned to the pen, is

   A. *foolish,* because the prisoners have not been out of the building and have been under surveillance at all times
   B. *sensible,* because the prisoners may have acquired contraband when they were out of the pen
   C. *foolish,* because the prisoners were searched very thoroughly the first time
   D. *sensible,* because prisoners in court pens should be searched regularly several times each day

9. Which one of the following statements about firearms is the MOST accurate?

   A. A correction officer's personal safety can be absolutely guaranteed only when he carries a gun.
   B. An armory tower is usually a very poor place for storing firearms.
   C. A supply of firearms coming into an institution should be clearly labeled.
   D. The best place for storing firearms is right next to the inmate housing area; for easy accessibility when needed.

10. The practice of receiving a new prisoner and admitting him to the institution without a complete strip shakedown is

    A. *desirable only* if the officer delivering the prisoner gives written assurance that the prisoner has been frisked and is free of contraband
    B. *not desirable* under any circumstance
    C. *desirable only* if the prisoner has been brought directly from another jail
    D. *not desirable* except with material witnesses

11. A superior officer should patrol at irregular and unexpected times throughout his tour.
This method of patrol is *preferable* to regular patrols at scheduled times MAINLY because

    A. the superior officer has greater flexibility in scheduling the day's activities
    B. patrols will not be forgotten or reduced if they become habitual
    C. officers on post know that the superior officer will be around to inspect their work
    D. it gives a truer picture of actual conditions on the different posts

12. A well trained correction officer, if (s)he is alert, will know at all times how many prisoners (s)he has and where they are.
    Of the following, the CHIEF implication of this statement for the supervisor is that the

    A. responsibility for the proper custody, security and control of inmates is primarily that of the line officer
    B. superior officer, as well as the officer, should know at all times how many prisoners each officer has in (her) his charge and where each is assigned
    C. superior officer should repeatedly test the alertness of subordinates by questioning them as to the number and the whereabouts of the prisoners under their supervision
    D. most thorough grounding of officers in proper methods of custody and security will be nullified if they are not also imbued with an understanding of the importance of being always attentive to duty

13. Of the following, the LEAST desirable procedure to follow in the control of contraband is to search

    A. cells at regular intervals in accordance with a fixed schedule
    B. both incoming and outgoing vehicles
    C. trustees often
    D. the visitor when an inmate is authorized to have an open type visit

14. In a well-run correctional institution, it should not be too difficult for an inmate to bring to the attention of the administration a matter that he considers important. However, a danger that MUST be guarded against in keeping communication between inmates and staff open is that

    A. inmates may gradually assume some staff functions
    B. introverted inmates may not utilize the established channels of communication
    C. there may be an accompanying weakening of inmate discipline
    D. certain classes of inmates may consume administrators' time needlessly

15. Extra security precautions are generally advisable in the supervision of prisoners at mess.
    This is so MAINLY because

    A. different classes of inmates mingle together freely at mess
    B. large numbers of prisoners are concentrated together in one place
    C. prisoners are usually dissatisfied with institution food
    D. prison riots may begin anywhere

16. In a certain correctional institution a superior officer discharging an inmate asked the latter some personal questions such as, *Where do your parents live?*, *What is your mother's name?*, etc.
    The purpose of asking these questions was PROBABLY to

    A. check the accuracy of the information on the discharge papers
    B. motivate the inmate to renew his family ties
    C. prevent a substitution of inmates
    D. show an interest in the inmate's welfare

17. Which one of the following is NOT a recommended procedure when searching a large group of inmates, such as a work detail?

    A. After search of inmates is completed, officer searches area where they were standing
    B. Each inmate in turn approaches officer for search, arms outstretched, back to officer
    C. First inmate searched starts a new line at a distance from those not yet searched
    D. Inmates in a circle, far apart from each other, the officer in the center where (s)he can see all the inmates

18. For a correction officer to keep a type of cover over the prison keys that (s)he carries is a

    A. *good idea*, it will prevent the inmates from studying the shapes of the keys
    B. *poor idea*, the inmates are likely to resent such extraordinary precautionary measures
    C. *good idea*, it will prevent loss of keys
    D. *poor idea*, it will cause a correction officer undue delay in reaching for a key in an emergency

19. As a general rule, delay by uniformed personnel in considering inmate complaints is

    A. *desirable*, it will discourage complaints
    B. *undesirable*, it may create inmate unrest
    C. *desirable*, most inmate complaints are not justified
    D. *undesirable*, the cause of the complaint may disappear if action is delayed

20. In every prison population, there are a few inmates, probably not over 5 percent of the total, who are constantly attempting to agitate trouble for the administration. These individuals are frequently model prisoners on the surface.
    Of the following, the MOST practical way to prevent these habitual agitators from causing any great amount of harm is to

    A. keep them under constant observation
    B. keep the rest of the inmates satisfied by providing good prison conditions
    C. let these troublesome inmates know that the administration knows who they are and that any attempt to start trouble will be dealt with swiftly
    D. segregate them

21. Of the following, the BEST justification for NOT keeping large amounts of gas munitions on hand at an institution is that

    A. a large supply creates a security problem
    B. additional supplies can be obtained quickly if trouble is suspected
    C. gas shouldn't be used in large quantities
    D. the effectiveness of gas munitions depreciates quickly

22. Which one of the following principles is LEAST desirable to follow in a good system of key control?

    A. A listing of all keys should be maintained which should include the trade name of the lock
    B. Keys should not be issued from several locations of an institution

C. No duplicate keys should be kept at the institution
D. The location of each lock for which there is a key should be recorded

23. Of the following, the BEST way for a superior officer to avoid *unintentional* infractions of the institution's rules by inmates is to

    A. enforce the rules uniformly and impartially
    B. make sure the officers know the rules, so they can enforce them
    C. post the rules conspicuously where they will always command the attention of inmates
    D. see that inmates are instructed thoroughly in these rules

24. For a superior officer to occasionally research a correction officer's detail of inmates after the latter has completed (her) his search, is a

    A. *desirable* practice because it discourages a lackadaisical attitude in the searching of inmates
    B. *undesirable* practice because it impairs the officer's confidence
    C. *desirable* practice because even the officer who consistently employs the most thoroughgoing methods of searching should be checked regularly
    D. *undesirable* practice because it weakens the officer's control of the inmates

25. Suppose that a study of prison inmates shows that the rate of recidivism increases as the number of the offense increases. For example, 10% of first offenders becomes second offenders, 30% of second offenders become third offenders, 70% of third offenders become fourth offenders, ect.
    If the findings of this study are valid, then it is MOST reasonable to assume that

    A. environment plays a minor role in the pre-disposition towards criminal behavior
    B. exposure to prison life inevitably leads to the commission of further crimes
    C. first offenders represent the most fruitful field for intensive rehabilitative efforts
    D. it would be desirable in an institution to house together offenders who have committed the same number of offenses

26. Which one of the following statements about the psychopathic or sociopathic personality is TRUE?

    A. All criminals are sociopathic in varying degrees.
    B. The sociopath is of average intelligence or higher.
    C. The sociopath has frequent guilt feelings about his non-conformist behavior.
    D. The sociopath responds well to psychotherapy or mental treatment.

27. A superior officer instructed subordinates *never, under any circumstances,* to use force against an inmate.
    The superior officer's instructions were

    A. *foolish,* the use of force against an inmate is justified in certain situations
    B. *sensible,* the use of force may accidentally cause the death of an inmate
    C. *foolish,* each correction officer should use common sense in each situation
    D. *sensible,* unless force is absolutely prohibited, some officers are bound to use it to excess

28. Which one of the following is LEAST characteristic of an inmate who has a paranoid personality?
    He

    A. forgets an imagined offense quickly
    B. thinks other people are hostile to him
    C. thinks other people are jealous of him
    D. tries to prove the institution is not well run

29. Model behavior in prison is NOT ALWAYS a good guide to the inmate's success on parole because

    A. adjustment to the complexities of civilian life is as difficult as adjustment to prison life
    B. experience has shown that parolees very often violate the terms of their parole
    C. inmates are individuals and generalized conclusions cannot be drawn regarding their behavior
    D. prison-wise inmates will often behave well in prison merely to hasten the date of release

30. The practice of using inmate trustees to perform responsible tasks in a correctional institution is GENERALLY considered by progressive prison administrators to be

    A. desirable only with inmates nearing the end of their sentence
    B. of doubtful value
    C. of value if used with discretion
    D. unacceptable

31. The one of the following that is CHARACTERISTIC of the schizoid type of personality encountered in correctional work is

    A. an exaggerated degree of socialization with other inmates
    B. assertiveness
    C. a tendency to become emotionally involved with certain inmates
    D. a tendency to excessive day-dreaming

32. It is generally considered UNDESIRABLE, as a disciplinary practice, to restrict an inmate's letter writing privilege unless the

    A. inmate is not unduly harmed by this restriction
    B. offense being punished is in violation of the regulations relating to this privilege
    C. restriction is for a short time
    D. restriction is used in conjunction with other forms of punishment

33. Of the following, one of the MAIN theories underlying the use of the indeterminate sentence is that the

    A. punishment should be adjusted to the severity of the offense
    B. rate of improvement should be a factor in determining the length of imprisonment
    C. sentencing of offenders should be left entirely to the discretion of the courts
    D. variation in sentence for the same offense is destructive of inmate morale

34. Since inmate programs of work, recreation, vocational training, etc. have not been effective in reducing crime or the rate of recidivism, they should be abandoned.
A basic WEAKNESS of this criticism is that it fails to take into account that these programs

    A. are also needed to keep inmates occupied
    B. are not intended to achieve the purposes stated
    C. can not influence the majority of criminals, since they are not apprehended
    D. have been tried for only a very short time

34.___

35. Contrasting the responsibility of prison management for rehabilitating inmates with its responsibility for secure custody and control of inmates, which one of the following statement is MOST accurate?

    A. Both responsibilities have equal priority.
    B. Good control can be consistently realized without rehabilitative treatment.
    C. Methods for effective rehabilitative treatment can operate only in an atmosphere where control is maintained.
    D. The more fundamental responsibility is the rehabilitation of inmates.

35.___

KEY (CORRECT ANSWERS)

1. A		16. C	
2. C		17. D	
3. A		18. A	
4. A		19. B	
5. B		20. B	
6. C		21. D	
7. D		22. C	
8. B		23. D	
9. C		24. A	
10. B		25. C	
11. D		26. B	
12. D		27. A	
13. A		28. A	
14. D		29. D	
15. B		30. C	

31. D
32. B
33. B
34. A
35. C

TEST 3

DIRECTIONS: Each question or incomplete statement is followed by several suggested answers or completions. Select the one that BEST answers the question or completes the statement. *PRINT THE LETTER OF THE CORRECT ANSWER IN THE SPACE AT THE RIGHT.*

1. In all probability, the behavior of a recalcitrant inmate serving an indefinite sentence would be MOST influenced by a threatened

   A. isolation and restricted diet
   B. loss of family visits
   C. loss of good time
   D. suspension of privileges

   1.____

2. Is it DESIRABLE for indeterminate sentence prisoners to be familiar with the general procedures of the parole board?

   A. *No,* it would lead to attempts by inmates to interfere with the parole board.
   B. *Yes,* it will lead to greater public acceptance of parole boards.
   C. *No,* parole board procedures and practices change from time to time.
   D. *Yes,* it would lessen prisoner resentment, caused by ignorance, against actions of the parole board.

   2.____

3. While we cannot tell to what extent individuals are predisposed toward crime at birth, there is no doubt that some are so formed that in an unfavorable environment they are more apt to be lead into crime than others.
   This statement suggests MOST NEARLY that

   A. all individuals have some pre-disposition toward crime from birth but most are able to overcome this
   B. if exposure to unfavorable environment were eliminated, crime would be eliminated
   C. it is possible to foretell criminal behavior
   D. under the same circumstances, some persons will react criminally because of hereditary factors, while others will not

   3.____

4. Of the following, the PRINCIPAL reason for controlling the amount of money an inmate may spend weekly for commissary items is, *generally,* to

   A. check gambling and attempts at bribery
   B. control smuggling of contraband
   C. keep the commissary staff at a moderate size
   D. make it easier to operate the commissary

   4.____

5. In prostitution cases, the courts have little choice but to decide whether the offense actually occurred as charged, rather than the more desirable alternative of determining whether the particular offender is a social misfit in need of rehabilitation.
   This statement *implies* MOST DIRECTLY that

   A. a very large proportion of women who are social misfits resort to prostitution
   B. the determination of whether a prostitution offender is a social misfit is up to the courts
   C. there is the wrong legal emphasis in prostitution cases
   D. with an effort at rehabilitation, prostitution would be eliminated

   5.____

6. Special privileges which are not open to all the inmates of a correctional institution must not be permitted to particular individuals.
   This statement implies that

   A. some classes of inmates should not be permitted special privileges
   B. any inmate should be able, by good conduct and proper attitude, to earn any privilege which another inmate enjoys
   C. no inmate should enjoy a privilege which all the other inmates do not also enjoy at the same time
   D. there should not be any special privileges for inmates to enjoy

7. Of the following, the MAIN drawback of placing *chief* or sole emphasis in a prison recreation program on active games and sports is that it

   A. deprives those not physically fit of the opportunity to participate
   B. fosters an unhealthy competitive spirit
   C. requires money for equipment
   D. requires the inmate to expend too much physical energy

8. The experience of several leading cottage type correctional institutions for women with inmate student government programs has shown them to be

   A. *desirable,* they develop a sense of group responsibility in the inmate
   B. *undesirable,* they tend to become a type of kangaroo court
   C. *desirable,* they have effectively fixed responsibility for the maintenance of discipline in each cottage on the cottage committee
   D. *undesirable,* they must be directed by staff, and inmates lose interest

9. Institutions for women have made notable contributions to correctional progress because public opinion has not stood in the way of experimentation with new methods and techniques by women superintendents.
   Of the following, the CHIEF reason for this attitude on the part of the public is, *probably,* that

   A. a more chivalrous attitude toward women is a cultural phenomenon of our society that has carried over into the public's attitude toward the heads of women's institutions
   B. the number of women offenders is smaller than the number of men offenders
   C. the public is not as well informed about women's institutions
   D. women offenders do not generally commit acts of violence or present a threat to the public in the same way as male offenders

10. Which one of the following statements about the homosexual inmate is LEAST accurate?

    A. Individuals who habitually engage in such conduct are quite easy to identify.
    B. Some, but not all such inmates, have certain distinctive mannerisms.
    C. Some inmates who engage in homosexual practice in prison are sexually normal outside of prison.
    D. When housed in dormitories with normal inmates, they will be deterred from engaging in homosexual practices with such inmates.

11. According to the Rules and Regulations, a superior officer is NOT required to

    A. be responsible for handling records, fines, bails, and entries in the register of prisoners when in charge of a tour
    B. be responsible for the identification and discharge of prisoners when in charge of a tour
    C. immediately send home a correction officer under her (his) command who reports to work intoxicated
    D. report in writing all latenesses of correction officers under (her) his command

12. A member of the immediate family of an inmate who is confined in an institution may visit the inmate *provided* said family member is NOT LESS THAN _____ years old.

    A. 16   B. 17   C. 18   D. 19

13. Assume that in a sampling of inmates, three-fifths are found to be over 30 years old. One-third of the remainder are under 20 years of age.
    Then, of all the inmates in this sampling, the NUMBER between the ages of 20 and 30 inclusive is, *most nearly*, _____ of the total

    A. 1/15   B. 4/15   C. 3/16   D. 2/7

14. Suppose your institution's census decreased 15% from 2000 to 2002, increased 10% from 2002 to 2004, and increased 5% from 2004 to 2006.
    The number of inmates in 2006 was, *most nearly*, what PERCENT of the number of inmates in 2000?

    A. 98%   B. 99%   C. 99.5%   D. 100%

15. According to the Rules and Regulations, prisoners sentenced in night court to one day are to be discharged

    A. on the day and hour specified by the judge
    B. after the court has adjourned
    C. at 9:00 a.m. the next morning
    D. at 4:00 p.m. the next afternoon

16. When an officer finds narcotics in the possession of an unauthorized person at an institution, the officer is required to take possession of the narcotics, place them in a sealed envelope or package, and make certain notations on the outside of such envelope or package. Such notations do NOT include the

    A. name of witnesses
    B. status of the person on whom the narcotics was found
    C. time the incident occurred
    D. type of narcotics that was found

17. Criminal court procedure provides for the

    A. more extensive use of probation with certain classes of minor offenders
    B. release on their own recognizance of certain offenders who cannot furnish bail
    C. setting up of a 24-hour arraignment part of criminal court in each borough
    D. speeding up court calendars by assignment of rotating panels of judges

18. A superior officer has been notified by a correction officer under his supervision that an inmate has committed an infraction of discipline important enough to necessitate action. The FIRST thing that the superior officer should do is to

    A. inform the disciplinary officer or board of the institution so that a hearing can be held quickly
    B. investigate the complaint to see if the facts warrant disciplinary action
    C. notify the inmate that he is in a punishment status pending a hearing
    D. place the inmate in segregation pending investigation

19. If a member of a work gang in an institution escapes, the officer in charge of the gang should FIRST

    A. inform his superior officer of the name and number of the escapee
    B. inform the Police Department of the escape
    C. line up all the remaining members of the work gang
    D. question the other inmates of the gang to find out who saw the inmate last, when, and where

20. Assume you are preparing a summary of all the inmates serving definite sentence in your institution, grouped according to length of sentence. You have the following totals: the number of inmates serving a definite sentence of more than 6 months; the number of inmates serving a definite sentence of more than 3 months; and the number of inmates serving a definite sentence of 3 months or less.
    To find what fraction the inmates serving more than 6 months constitute of all the inmates serving a definite sentence, you should

    A. divide the number of inmates serving more than 6 months by the number serving 3 months or less, then by the number serving more than 3 months, and add the two
    B. divide the number of inmates serving more than 6 months by the sum of the inmates serving 3 months or less and the inmates serving more than 3 months
    C. divide twice the number of inmates serving more than 6 months by the total of all the inmates serving definite sentences
    D. subtract the number of inmates serving more than 6 months from the total of all the inmates serving definite sentences and then divide by the total number of inmates serving definite sentence

21. According to the Rules and Regulations, the officer on duty is NOT required to inspect an inmate placed in isolation or solitary confinement more often than

    A. once a day   B. once every hour
    C. twice a day   D. twice every hour

22. A superior officer is instructing a correction officer assigned to a court pen in the proper procedure for the receipt of new or direct admissions from the police.
    The superior officer need NOT instruct the correction officer to

    A. ask the patrolman to sign his name and write his precinct or command in the proper section on the back of the commitment
    B. require the prisoner to sign his name on the commitment while the patrolman is there

C. take a print of the prisoner's left index finger on the commitment
D. tell the patrolman the reason for the procedures the correction officer must follow before assuming custody of the prisoner

23. Unless otherwise stated on the commitment papers, an inmate in an institution on two separate commitments MUST serve the sentences consecutively *if* the sentences are

   A. being served in default of payment of respective fines
   B. for the same offense
   C. from the same court
   D. from the same court and the court did not indicate the order in which they are to be served

24. When contraband is found on a prisoner who is received from the police at a court detention pen, the correction officer should

   A. deliver the contraband to the property clerk of the court
   B. notify the person designated by the prisoner to pick it up
   C. take charge of it pending dispostion of the case
   D. have the police officer take it from the prisoner

25. The Department of Correction will conduct a lineup for the purpose of identification of an inmate at the written request of the Police Department or Office of the District Attorney. Which one of the following is NOT a part of the lineup procedure as conducted by the Department of Correction?

   A. A record is kept of the names of all inmates presented at the lineup.
   B. The suspected inmate must be advised of the reason he is being called.
   C. The names of any police officers present during the lineup must be recorded.
   D. Each individual lineup is made up of nine inmates, including the person suspected.

26. Which one of the following is part of the standard operating procedure whenever a payment for a fine is made at an institution of the Department?

   A. A certified or teller's check will be accepted in payment.
   B. The duplicate copy of the receipt is given to the person paying the fine.
   C. The payment will be accepted even if other detainers exist in the case.
   D. The serial numbers of all bills received in payment must be entered on the receipt form.

27. A superior officer is explaining security precautions to an officer who is to escort an inmate to a public clinic for required treatment.
The superior officer should instruct the officer to

   A. call him (her) for permission to remove the inmate's handcuffs if there is an emergency and the inmate's life is in danger
   B. keep the inmate handcuffed at all times and under no circumstances remove the handcuffs
   C. remove the inmate's handcuffs while the inmate is being treated by the physician
   D. telephone him (her) for security instructions to be taken if the doctor asks that the handcuffs be removed

28. When a prisoner is to be discharged from a court detention pen, the name of the prisoner and the statement of charge on the order of discharge must be compared with this information on the commitment.
However, if the prisoner was transferred to the court pen from an institution of the Department, this comparison is *also* to be made with the information on the

   A. accompanying card
   B. inmate detention record
   C. inmate identification card
   D. records and statistics card

29. Suppose that an inmate's date of release falls on Independence Day, Monday, July 4. The inmate should be discharged

   A. the day before
   B. two days before
   C. three days before
   D. the day after

30. Which one of the following statements about the *Manhattan Bail Project* is NOT true?

   A. Its work has been taken over by the Office of Probation.
   B. It was a project launched by the Vera Foundation.
   C. Of the cases released on recognizance and later convicted, the majority received suspended sentences.
   D. Only 25% of the defendants released on recognizance failed to return to court when required.

31. While the available data reveal that the typical offender in the institutions of the Department of Correction has a background of family failure, the rehabilitative efforts of the Department must nevertheless be directed toward the offender as an individual, rather than toward the family. This is so MAINLY because

   A. family patterns cannot be influenced
   B. it has not been proven that there is any direct relationship between environment and criminal behavior
   C. the Department of Correction does not have the capability to reach out and change the family background
   D. the typical offender does not have any firm family ties

32. In a correctional institution, it is usually desirable to vest responsibility for the general enforcement of discipline and the administration of punishment in a single disciplinary officer, who is usually the head of the institution or one of (her) his deputies.
This system for the enforcement of discipline is *desirable* MAINLY because

   A. discipline, if inflexible, will do more harm than good
   B. greater uniformity in the enforcement of discipline and the application of punishments will result
   C. the list of infractions and punishments should be well publicized
   D. the officer responsible for the enforcement of discipline should not be too far removed from the offender

33. SUPERVISION IN THE ADMINISTRATION OF JUSTICE was written by   33._____

    A. Paul B. Weston
    B. Elmer H. Johnson
    C. Vernon Fox
    D. Sanford Bates

34. INTRODUCTION TO CORRECTIONS was written by   34._____

    A. Paul B. Weston
    B. Elmer H. Johnson
    C. Vernon Fox
    D. Sanford Bates

35. JOTTINGS ON JAILS AND JAILERS is   35._____

    A. a feature of the American Journal of Correction
    B. a publication of the State Department of Correction
    C. the title of a magazine on correction
    D. the title of a recent book by a well-known retired warden

KEY (CORRECT ANSWERS)

1.	C	16.	D
2.	D	17.	C
3.	D	18.	B
4.	A	19.	C
5.	C	20.	B
6.	B	21.	D
7.	A	22.	D
8.	A	23.	A
9.	D	24.	D
10.	A	25.	B
11.	C	26.	C
12.	C	27.	D
13.	B	28.	A
14.	A	29.	C
15.	B	30.	D

31. C
32. B
33. A
34. C
35. A

EXAMINATION SECTION
TEST 1

DIRECTIONS: Each question or incomplete statement is followed by several suggested answers or completions. Select the one that BEST answers the question or completes the statement. *PRINT THE LETTER OF THE CORRECT ANSWER IN THE SPACE AT THE RIGHT.*

1. Of the following, the MOST serious problem that faces the commanding officer in the supervision of new correction officers is that, for the most part, these officers

    A. are afraid to face up to the responsibilities of their position
    B. are over-confident and have a *know-it-all* attitude
    C. have accepted this employment only as a stopgap until they find other work
    D. have had no extensive formal training in this field of work

    1.____

2. An employee's performance should be evaluated quarterly during the probationary period and at least once a year after the probationary period.
   Of the following, the CHIEF justification for the less frequent formal evaluation of employee performance after the probationary period is that

    A. over-supervision of experienced employees is unnecessary and undesirable and may create resentment on the part of the employee
    B. the employee has already proven himself satisfactory by passing his probationary period
    C. the older employee reacts more quickly and responsively to supervision
    D. the supervisor has already achieved a considerable degree of familiarity with the employee's capabilities, performance, and need for further training

    2.____

3. It has been suggested that the in-service training of employees in the correctional field be continued from the time of their employment until the time of their leaving the department.
   Of the following, the CHIEF justification for such a continuous program of in-service training is that

    A. a person's capacity for learning increases with age
    B. because of a natural tendency to forget what one has learned and not put into practice, training must be repeated at regular intervals
    C. employees usually are capable of further development on the job during the entire period of their employment
    D. for learning to be effective, successive stages in the learning process must be correlated and coordinated

    3.____

4. Of the following, the CHIEF advantage of rotating the qualified staff of a correctional institution among the various job assignments is the

    A. development of versatility in staff members
    B. elimination of jealousy among employees
    C. establishment of bases upon which to formulate work norms
    D. lessening of the undesirable trend toward increasing specialization

    4.____

5. It has been stated that the key to successful application of the majority of standards that have been set for an adult correctional institution is the proper organization, selection, training, and assignment of the staff.
   Of the following, the CHIEF justification for this statement is that

   A. proper selection, training, organization, and assignment of staff are often a neglected phase of institutional management
   B. proper staffing is the most complex aspect of correctional institution management
   C. staff selection, training, organization, and assignment is a continuous process
   D. the staff is the medium through which these standards must be implemented

6. Of the following, the MOST important reason why supervisors should give careful consideration to the techniques they utilize for assignment of employees to specific jobs is that

   A. an opportunity is thus offered the supervisor for periodic evaluation of the qualifications and work performance of all employees
   B. efficiency of employees is dependent in part on the techniques used by supervisory officers for selection of employees for assignments
   C. requests of employees for change in work assignments may indicate dissatisfaction with present conditions
   D. standardized techniques for the selection of employees for specific job assignments have not yet been developed

7. In the selection and appointment process for correction officers, particular care is taken to screen out the neurotic and unstable. Suppose, however, that in spite of this, as a result of your observations during the probationary period you are convinced that a new officer appointed to your command has a neurotic and unstable personality
   Of the following, the BEST action for you to take as commanding officer is to

   A. give restrictive assignment and close supervision to this officer unless the need for more drastic action is indicated at a later date
   B. help the employee to correct this undesirable trait by giving proper and continuous training
   C. recommend that the employee be dropped at the end of the probationary period
   D. refer the employee for appropriate medical care

8. Attempts to apply police training to prison personnel will have unsatisfactory results.
   Of the following, the MOST probable cause of these poor results would be the

   A. difference in emphasis of the two fields of work
   B. failure to properly integrate classroom teaching with practical work
   C. poor quality of the instruction
   D. shortness of the training period generally used

9. Of the following, the LEAST desirable use of a new officer's probationary period by the commanding officer is to

   A. carefully check and evaluate performance of work assigned
   B. instruct the officer in the proper performance of assigned duties
   C. observe whether the officer is capable of performing the duties of the job efficiently
   D. train the officer for promotion to the next higher rank

10. The statement has been made that correction officers have a tendency to get into a rut. If this statement is valid, the one of the following actions by an officer which BEST illustrates this tendency is:

    A. Continuing in the same assignment for several years without being motivated to task for a change in assignment
    B. Performing an act of alertness or heroism after the incident which might have been prevented by such act has already been precipitated
    C. Releasing an inmate after partial identification, taking for granted that it must be the correct inmate
    D. Using the standard, approved methods of conducting tier searches for contraband instead of trying to devise more ingenious and novel methods

11. A superior officer, investigating why an order had not been carried out, was told by the officers concerned that they had not realized that what the superior officer intended as an order.
    This incident illustrates MOST directly an order that was NOT

    A. concise
    B. possible of performance
    C. recognizable as an order
    D. reviewed after issuance of the order

12. In explaining to a subordinate the importance of the tier officer's initial contact with a new admission, the superior officer should stress MOST the

    A. constructive influence this initial contact can have on the inmate's future adjustment to confinement
    B. desirability of getting the inmate to talk freely and without interruption
    C. harmful effect on the inmate's morale of a businesslike approach to the conduct of this initial interview
    D. value of this initial interview in impressing the inmate with the fact that violations of the rules will not be tolerated

13. In explaining to a group of new officers the reasons why their position is so important in the operations of the department, the commanding officer should emphasize MOST the fact that

    A. the inmate's attitude to the officer is basically a hostile one
    B. the largest number of uniformed personnel is in the rank of correction officer
    C. the officer represents the most frequent, direct contact of the department with the inmate
    D. this is the rank from which the administrative positions in the department will be filled

14. Each job assignment of personnel in the institution should be carefully described in writing, setting forth the duties, responsibilities, and special requirements of the particular job assignment.
    Of the following, the CHIEF advantage of this procedure is that

    A. a change in administration or supervision will not interfere with the orderly running of the institution
    B. defects in administrative organization will become apparent

C. employees will have a ready means of knowing what is expected of them in their particular assignments
D. it will be possible to transfer employees more freely from one job assignment to another

15. If, as commanding officer, you find that there occur a considerable number of minor, apparently unintentional infractions of rules by inmates on one officer's post, the BEST action of the following for you to take FIRST would be to

    A. determine whether the inmates on this post have a clear understanding of the rules and what constitutes violation of the rules
    B. find out the basic causes of inmate dissatisfaction on this post and correct them
    C. give this officer additional training in proper techniques for maintaining stricter discipline on the post
    D. investigate whether it would be advisable to assign a more competent officer to this post

16. Suppose you learn that an officer under your command intends to file an official complaint against an inmate for committing an infraction of the institution's rules. Of the following, the BEST action for you to take as commanding officer is to

    A. advise the officer that the filing of official complaints should be reserved for the most serious infractions only
    B. determine if the infraction is serious enough to warrant an official complaint
    C. make an inspection to determine whether discipline on the post is otherwise satisfactory
    D. support the officer in the interest of maintaining institution discipline and morale

17. Suppose it comes to your attention that an officer under your supervision does not give prompt consideration to all complaints and requests of inmates.
    Of the following, the BEST action for you as commanding officer to take is to

    A. discuss with the officer the harmful effect such action can have on inmate morale
    B. explain to the officer that action on complaints must be differentiated from action on requests
    C. order the officer to comply with all inmate complaints and requests promptly
    D. warn the officer and give closer supervision as something serious might result from this method of work

18. In explaining to a correction officer why an unvaried routine in the conduct of tier post inspections is not desirable, a superior officer should stress MOST the fact that

    A. a method of work that may be entirely acceptable in one situation generally proves to be unacceptable when transferred without modification to a different work situation
    B. inmates seeking to violate the institution's rules make a study of the officer's habits so that they can time their activities to forestall detection
    C. it is important to have a clear understanding of the purposes of the tier post inspection in order to be able to carry it out efficiently and intelligently
    D. the discovery of contraband is not the sole purpose of a tier post inspection

19. A superior officer instructed subordinates in the meaning of parole, the conditions under which it is granted, and in the rules and practices of parole supervision.
The superior officer's action was

   A. *necessary and desirable*; the entire prison staff should have an understanding of parole if the indoctrination and orientation of the inmates with respect to parole is to be well done
   B. *unnecessary and undesirable*; only occasionally does a member of the superior officer's staff have any responsibilities directly connected with the parole function
   C. *necessary and desirable*; while the staff generally has no concern with parole matters and problems, they should have a well-rounded background which includes a knowledge of related agencies
   D. *unnecessary and undesirable;* the parole function is the responsibility of another agency

20. Of the following, the LEAST important rule for a superior officer to stress when instructing an officer in the fundamentals of making a count of prisoners is:

   A. Count each tier of a cell block separately and make a temporary note of the count for each tier
   B. Do not speak to prisoners or to other personnel when making a count
   C. See flesh or movement or hear prisoners speak before recording them as counted
   D. Speak the number out loudly as you count each inmate so that you can actually be heard making the count

21. A superior officer instructed a group of new officers that, before beginning their tier count when coming on duty, they should get the off-going officer's last count and use this as a check when making their count.
The superior officer's instructions were

   A. *good* because a new officer should receive assistance from an experienced officer
   B. *poor* because errors in the previous count may be unconsciously duplicated
   C. *good* because both counts must agree
   D. *poor* because the on-coming officer is not in any way responsible for the off-going officer's count

22. A commanding officer instructed subordinates that, at all times, the tier officer going off duty was to notify the on-coming officer of any inmate who should be particularly watched.
The commanding officer's instructions were

   A. *good* because the on-coming officer will not be surprised if any inmate behaves strangely
   B. *poor* because alertness and initiative on the part of the on-coming officer may be reduced
   C. *good* because the on-coming officer will benefit from the experience and observation of the off-going officer
   D. *poor* because all inmates should be given careful and close custody and supervision

23. Of the following, the technique that is likely to contribute MOST to the successful control of suicides in a command is for the commanding officer to

    A. explain to subordinates some of the most common methods by which inmates commit suicide
    B. keep subordinates informed of the latest statistics on suicides in the department's institutions as a sobering reminder that constant attention to duty is required
    C. stress to subordinates repeatedly the serious effect on the institution of a successful suicide
    D. train subordinates in spotting the inmates who may be potential suicides

24. A commanding officer stated to a group of newly-appointed correction officers: *I cannot emphasize to you too much the importance of frequent patrol of your post.*
    The commanding officer MOST probably placed such great emphasis on the importance of frequent patrol for the reason that

    A. many commanding officers neglect to develop in their subordinates a proper understanding of and technique for the post patrol
    B. most officers do not patrol often enough
    C. patrol is the best way for an officer to keep in touch with what is happening on his post
    D. patrol is the best way of developing regular habits of work in a correction officer

25. Suppose that two experienced officers assigned to a tier post report to you that they suspect there is contraband hidden on the post but that they have been unable to locate it in spite of several searches.
    As their superior officer, the BEST thing for you to do at this time is to

    A. advise the officers to continue to be on the alert and to make several more searches at unexpected times
    B. explain to the officers that it is pointless to persist in these suspicions when they have not been substantiated by the facts
    C. organize and supervise a special search of the tier with a selected group of officers
    D. review the techniques employed by the officers in conducting these searches and point out why they are faulty

KEY (CORRECT ANSWERS)

1. D
2. D
3. C
4. A
5. D

6. B
7. C
8. A
9. D
10. C

11. C
12. A
13. C
14. C
15. A

16. B
17. A
18. B
19. A
20. D

21. B
22. C
23. D
24. C
25. C

TEST 2

DIRECTIONS: Each question or incomplete statement is followed by several suggested answers or completions. Select the one that BEST answers the question or completes the statement. *PRINT THE LETTER OF THE CORRECT ANSWER IN THE SPACE AT THE RIGHT.*

1. A cautious and observant officer seldom becomes involved in litigation initiated by an inmate who is injured during confinement on a tier.
   This statement is MOST probably based on the principle that such an officer will

   A. avoid and prevent situations which might cause injury to an inmate
   B. avoid any and all disputes with inmates
   C. be able to persuade the inmate that litigation is not justified
   D. make sure that any injury to an inmate is the result of the inmate's own negligence

   1.____

2. Of the following, the factor that contributes MOST to making the problem of custodial supervision in a prison so difficult is the

   A. few troublesome inmates who do not adjust
   B. lack of adequate space and facilities
   C. shortage of staff
   D. unnatural environment of a prison

   2.____

3. A superior officer is summoned by a correction officer to the cell of a newly committed inmate who has been taken suddenly ill. After observing the inmate, the superior officer thinks that the inmate's condition is due to nervous excitement resulting from commitment to the institution.
   The superior officer should

   A. speak quietly to the inmate until a normal condition is restored
   B. give the inmate a mild sedative
   C. make the inmate comfortable and instruct the officer to keep a close watch
   D. secure medical assistance for the inmate

   3.____

4. Of the following, the type of inmate in whom arrest and confinement are likely to cause the GREATEST emotional shock is the

   A. adolescent offender
   B. adult of established family in the community
   C. mental defective
   D. recidivist who was confident of not getting caught

   4.____

5. The maintenance of the personal cleanliness of inmates through the medium of regular bathing assumes added importance in a prison MAINLY for the reason that

   A. it is another procedure by which the possession of contraband by inmates can often be discovered
   B. most inmates have not developed proper habits of cleanliness
   C. personal body cleanliness is important in all individuals, including prison inmates
   D. the confining nature of institutional life necessarily brings inmates into close daily contact with each other

   5.____

6. From the standpoint of custody, the first concern of the correction officer in the court pen should be to lock the inmate in the pen as soon as possible.
   Of the following, the CHIEF justification for this statement is the fact that the officer

   A. can more easily take an accurate count of inmates confined in the pen
   B. can then give undivided attention to other important duties
   C. does not know how soon the inmate will have to be produced in court again
   D. may be the only obstacle between the inmate and escape

7. In the event that an officer discovered an attempted suicide by an inmate, the FIRST thing the officer should do is

   A. administer first aid
   B. gather all the evidence
   C. go to summon the institution physician
   D. notify the head of the institution

8. When an inmate commits a serious infraction of discipline, the commanding officer is required to investigate the incident as soon as practicable, but not later than the same day.
   Of the following, the CHIEF justification for such prompt investigation is that

   A. an investigation delayed is usually forgotten
   B. memory of the incident will be more accurate in the minds of participants and witnesses
   C. the inmate will be impressed with the seriousness of the offense
   D. the various participants and witnesses concerned in the incident will have less opportunity to prepare false versions of what actually happened

9. An officer should NOT use force toward an inmate for the purpose of

   A. compelling obedience to an order
   B. curbing a riot
   C. protecting the inmate's life
   D. self-defense

10. Cell location is an important factor in the custody and security of inmates who may be potential suicides PRIMARILY for the reason that

    A. cell location has an important effect on the morale of the inmates
    B. in some cells, it is easier to conceal contraband
    C. the ease of committing suicide varies from cell to cell
    D. the officer can keep certain cells under close observation more easily

11. Familiarity with the statistical information about suicides and attempted suicides in the institutions of the department is of value to the superior officer MAINLY because such information

    A. can assist the superior officer in personally detecting and preventing a greater number of suicides
    B. can be used as a basis of comparison with what is happening on the superior officer's command

C. can be used as an aid in training subordinates in the detection and prevention of suicides
D. gives the superior officer a broader understanding of the success of the department in carrying out its objectives

12. In the institutions of the department, special security procedures are observed with an inmate sentenced to death or to a long term in a state prison.
Such special procedures are advisable MAINLY for the reason that the

   A. department is only temporarily responsible for someone who is actually a prisoner of the state
   B. inmate's friends and accomplices on the outside may attempt to free the inmate by force
   C. isolation of such inmate from the rest of the prison population is not practicable
   D. severity of the sentence may impel such inmate to commit some desperate act

13. An ADVANTAGE of frequent special tier searches for contraband, although often no contraband may be discovered in such searches, is that

   A. inmates are placed on notice that contraband will not be tolerated in the institution
   B. negligence on the part of the tier officer with respect to contraband control does not have serious results
   C. officers are given training in military discipline
   D. responsibility for contraband control on the post is shared equally by superior and subordinate

14. When assigned to duty in a large mess hall during inmate mess, it is important for officers to station themselves in such a way that they can see and be seen by their superior at all times.
This statement is justified MAINLY for the reason that the

   A. inmates will not attempt to create any disturbance when they see that the officers and their superior are in ready communication with each other
   B. officers will be able to show their superior that they are performing their jobs properly
   C. officers will be able to tell if the superior has left the mess hall
   D. superior, who may be far away from the officers, might suddenly find it necessary to transmit an order to them quickly by means of a signal

15. The sole value of the maintenance of proper sanitation procedures on a tier post is the protection of the health of the inmates and of the prison personnel.
This statement is

   A. *correct* because the health of inmates and personnel must be protected at all times in the interest of proper institutional administration
   B. *incorrect* because proper post sanitation also has other values, such as morale building
   C. *correct* because the poor physical and moral condition of many inmates creates an undue amount of sanitation problems
   D. *incorrect* because there has been no positive evidence that cleanliness on a tier post actually affects health

16. The primary function of the prison is the safekeeping of the prisoners committed to the prison.
    This statement is

    A. *invalid* because it ignores the latest concepts in correctional work, which emphasize the rehabilitative potentialities of imprisonment
    B. *valid* because statistics on recidivism show that it is the only function capable of realization
    C. *invalid* because the prison has several functions, each of which is greatly important
    D. *valid* because the prison is legally responsible for the safe custody of the prisoners committed by the courts until the expiration of their sentences

16.____

17. In its inmate treatment program, a correctional institution should operate on the philosophy that well-adjusted people do more than merely sleep, eat, and work.
    Of the following, the MOST valid inference based on this statement is that an additional important function of the correctional institution is to

    A. give inmates an insight into the problems and conflicts of well-adjusted people
    B. prepare inmates for employment in useful work
    C. train inmates in proper use of leisure time
    D. train inmates to strike a proper balance between work and rest

17.____

18. All the processes in a correctional institution should be directed toward educating the individual for successful community living.
    Of the following, the factor that contributes MOST to making this task a difficult one is the

    A. absence of a clear definition as to what constitutes successful community living
    B. conflict of interest between community and institution
    C. competitive nature of modern-day community life
    D. need to change unacceptable behavior patterns into patterns acceptable to the community

18.____

19. It has been recommended that the work-week of inmates employed in a program of prison industries be the same as the work-week for similar employment in private industry. From the standpoint of the major objectives of a prison industries program, the adoption of this recommendation is desirable MAINLY for the reason

    A. it will make possible the inclusion of a wider variety of employments in the prison industries program
    B. it will tend to make the deterrent objective of imprisonment more effective
    C. the prison industries will then be more profitable to operate since production will be greater
    D. the rehabilitative process will be aided if conditions of work approach those in real life

19.____

20. The work assignment of inmates should be based on other factors in addition to their request for particular assignments.
    Of the following, the LEAST important reason for this is that the inmates may

20.____

4 (#2)

33

A. have questionable motives for requesting particular assignments
B. make a better adjustment to their assignments if they are in accord with their wishes
C. request assignments for which no additional institutional help is required
D. not be fitted for the work requested

21. Classification is a dynamic process. According to this statement, it would be MOST reasonable to assume that, in the classification process,

   A. an inmate's treatment program should be modified in accordance with the changing needs of the inmate
   B. an inmate's treatment program should be carefully planned to avoid the need for changes, or the inmate's cooperation will be lost
   C. interference with, or interruption of, an inmate's treatment program will have serious results
   D. there are very many contributing elements, all equally important, and all of which must operate at maximum efficiency

22. The present trend in penology is to liberalize visiting privileges for inmates as much as possible. However, the MOST important factor that keeps many prison officials from going along with this trend is the fear that liberal prison-visiting will

   A. increase the danger of the introduction of contraband into the prison
   B. interfere with the operation of normal prison routines
   C. lead to a breakdown of prison discipline
   D. require major alteration in existing prison facilities for visiting

23. An IMPORTANT rule to be observed in the carrying out of an institutional program of inmate activities and privileges is :
Do not

   A. curtail or revoke any inmate activity or privilege after it has been instituted
   B. give privileges to one inmate which cannot be earned in the proper way by any other inmate
   C. make any activity or privilege too pleasurable for the inmate
   D. use the program as an aid to the maintenance of discipline

24. Of the following, the MOST important reason for issuing standard prison clothing to all inmates of a sentence institution, rather than permitting them to wear their own civilian clothing, is that it

   A. contributes to the maintenance of better discipline among inmates
   B. eliminates economic differences among inmates which might otherwise lead to friction
   C. is virtually impossible to properly search and sterilize all civilian clothing of all inmates
   D. make it easier for the public to recognized an escaped inmate

25. With respect to the operation of a parole system, correctional authorities generally OPPOSE the
    A. application of strict rules forbidding the parole of persons convicted of certain serious offenses, such as first degree murder and kidnapping
    B. principle that prisoners released from long-term institutions after earning sufficient good time should be released on parole
    C. release of short-time prisoners on parole
    D. requirement of service of a minimum period of imprisonment of reasonable proportions before an inmate becomes eligible for parole

KEY (CORRECT ANSWERS)

1. A
2. D
3. D
4. B
5. D

6. D
7. A
8. B
9. A
10. D

11. C
12. D
13. A
14. D
15. B

16. D
17. C
18. D
19. D
20. B

21. A
22. A
23. B
24. B
25. A

TEST 3

DIRECTIONS: Each question or incomplete statement is followed by several suggested answers or completions. Select the one that BEST answers the question or completes the statement. *PRINT THE LETTER OF THE CORRECT ANSWER IN THE SPACE AT THE RIGHT.*

1. It is generally agreed among penologists that the system of communication in an institution should make it possible for any inmate to bring what seems to him an important problem to the attention of an appropriate staff member with the least possible delay. However, a DANGER to be guarded against in this connection is

   A. the artificial separation of lines of authority
   B. a sudden breakdown of administrative control
   C. a lack of coordination between professional and custodial staff
   D. the misuse of the privilege by unstable inmate personalities

2. The one of the following which is NOT an advantage of removing certain classes of inmates from the regular type of prison to outside work on camps and farm colonies is the

   A. ending of direct contact between these inmates and the more undesirable elements in a prison
   B. gradual easing of some of the tensions of prison life for these inmates
   C. removal of the stigma of a prison sentence from these inmates
   D. reduction of inmate idleness in the regular prison

3. The suggestion has been advanced that in correctional systems the parole board be made a part of the department of correction.
   Of the following, the CHIEF argument in support of this suggestion is:

   A. The fullest independence of the parole function and freedom of interference or influence from any source is desirable
   B. Lay persons are not sufficiently familiar with correctional problems and procedures to be able to perform this function effectively
   C. Since parole is really an extension of the sentence begun in the correctional institution, close integration of the two services is logically desirable
   D. The number of persons placed on parole is not sufficiently large to make administratively feasible the existence of an independent agency

4. It has been stated that the quality of the staff in a correctional institution is more important than the physical facilities of the institution.
   This statement is MOST probably based on the belief that

   A. a basic change in the character of the inmate can be brought about only as a result of the influence and guidance of the staff
   B. a competent staff can achieve excellent results without regard to the physical facilities available
   C. no institution can be run without a staff
   D. the physical facilities of an institution are not important when the staff is highly competent

5. In the *cottage* type of correctional institution for women, it is usually considered unnecessary and inappropriate to have disciplinary and custodial controls of the kind customarily found in an institution for men.
   Of the following, the factor that is LEAST significant in contributing to this difference in this type of women's institution is the

   A. comparative openness of the cottage type institution
   B. difference in preparation and training of the staff
   C. more personal and closer relationship between inmates and staff
   D. small inmate population

6. A feature that makes the *cottage* type institution particularly suitable for female offenders is the

   A. extensive facilities it has for outdoor recreation
   B. opportunities it affords for homemaking activities
   C. practicability of locating near urban centers
   D. privacy offered each individual inmate

7. All correctional institutions for women must accept offenders ranging in age from girls to senile women, and presenting a wide range of sentences and offenses, backgrounds, and training and treatment needs.
   This is so MAINLY for the reason that

   A. female offenders, no less than male offenders, are necessarily different in their characteristics and backgrounds
   B. there is an absence and lack of understanding of modern classification procedures
   C. sentencing is a function of the courts, which are neither greatly concerned with nor very much aware of the problem of the correctional administrator
   D. the comparatively small number of women prisoners does not make economically feasible the establishment of diversified institutions for women

8. In the carrying forward of a vocational training program in a women's correctional institution, it will MOST likely be found that those women who have never engaged in systematic training of any kind will

   A. be least eager to participate
   B. be the best learners
   C. have a short interest and concentration span
   D. not make suitable material for such a program

9. Of the following, it is MOST important that the outdoor recreation provided in a correctional institution for women be, so far as possible,

   A. of a competitive, group nature
   B. of the same basic kind and variety as the outdoor recreational activities in an institution for men
   C. of the type that the women can engage in after leaving the institution
   D. limited to non-strenous activities

10. Of the following, a course that it is particularly important to include in the education program of a correctional institution for women, more so than in a similar program of a correctional institution for men, is a course in

   A. bookkeeping
   B. child guidance
   C. office practice
   D. 3 R's

11. In a correctional institution, inmate discipline is directly associated with morale.
   Of the following, the CHIEF implication of this statement for the commanding officer is that

   A. disciplinary problems are best solved by increasing the inmate's morale
   B. where morale is high, discipline will be maintained more easily
   C. where morale is low, discipline will be found to be lax
   D. where strict disciplinary measures are enforced, morale will be high

12. So small a percentage of all offenders are caught and convicted that what happens to them can have little effect on the great body of potential and actual violators of the law. This statement places GREATEST doubt on the value of _____ as an objective of imprisonment.

   A. deterrence
   B. punishment
   C. reformation
   D. rehabilitation

13. Suppose that case studies show that rejection by members of an inmate's family has a depressing effect on the inmate's morale.
   This fact can be used MOST constructively in correctional work to

   A. allow additional privileges to inmates with close family ties
   B. bring family influences to bear in assisting in the inmate's rehabilitation
   C. deny mail and visiting privileges for disciplinary reasons only as a last resort
   D. reveal other media that can be employed to boost the morale of an inmate with no family ties

14. It has been stated that, in the final analysis, the soundest security measure of all is the existence of a positive program of inmate activities.
   Of the following, the CHIEF justification for this statement is the fact that

   A. a good program of inmate activities will point up the need for correction of certain security weaknesses which might not otherwise be apparent
   B. inmates engaged in such a program of activities seldom resort to disturbances or escape attempts
   C. security without rehabilitation through an inmate program is not a lasting solution to the crime problem
   D. since security is the primary responsibility of the institution, it must be guaranteed by all institutional programs

15. To say that an inmate is psychotic implies MOST directly that the inmate

   A. has a split personality
   B. has suicidal tendencies
   C. is mentally deranged
   D. is of low mentality

16. It is a function of the Grand Jury to

A. determine whether a crime has been committed
B. determine whether a defendant is guilty of a crime
C. secure the evidence necessary to bring an accused to trial
D. take testimony from the district attorney and his witnesses as well as from the defendant and his witnesses

17. Of the following, the factor that is LEAST significant in making the problem of custody and control in a trial prison more difficult than in a sentence prison is the   17.____

    A. comparative absence of program for inmates in a trial prison
    B. different educational and social background of inmates in a trial prison
    C. different legal status of trial inmates
    D. heterogeneity of inmates in a trial prison

18. Of the trial inmates confined in the detention prisons, a comparison of inmates charged with misdemeanors with inmates charged with felonies shows that, generally, those charged with   18.____

    A. felonies are confined for shorter periods of time while awaiting trial
    B. misdemeanors are easier to control as a group
    C. felonies are in poorer physical condition
    D. misdemeanors have a lower rate of recidivism

19. With respect to communication between trial inmates and their relatives or friends on the outside, the commanding officer should advise correction officers that   19.____

    A. they must closely supervise all telephone calls made by trial inmates
    B. they must make all the entries on the telephone message form carefully as it is a permanent record
    C. inmates who do not have the money to pay for a call must be given stationery to communicate by mail
    D. the right of such communication is guaranteed to trial inmates by law

Questions 20-25.

DIRECTIONS: For each book title in Column I below, select the author of the book from Column II; then write the capital letter preceding the author's name in the appropriate space at the right.

Column I

Column II

20. CONTEMPORARY CORRECTION

    A. Alexander, Myrl E.
    B. Barnes, Harry E.

    20.____

21. CRIMINOLOGY, A CULTURAL INTERPRETATION

    C. Fenton, Norman
    D. Glueck, Sheldon and Eleanor

    21.____

22. FIVE HUNDRED DELINQUENT WOMEN

    E. Lindner, Robert M. and Seliger, Robert V.
    F. MacCormick, Austin H.

    22.____

23. JAIL ADMINISTRATION

    G. Pigeon, Helen D.
    H. Scudder, Kenyon J.

    23.____

24. PRINCIPLES AND METHODS IN DEALING WITH OFFENDERS   J. Taft, Donald R.   24.____

25. PRISONERS ARE PEOPLE   K. Tappan, Paul W.   25.____

KEY (CORRECT ANSWERS)

1. D   11. B
2. C   12. A
3. C   13. B
4. A   14. B
5. B   15. C

6. B   16. A
7. D   17. B
8. C   18. B
9. C   19. D
10. B   20. K

21. J
22. D
23. A
24. G
25. H

EXAMINATION SECTION
TEST 1

DIRECTIONS: Each question or incomplete statement is followed by several suggested answers or completions. Select the one that BEST answers the question or completes the statement. *PRINT THE LETTER OF THE CORRECT ANSWER IN THE SPACE AT THE RIGHT.*

1. In the ten years from 1970 to 1980, in the nation as a whole, the

    A. number of major crimes remained constant but the number of lesser offenses increased markedly
    B. percentage increase in population was greater than the percentage increase in major crimes
    C. percentage increase in population was smaller than the percentage increase in major crimes
    D. percentage increase in population equaled the percentage increase in major crimes

1._____

2. According to figures released, major crimes in the period of 1980-1985, compared with the period of 1975-1980,

    A. decreased slightly
    B. remained steady
    C. showed an increase of less than one quarter
    D. showed an increase of more than one third

2._____

3. During the late 60's, major prison riots occurred in the states of

    A. New York and New Jersey
    B. Michigan and Ohio
    C. New Jersey and Washington
    D. Washington and Michigan

3._____

4. The Annual Congress of Correction is held every year in a

    A. city   B. town   C. village   D. seaport

4._____

5. The book MY SIX CONVICTS

    A. has its setting in a state prison
    B. is a completely factual autobiography
    C. was unfavorably received by penologists
    D. was written by a former warden

5._____

Questions 6-10.

DIRECTIONS: For each book in Column I, select the author of the book from Column II; then write the letter preceding the author's name in the appropriate space at the right.

41

COLUMN I	COLUMN II
6. Jails - Care and Treatment of Misdemeanant Prisoners in the United States	A. Barnes, Harry E. and Teeters, Negley K.
7. New Horizons in Criminology	B. Glueck, Sheldon and Eleanor
8. Probation and Parole	C. Harris, Mary B
9. The Training of Prison Guards in the State of New York	D. Monahan, Florence
	E. Pigeon, Helen D.
10. Women in Crime	F. Robinson, Louis N.
	G. Wallack, Walter M.

11. A person with a *psychopathic personality* is

   A. consistently abnormal in his behavior
   B. feebleminded
   C. insane and has criminal tendencies
   D. psychotic

12. A person is considered to be of normal intelligence if his IQ or intelligence quotient falls within the range of

   A. 60-80   B. 70-90   C. 80-100   D. 90-110

13. The term *malingerer* is MOST correctly applied to an inmate wh

   A. bears an officer a grudge for a long time
   B. is a habitual liar
   C. pretends to be ill in order to avoid working
   D. takes a long time to recover from an illness

14. The MOST accurate of the following statements about the County Grand Jury is:

   A. Considers evidence to determine if a crime has been committed
   B. Is composed of 12 persons
   C. Is sworn in for an indefinite period of service
   D. Serves at the call of the Chief Magistrate and the District Attorney

15. The one of the following which is NOT a function of the Criminal Courts in the city is

   A. holding a defendant charged with a misdemeanor for the Court of Special Sessions if the evidence indicates that he has committed the crime charged
   B. sitting as a Court of Special Sessions in certain misdemeanor cases
   C. trying defendants charged with felonies
   D. trying defendants charged with minor traffic violations

16. In the city, the Night Court is a branch of

   A. County Court   B. Supreme Court
   C. Civil Court   D. Criminal Court

17. Members of the uniformed force of the Department of Correction are designated as peace officers by the

    A. Administrative Code
    B. City Charter
    C. Code of Criminal Procedure
    D. Penal Law

18. In the city, jurisdiction over court detention pens is vested in the Department of Correction by the

    A. Administrative Code   B. City Charter
    C. Correction Law   D. Penal Law

19. Of the following State institutions, the one which houses MAINLY female defective delinquents is the

    A. Albion State Training School
    B. Institution for Defective Delinquents at Napanoch
    C. Westfield State Farm
    D. Woodbourne Institution for Defective Delinquents

20. According to the Penal Law, escape from lawful imprisonment is always a

    A. felony
    B. felony if the imprisonment was for a felony
    C. misdemeanor
    D. misdemeanor if the imprisonment was for a felony

21. A writ or order by a Magistrate, Justice or other competent authority and addressed to an officer requiring him to arrest the person named therein and bring him before the Court to be examined regarding the offense with which he is charged. The preceding definition refers MOST directly to a

    A. certificate of reasonable doubt
    B. mandamus
    C. warrant
    D. writ of habeas corpus

22. From 2000 to 2005, inclusive, the inmate census in the Department

    A. decreased steadily   B. fluctuated up and down
    C. increased steadily   D. remained almost constant

23. In 2005, the average daily inmate census in the Department was between

    A. 5,500 and 10,000   B. 4,500 and 5,500
    C. 3,500 and 4,500   D. 2,500 and 3,500

24. The MOST accurate of the following statements about the offenses for which prisoners were sentenced to the institutions of the Department last year is that the

    A. largest number of male commitments was for disorderly conduct whereas the largest number of female commitments was for vagrancy (prostitution)
    B. largest number of male commitments was for vagrancy whereas the largest number of female commitments was for disorderly conduct

C. number of women committed for drug offenses was about 50% of the number of men committed for drug offenses
D. second largest number of male commitments was for gambling whereas the second largest number of female commitments was for petty larceny

25. Of the inmates committed to the Department last year, the average age of the inmates committed to the workhouse as compared to the average age of the inmates committed to the penitentiary was

    A. higher
    B. higher for male commitments but lower for female commitments
    C. lower
    D. neither higher nor lower

26. Of all the inmates sentenced to the institutions of the Department last year, those who had any education beyond the elementary school constituted between

    A. 15% and 20%   B. 10% and 15%
    C. 5% and 10%   D. 0% and 5%

27. Last year, the average rate of recidivism among workhouse and penitentiary inmates (men and women) in the institutions of the Department was

    A. between 50% and 60%
    B. less than 30%
    C. more than 30% but less than 55%
    D. more than 60% but less than 75%

28. Of all workhouse sentences to the Department in 1985, definite workhouse sentences of 6 months or less (men and women) constituted

    A. between 75% and 80%   B. between 80% and 90%
    C. less than 75%   D. more than 95%

29. During the fiscal year 1984-1985, the average daily food cost per prisoner in the institutions of the Department was between

    A. 50? and $1.00   B. $1.00 and $2.00
    C. $2.00 and $3.00   D. $3.00 and $4.00

30. In the detention prisons of the Department, persons charged with felonies GENERALLY constitute

    A. about half of the inmate population
    B. a majority of the inmate population
    C. a minority of the inmate population
    D. less of a discipline problem than persons charged with misdemeanors

31. A uniformed member of the city police department may interview a trial inmate in a Department of Correction institution if he presents a

    A. police department form properly filled out and a special Department of Correction pass
    B. police department form properly filled out and signs a consent form which is also signed by the inmate

C. special Department of Correction pass and a consent form signed by himself and the inmate
D. special Department of Correction pass and a letter of authorization signed by the police commissioner or his authorized representative

32. When an inmate enters the custody of the Department, certain forms are filled out. Of these forms, the ones which must always accompany the inmate while he is in the custody of the Department are the _____ card and _____ card.

    A. commitment; accompanying
    B. commitment; pedigree
    C. registration; accompanying
    D. registration card, accompanying; commitment

33. A correction officer in charge of a court detention pen should be instructed by the captain that when a police officer delivers a prisoner to the court pen, the correction officer should

    A. enter in the *police blotter* the name, shield number, command and time of arrival of the police officer and the prisoner's name and sex
    B. fill out an arraignment card and complaint form
    C. require the police officer to present a valid commitment signed by a Magistrate
    D. search the prisoner and turn over to the police officer any articles of contraband

34. In the Department, *jail time* is

    A. figured from the day of admission on a charge to and including the day of sentence
    B. not considered in determining the length of custody under an indefinite sentence
    C. not deducted from the time to be served if the sentence includes an alternative fine
    D. the amount of time in days that an inmate has been confined in the custody of the Department

35. The LEAST accurate of the following statements is that a

    A. commitment under an alternate sentence of a fine or a definite term can be made both to the workhouse and to the penitentiary
    B. maximum workhouse definite sentence is for a longer period than a maximum penitentiary definite sentence
    C. maximum workhouse indefinite sentence is for a shorter period than a maximum penitentiary indefinite sentence
    D. minimum penitentiary definite sentence is for a longer period than a minimum workhouse definite sentence

36. The LEAST accurate of the following statements about time off for good behavior in the institutions of the Department is that

    A. penitentiary definite sentences of 3 months or more are allowed 5 days good time per month
    B. penitentiary indefinite sentences are allowed 5 days good time per month
    C. workhouse definite sentences of 30 days or more, where no alternative fine is imposed, are allowed 5 days good time per month
    D. workhouse indefinite sentences are allowed 5 days good time per month

37. If an inmate is committed to the Department by a judge for more than one charge, 37.____

    A. all charges must be stated on the one commitment
    B. duplicate records must be kept at the institution for each charge
    C. separate commitments are always required for each charge
    D. separate commitments are required only if the inmate must answer to each charge in a different court

38. A *short commitment* is a commitment issued by a judge wherein the defendant is 38.____

    A. held for future action in the Criminal Courts
    B. held for the Court of Special Sessions
    C. held for the Grand Jury
    D. sentenced by the judge for the offense committed

39. A defendant was committed to the Department by a judge for a future hearing. After the hearing, the defendant was re-committed for another hearing by a judge. In this case, 39.____

    A. a new commitment must be issued by the judge
    B. the issuance of a new commitment is at the discretion of the judge
    C. the original commitment is designated as the superseding commitment
    D. the original commitment is still valid

40. When the arresting officer calls for an inmate to produce the inmate in court to answer to the charge, it is important that he be informed by the pen officer of any warrants against the inmate MAINLY because 40.____

    A. it may be necessary to produce the warrants in court together with the inmate
    B. the inmate may be released on the original charge
    C. the warrants may be for more serious offenses than the present arrest
    D. this information will help to identify the inmate

41. When a prisoner is committed on a direct admission, the officer at the detention pen is required to note on the back of the commitment the condition of the inmate at the time when taken into custody by the Department. Of the following, the PRINCIPAL reason why this information is important is that 41.____

    A. a comparison can be made at the time of release to see if any improvement has been made
    B. drug addicts and alcoholics can be noted and segregated
    C. it may influence the determination as to which institution the inmate is to be transferred
    D. subsequent charges that an inmate was mistreated while in the Department's custody can be refuted

42. The pen officer shall make a thorough inspection of the court pens at the beginning of the tour every day. In the court pens operated by the Department, this thorough inspection is very important MAINLY because the pens are 42.____

    A. directly accessible from the street
    B. not escape-proof
    C. not under the supervision of Department of Correction personnel at all times
    D. very antiquated for the most part compared with other facilities for housing prisoners

43. When opening or closing a mechanically operated cell door, the officer should, after setting the door in motion, stop such motion for a fraction of a second and then complete the movement of the door. Of the following, the BEST reason for operating a mechanical cell door in the manner described in the statement is that the

    A. door will not function properly unless it is operated in this way
    B. obstructions in the path of the door can be removed in time
    C. officer can observe if the door is operating properly
    D. fast inmate is warned to get in or out of the cell immediately

43.____

44. Detention prisons house mainly prisoners awaiting trial, A house gang of sentenced inmates is often transferred to a detention prison to do maintenance work throughout the institution. Of the following, the GREATEST potential danger from such a house gang is that its members will

    A. gain control over inmates awaiting trial by claiming to be *in the know*
    B. have too many opportunities for escape
    C. pass contraband to inmates awaiting trial
    D. upset prison discipline by fighting with inmates awaiting trial

44.____

45. It is important that the tier officer be notified as soon as possible of any change in an inmate's court status MAINLY because

    A. a change in an inmate's court status may necessitate a change in custodial supervision
    B. prison records to be of value must be accurate and up-to-date
    C. subordinates should not be able to justify errors
    D. of judgment on the grounds of ignorance of the facts
    E. the tier officer, who supervises many inmates, may find it difficult to remember every detail of each inmate's status

45.____

46. The importance of full and complete fact-finding by the correction officer assigned to getting the newly admitted prisoner's pedigree cannot be too greatly stressed. Of the following, the BEST justification for this statement is that

    A. a job worth doing at all is worth doing well
    B. the correction officer will be held responsible for the completeness and correctness of the information obtained
    C. the information so obtained will be used to identify the inmate in the future
    D. incomplete information is of little value

46.____

47. Department procedure requires the keeping of complete and permanent records of all telephone calls made by inmates. Of the following, the BEST justification for this requirement is that

    A. an excessive number of calls by any inmate will be revealed and can be investigated
    B. attempts by inmates to communicate illegally with outside persons can be controlled
    C. the records can be used to refute charges by an inmate that the privilege of making telephone calls was denied
    D. while an inmate may make only one free call, other calls paid for by the inmate are not limited to number

47.____

48. When a police line-up is conducted for the purpose of identification of an inmate by a witness, it is MOST desirable that the

   A. inmates selected for the line-up be informed of the reason for their selection
   B. inmate to be identified be dressed in the clothes worn on admission to the institution
   C. other inmates in the line-up be of a different general appearance than the inmate to be identified
   D. police officer who brought the witness to the institution be present at the line-up at the time the identification is made

49. The presence of any sanitation equipment, such as mops and buckets, in the cells of inmates is prohibited. Of the following, the BEST justification for this rule is that

   A. many inmates are not concerned about taking good care of prison equipment
   B. such equipment should be available for use by all inmates
   C. the presence of such equipment in cells detracts from the neat appearance of the institution
   D. the ready availability of such equipment may tempt an inmate to use it in an attack

50. The newly sentenced inmate in the institutions of the Department is usually more relaxed mentally than the inmate awaiting trial. Of the following, the MAJOR reason for this is that the newly sentenced inmate

   A. has formed friendships with other inmates in similar circumstances
   B. is able to receive regular visits from family members
   C. is no longer uncertain as to the immediate future
   D. realizes that good behavior may earn a reduction in time

KEY (CORRECT ANSWERS)

1. C	11. A	21. C	31. B	41. D
2. D	12. D	22. C	32. D	42. C
3. A	13. C	23. A	33. D	43. B
4. A	14. A	24. A	34. C	44. C
5. C	15. C	25. A	35. B	45. A
6. F	16. D	26. D	36. A	46. C
7. A	17. C	27. C	37. C	47. C
8. E	18. B	28. D	38. A	48. B
9. G	19. A	29. D	39. A	49. D
10. D	20. B	30. B	40. B	50. C

TEST 2

DIRECTIONS: Each question or incomplete statement is followed by several suggested answers or completions. Select the one that BEST answers the question or completes the statement. *PRINT THE LETTER OF THE CORRECT ANSWER IN THE SPACE AT THE RIGHT.*

1. Of the following, the PRIMARY factor governing the assignment of an inmate to work in a penitentiary should be   1.____

    A. his intelligence
    B. his previous work experience
    C. his vocational plans after release
    D. the special training he requires
    E. the degree of custody required

2. Shackles, the lock step, prison stripes, and enforced silence are almost entirely out of vogue. Of the following, the CHIEF objection to such correctional procedures is that they   2.____

    A. are difficult to enforce
    B. are detrimental to the inmate after release from prison
    C. make prison discipline more difficult to control
    D. require a large and well trained staff if they are to be utilized effectively
    E. are very unpopular with inmates

3. The releasing officer questioned the prisoner about to be released concerning such personal details as the address of his mother and his father's first name. Of the following, the BEST explanation of the releasing officer's behavior is that   3.____

    A. there were probably errors in the prison records
    B. prisoners often change their stories after a period of time
    C. it sometimes happens that the wrong prisoner is released
    D. rehabilitation of an inmate requires personal attention at every stage of the correctional process
    E. prisoners are occasionally not sufficiently well oriented to be released

4. Frequently, the man who makes an ideal inmate in the penitentiary does not make an ideal parolee when released. Of the following, the BEST justification for this statement is that   4.____

    A. adjustment to prison life is in many respects more complex than adjustment to civilian life
    B. high moral standards tend to remain well established once they have been developed
    C. prison-wise inmates are often on their best behavior while they remain in prison
    D. prison constitutes an acid test and no man is ordinarily paroled unless he passes this test
    E. there is no such thing as an ideal inmate, each inmate is an individual

5. Suppose that a judge, on the basis of the chief medical officer's petition and the examiner's certificate of lunacy, signs an order for the transfer of an inmate to a state hospital for the criminally insane. The inmate must be transferred within   5.____

A. 24 hours after receipt of the order
B. 15 days after the signing of the order
C. 48 hours after receipt of the order
D. 10 days after the signing of the order
E. a reasonable period of time fixed at the discretion of the warden

6. The one of the following items of information concerning an inmate which is NOT recorded on the BACK of the commitment when the inmate is received at a correctional institution is the

   A. name of the committing judge
   B. age of the inmate
   C. religion of the inmate
   D. name of the nearest relative of the inmate
   E. apparent physical condition of the prisoner

7. Of the following, the MOST accurate statement concerning bonds, notes, or certificates accepted for bail at a city prison is that

   A. one bond, note, or certificate may be accepted for two or more cases
   B. registered bonds may be accepted
   C. part cash and part securities may be accepted
   D. bonds, notes, or certificates may be accepted only in such denominations as to make the sum of the bail in each case
   E. securities must be in coupon or bearer form only, with all coupons detached

8. The one of the following cases in which probation is likely to be MOST effective is the case of the

   A. sex pervert
   B. elderly recidivist
   C. chronic alcoholic
   D. young first offender
   E. young hardened criminal

9. The common age limits for reformatories are USUALLY

   A. 16 to 30
   B. 12 to 18
   C. 19 to 25
   D. 12 to 40
   E. 19 to 21

10. The one of the following which is NOT a type of commitment received at city prisons is

    A. Short Form
    B. Magistrates' General
    C. Mental Observation
    D. Material Witness
    E. Bail Surrender

11. MOST of the writs of Habeas Corpus served upon the warden of Riker's Island are returnable in

    A. Felony Court
    B. the Court of Appeals
    C. Criminal Court
    D. the Appellate Division
    E. the Supreme Court, Bronx County

3 (#2)

12. Henry Doe is sentenced on April 4, 2008 in the Supreme Court for the crime of second degree assault, to serve 6 months in the penitentiary. He is received at the penitentiary on April 6, when the sentence begins. He has spent twenty days in jail awaiting trial. The length of time on which commutation is allowed is _____ months _____ days.   12._____

　　A. 5; 9　　　B. 5; 28　　　C. 6; 0　　　D. 6; 2　　　E. 6; 20

13. Suppose that John Doe is sentenced on June 16, 2008 on a paternity charge to serve one year in the workhouse, or place a bond of $500. Of the following, the MOST accurate statement under these circumstances is that   13._____

　　A. he will be discharged on June 17, 2008 if no bond is placed
　　B. he will be allowed 5 days off for each month of good behavior
　　C. he will be allowed 2 days a month good time for good behavior
　　D. a minimum of at least 30 days must be served even if bond is placed
　　E. the institution is not empowered to accept a cash bond in this type of case

14. Henry Doe is sentenced on September 1 to serve 5 months and 29 days in the workhouse for disorderly conduct. With full time off for good behavior, his time will be up on _____ of the following year.   14._____

　　A. January 28　　　B. February 4　　　C. February 9
　　D. February 20　　　E. March 1

15. Of the following, the LEAST accurate statement concerning the time served by an inmate is that   15._____

　　A. should the day of discharge fall on a Sunday, the inmate is discharged the day before
　　B. should the day of discharge fall on a holiday, the inmate is discharged the day before
　　C. no credit is allowed for time awaiting trial in any fine case
　　D. time served in a fine case may be prorated on the basis of the amount of fine paid
　　E. good time is allowed only on a sentence of 30 days or more

16. Of the following, the MOST accurate statement concerning the time to be served before an inmate may be released on parole is that in the case of   16._____

　　A. penitentiary indefinite sentences, the date of discharge is fixed by the committing judge
　　B. workhouse indefinite sentences, the date of discharge is fixed by the committing judge
　　C. penitentiary indefinite sentences the time to be served is fixed by the Parole Commission with the written consent of the committing judge
　　D. reformatory cases, the time to be served is fixed by the committing judge
　　E. penitentiary definite sentences, the time to be served is fixed by the Parole Commission

17. The approval of the Governor of the State must be received before release or discharge, with commutation for good time, of _____ cases.   17._____

　　A. penitentiary definite　　　B. penitentiary indefinite
　　C. workhouse definite　　　D. workhouse indefinite
　　E. both penitentiary indefinite and workhouse indefinite

18. The *Auburn System* refers MOST accurately to the practice of 18.____

    A. having inmates work in shops during the day and keeping them in individual cells at night
    B. keeping prisoners in solitary confinement most of the time
    C. classifying and segregating prisoners according to their needs
    D. establishing inmate councils elected by the inmates themselves
    E. establishing minimum security institutions without walls

19. The indeterminate sentence applies to the vast majority of penitentiary commitments and 19.____
    to a relatively small number of workhouse sentences. Penitentiary indeterminate sentences are for a maximum of _____ years.

    A. 1   B. 2   C. 3   D. 4   E. 5

20. The *Bertillon record,* in connection with a newly received inmate, refers MOST accurately 20.____
    to his

    A. medical history   B. court record
    C. commitment papers   D. physical measurements
    E. fingerprints

21. Of the following, the MOST accurate statement concerning sentences in the city is that 21.____
    _____ sentences are _____ only.

    A. workhouse; definite   B. penitentiary; indefinite
    C. workhouse; indefinite   D. penitentiary; definite
    E. reformatory; indefinite

22. Walkill is BEST described as a(n) 22.____

    A. major receiving institution for the western part of the state
    B. institution for mental defectives
    C. institution for the criminally insane
    D. centralized prison hospital
    E. institution for the re-training of men about to be released

23. The State *Use* Plan refers MOST accurately to 23.____

    A. vocational guidance for juvenile delinquents
    B. inspection of local correctional institutions by the State
    C. disposal of goods manufactured by prison labor
    D. a method of classifying prisoners
    E. determination of the actual length of indeterminate sentences

24. The non-self-contained gas mask used in the Department of Correction is LEAST effec- 24.____
    tive

    A. against phosgene gas
    B. against chlorine gas
    C. against carbon monoxide gas
    D. in an atmosphere containing less than 16% oxygen
    E. in an atmosphere containing more than 50% of combined poisonous gases

25. Suppose that a correction officer has been exposed to tear gas. As his superior officer, you should recommend that he bathe his eyes with a solution of

   A. baking soda
   B. gentian violet
   C. boric acid
   D. tannic acid
   E. epsom salts

26. The use of the liquid type of tear gas has been discontinued in the Department of Correction in favor of the crystal type CHIEFLY because the liquid type

   A. will not rise more than 12 or 15 feet above the ground
   B. forms a vapor which is heavier than air
   C. is too mild to be greatly effective
   D. deteriorates rapidly in storage
   E. is too heavily concentrated

27. Prison officers must constantly exercise vigilance that poisonous insecticides are not stored, even temporarily, near foodstuffs. The one of the following insecticides to which the above statement is ESPECIALLY pertinent is

   A. sodium fluoride
   B. red squill
   C. finely powdered borax
   D. a spray made with odorless kerosene
   E. a spray made with pyrethrum

28. In the city, a self-committed drug addict MOST usually serves a term of

   A. 30 days
   B. 60 days
   C. 100 days
   D. 6 months
   E. 8 months

29. The number of days per month commutation for good behavior allowed by law to penitentiary definite cases in the State is

   A. 1   B. 3   C. 5   D. 7   E. 10

30. It is desirable that courts have discretion in determining penalties in criminal cases MAINLY in order to

   A. make the punishment fit the gravity of the crime
   B. deter possible offenders
   C. curb interference from the courts
   D. encourage more widespread use of probation
   E. adjust the punishment to the crime, the offender, and the circumstances

31. Inmate John Jones is aged 45. He has had only two years of elementary school and is unable to read or write. Because of this disability, he is shy and lacks confidence in himself. For the correction officer assigned to classification to recommend that this inmate be given additional schooling would be

   A. *foolish*; he is obviously too old
   B. *wise*; he has insufficient education to make a good moral adjustment
   C. *foolish*; his intelligence is obviously too low
   D. *wise*; his confidence in himself would be increased
   E. *foolish*; he has already had more years of education than he can expect to obtain in prison

32. The correction officer will usually find correlation of human traits rather than compensation. On the basis of this statement, the correction officer should expect a mentally defective prisoner to be

    A. talented in some single respect
    B. able to learn a skilled trade in prison more easily than a highly intelligent prisoner
    C. less adept at manual skill than a highly intelligent prisoner
    D. well adjusted from a personality viewpoint
    E. equally competent in all respects

33. A representative group of young criminals in a certain state were found to be normal in intelligence, but 86% were retarded from one to six grades in school. Of the following, the BEST inference from these data is that

    A. lack of intelligence is highly correlated with delinquency
    B. criminals should be removed from the school system as soon as possible
    C. educational maladjustments are closely associated with delinquency
    D. the usual rate at which criminals progress educationally represents the limit of their learning powers
    E. in virtually any group of young persons there is little relationship between intellectual capacity and scholastic achievement

34. Many years ago, the establishment of the Children's Court was hailed as the solution to juvenile delinquency. And yet, the rate of juvenile delinquency has continued to increase. The one of the following which is LEAST valid as a possible explanation of the apparent failure of Children's Courts to reduce the rate of juvenile delinquency is that

    A. the emphasis has been chiefly on correction after the crime rather than on crime prevention
    B. inadequate funds and facilities have been provided for these courts
    C. the number of children in the population has increased in proportion to the population increase
    D. there has been a general crime increase over a period of years due to general social insecurity
    E. insufficient attention has been given to the remedying of environmental and family conditions leading to crime

35. To base a generalization regarding the causation of criminal behavior on a comparison of prison inmates with a civilian group is defective MAINLY because

    A. prison inmates comprise those criminals who have been convicted
    B. quantitative analysis is a misleading type of approach
    C. prison inmates do not include misdemeanants
    D. generalizations tend to be meaningless abstractions
    E. causation of criminal behavior is an individual matter

36. The purpose of a prison is the keeping in custody of individuals who may, because of their criminal behavior, be a menace to the persons and property of free citizens. This function of the correctional institution, however, is only half the job. Of the following, the CHIEF implication of the above statement is that

A. individuals may be expected to show criminal behavior even in prison
B. criminal behavior is a menace to the person and property of free citizens
C. the chief purpose of a prison is accomplished when the prisoner is removed from society
D. persons who are truly a menace to society have little chance for rehabilitation
E. influences must be brought to bear on the prisoner which will tend to prevent him from resorting again to criminal behavior when released

37. The one of the following parole procedures which has proven MOST effective in preventing recidivism is that

    A. no person is paroled unless he has served at least half his sentence
    B. every person paroled is required to write his parole officer at least once every three months
    C. no person is paroled unless he has a job waiting for him
    D. no person is paroled who has a record of a previous conviction
    E. a juvenile delinquent is paroled only in the custody of his parent or guardian

38. One can only see what one observes, and one observes only things which are already in the mind. Of the following, the CHIEF implication of this statement for the correction officer is that

    A. observation, to be effective, should be directed and conscious
    B. all aspects of a situation, unless the correction officer exercises caution, are likely to strike him with equal forcefulness
    C. memory is essentially perception one step removed from observation
    D. observation should be essentially indirect if it is to be accurate
    E. the mind observes and remembers each object seen, whether consciously or not

39. A promise to a subordinate is more important in a system of discipline than a promise to a superior. Of the following, the BEST justification for the above statement is that

    A. subordinates are generally in no position to make promises to superiors
    B. there is no obligation to make promises to subordinates
    C. discipline cannot be maintained if promises are broken
    D. discipline rests essentially on the respect of subordinates for their superior
    E. superiors are in a position to order whatever action is required

40. Suppose that you are a supervisor. A correction officer under your supervision submits to you a written recommendation concerning administrative procedure. You believe that the objective is worthwhile, but that certain precautions are necessary. Of the following, the BEST action for you to take is to

    A. submit the correction officer's memorandum to the warden, along with a statement of your own opinion
    B. submit the correction officer's memorandum to the warden without additional comment
    C. advise the correction officer to submit his memorandum to the warden directly
    D. advise the correction officer to withdraw his memorandum
    E. rewrite the correction officer's memorandum to include the necessary precautions and submit it to the warden as your own recommendation

KEY (CORRECT ANSWERS)

1.	E	11.	E	21.	E	31.	D
2.	B	12.	A	22.	E	32.	C
3.	C	13.	E	23.	C	33.	C
4.	C	14.	B	24.	D	34.	C
5.	D	15.	D	25.	C	35.	A
6.	A	16.	C	26.	D	36.	E
7.	D	17.	A	27.	A	37.	C
8.	D	18.	A	28.	C	38.	A
9.	A	19.	C	29.	E	39.	D
10.	E	20.	D	30.	E	40.	A

TEST 3

DIRECTIONS: Each question or incomplete statement is followed by several suggested answers or completions. Select the one that BEST answers the question or completes the statement. *PRINT THE LETTER OF THE CORRECT ANSWER IN THE SPACE AT THE RIGHT.*

1. While delegation of responsibility is undesirable, delegation of authority is wise. The supervisor who is a competent officer should realize that this statement is essentially

   A. *false,* because neither authority nor responsibility should be delegated by a supervisor
   B. *true,* because a supervisor should be responsible for his men but cannot be on hand to make all decisions
   C. *false,* because only the person ultimately responsible for an action should be expected to make decisions
   D. *true,* because the authority of a supervisor is specifically set forth in the Rules and Regulations
   E. *true,* because each supervisor is ultimately responsible for the work of the correction officers he supervises

2. Of the following, the LEAST accurate statement concerning the supervision of correction officers is that

   A. mistakes should generally be corrected as soon as detected
   B. it can be assumed that nearly all correction officers can analyze their own weaknesses
   C. misunderstandings are often due to the failure of superior officers to explain instructions properly
   D. repetition of a wrong procedure serves to fixate the habit
   E. it is good practice not only to call the attention of a correction officer to his mistakes, but to show him how to correct them

3. A correction officer, it is true, must obey orders implicitly, but this fact places a definite responsibility upon the supervisor. Of the following, the MOST accurate statement of the responsibility referred to in the above quotation is that a supervisor should

   A. issue orders in a manner commanding obedience
   B. demonstrate immediately to the correction officers the reasonableness of every command he issues
   C. issue direct commands only as a last resort
   D. be on hand to assist in carrying out every order he issues
   E. issue only orders which can be justified by him

4. Suppose that a correction officer newly assigned under your command appears to lack confidence in the performance of his duties. Of the following, the BEST action for you as a supervisor to take is to

   A. warn him that he is being observed constantly and that the poor quality of his work is being given special consideration
   B. give him an assignment which you believe he will be able to perform well
   C. assign him to exceptionally difficult tasks which you believe will constitute a definite challenge to him

D. have him observe the other correction officers at their work for a few months until his confidence improves
E. assign him to tasks on which he will be required to work alone

5. Of the following, the LEAST effective method that can be employed by a supervisor instructing the correction officers under his command in the proper discharge of their duties is to

    A. observe the mistakes a correction officer makes during his tour of duty and then discuss these mistakes with him individually
    B. discuss with the correction officers hypothetical situations which may occur in their work
    C. question the correction officers frequently on provisions of the Rules and Regulations relating to their work
    D. refer a correction officer to the proper provisions of the Rules and Regulations whenever it appears that the situation requires their application
    E. discuss the mistakes made by a correction officer with the other correction officers under your supervision, emphasizing both the kind of mistakes made and the person making them

6. Assume that you are a supervisor and that a correction officer with a long and excellent record has recently begun to exhibit laziness and lack of interest in his work. Of the following, the BEST course of action for you as his superior officer to follow is to

    A. call the attention of the other men specifically to this case to demonstrate that good work requires constant, diligent application
    B. start disciplinary action immediately against this correction officer as you would against any other
    C. overlook the matter until the correction officer again demonstrates his usual high quality of work
    D. interview the correction officer and attempt to determine the reason for his unusual behavior
    E. point out to the correction officer at the earliest opportunity that his excellent record is no excuse for incompetence and threaten disciplinary action unless he improves

7. The correction supervisor should realize that the best correction officer is not necessarily the one who leaps most quickly to execute an order, nor even the one who executes an order most efficiently. Of the following, the BEST justification for the above statement is that

    A. on many occasions, correction officers must show initiative in working without orders
    B. some correction officers work faster than others
    C. on some occasions, an order is executed rapidly, but inefficiently
    D. the correction officer who is really competent, when given an order, is cautious to think carefully before performing hasty action
    E. the correction officer who acts first may not be the one to finish first or to do the best job

8. A few men may be born leaders, but all of you new correction supervisors will soon find that command is essentially a habit. Of the following, the CHIEF implication of this statement is that

   A. relatively few men have the ability to become outstanding leaders and commanders
   B. the respect and confidence of his men can be developed by conscious effort on the part of a correction supervisor
   C. discipline is so well developed in a prison force that correction officers will obey the command of a supervisor as a matter of habit
   D. the correction officers who have been longer on the job and have more firmly fixed habits will probably make the better supervisors
   E. a new supervisor will probably make a better adjustment if placed with an older group of correction officers whose habits are more firmly fixed

9. Correction officers will rarely bear a grievance about a competent supervisor but something can be learned from every grievance situation that does occur if the supervisor is sufficiently alert and open-minded to accept responsibility for his own mistakes and to see the viewpoint of the men who bring up the grievance. Of the following, the MOST accurate statement on the basis of the above quotation is that

   A. grievances can usually be avoided by open-mindedness concerning the duties of the men
   B. satisfactory handling of grievances is essentially a matter of allocating responsibility between superiors and subordinates
   C. a supervisor should always attempt to understand the reason for every grievance brought to him by his men
   D. grievances can always be settled to the satisfaction of the men if the supervisor merely takes the trouble to see their viewpoint
   E. a supervisor should accept responsibility for his own mistakes but not for the mistakes of his men

10. Of the following, the BEST justification for having the limits of authority and responsibility clearly defined in an organization such as the Department of Correction is that

    A. responsibility is most properly mutual and interrelated
    B. every correction supervisor should probably be given some training in supervisory techniques
    C. some correction supervisors may be more competent than others
    D. every organization will probably benefit by exchange of viewpoints at parallel levels of authority
    E. overlapping authority will probably lead to conflicts

11. It is impossible to draw up a list of qualifications and maintain that the person who has these qualifications will make a successful correction supervisor. Of the following, the CHIEF justification for this statement is that

    A. the qualifications contributing to competence as a correction supervisor are probably independent in nature
    B. success as an officer is a temporary rather than a universal trait
    C. leadership is a habit rather than an acquirable skill

D. the qualities of a competent officer are often intangible and difficult to define
E. the qualifications necessary for competence in a correction supervisor are easily detected but difficult to substantiate

12. It has been suggested that the Rules and Regulations, when describing a recommended procedure, should state the reason for the recommendation. Of the following, the BEST justification for this suggestion is that

    A. correction officers should be sufficiently intelligent to understand the significance of their actions
    B. the Rules and Regulations are most accurately viewed as an official training document
    C. performance on the job is most likely to be efficient if based on understanding
    D. varied associations improve the recall of information
    E. discipline is improved if recommended procedures are specific and definite

13. Suppose that you are a correction supervisor. A newly appointed correction officer reports to you for duty. Of the following, the BEST procedure for you to follow to assure rapid orientation of this correction officer to his work is to

    A. ask him to give a brief survey of his qualifications for the job
    B. observe him carefully as he performs the routine aspects of his duties
    C. make a careful study of his previous work record before coming to the Department
    D. review with him the important elements of the job he will be required to perform
    E. question him at length concerning his knowledge of the inmates under his supervision

14. A newly appointed correction supervisor should be cautioned to avoid close familiarity with one of the correction officers under his command CHIEFLY because

    A. good discipline requires prompt obedience to commands
    B. respect for a superior officer must be implicit
    C. familiarity creates the impression of special favors
    D. the relationship between correction supervisors and correction officers is necessarily a close one
    E. a new correction supervisor can hardly be expected to be fully acquainted with the capabilities of his men

15. Assume that you are a correction supervisor. The CHIEF objection to allowing newly appointed correction officers under your supervision to learn how to perform their duties properly on the basis of their own experience is that a correction officer

    A. is likely to learn best when he is allowed to exercise originality
    B. will rarely forget a lesson learned through hard experience
    C. will learn more quickly when he is guided
    D. will be assigned only relatively routine jobs during his initial training period
    E. is likely to remember best what he learns first

16. The correction supervisor must enforce strict discipline, but he must not be devoid of personal sympathy or understanding. This statement is BEST illustrated by the correction supervisor who

    A. issues commands that are clear and understandable
    B. treats all correction officers equally regardless of personal sympathy
    C. defends impartially the actions of those men who are loyal to him
    D. understands the necessity of being military and commanding in bearing
    E. investigates the reasons for a correction officer's infractions of regulations

17. If the medical examiner's report on an inmate indicates that the inmate has *schizoid* tendencies, the one of the following types of behavior which the supervisor may MOST reasonably expect the inmate to demonstrate 'is

    A. epileptic fits
    B. withdrawal from reality
    C. sleepwalking
    D. incontinence
    E. constant aggressiveness

18. Of the following, the CHIEF distinction between a psycho-neurotic and a psychotic is that a psychoneurotic usually

    A. is suspicious and unfriendly whereas a psychotic is genial and happy
    B. has high intelligence whereas a psychotic has low intelligence
    C. requires the attention of a psychiatrist whereas a psychotic should be treated by a doctor
    D. suffers delusions whereas a psychotic does not suffer delusions
    E. is well-oriented to his surroundings whereas a psychotic lacks orientation

19. Of the following, the MOST accurate statement concerning the riot gun stocked by the city Department of Correction is that it

    A. is about 45" in length
    B. fires a .45 inch calibre cartridge
    C. is single action in type
    D. weighs about 7 1/2 pounds
    E. has an automatic device which ejects the cartridge case after each shot

20. Always use a brass rod when cleaning a revolver. Of the following, the BEST justification for the above statement is that

    A. a brass rod will not wear the bore around the muzzle
    B. brass rods are rigid and inflexible
    C. revolvers are rarely cleaned from the muzzle end
    D. brass can be tooled with great accuracy
    E. brass is a very hard alloy

21. The correction officer should know that the term *double action,* with reference to a revolver, means MOST NEARLY that

    A. the shell of a fired shot is ejected and a fresh cartridge is pushed from the magazine at the same time
    B. pulling the trigger cocks the hammer and presents a fresh cartridge for firing
    C. the revolver has both safety and automatic firing action
    D. the revolver can fire with or without automatic shell ejection
    E. pulling the trigger ejects the empty cartridge

22. A tourniquet is always a dangerous instrument and should be used with caution. Of the following, the CHIEF danger in the use of a tourniquet is   22._____

    A. shock
    B. increased venous bleeding
    C. blood clotting
    D. uninterrupted arterial bleeding
    E. gangrene

23. The correction officer must be able to detect the difference between sunstroke and heat exhaustion because different treatment is required. The one of the following symptoms which is MOST usually found in heat exhaustion rather than sunstroke is   23._____

    A. red face
    B. hot skin
    C. strong pulse
    D. very high temperature
    E. profuse sweating

24. All court pens in the city are under the jurisdiction of the Department of Correction. The jurisdiction cited in the above quotation is provided by   24._____

    A. an ordinance of the city
    B. the Rules and Regulations of the Department of Correction
    C. the charter of the city
    D. the Penal Law of the State
    E. a ruling of the Chief Magistrate of the city

25. The one of the following which is NOT a provision of the Constitution of the State regarding the administration of correctional institutions in the city is that   25._____

    A. no person may lose a residence by being held in a correctional institution
    B. a city may maintain a correctional institution
    C. a prisoner may be assigned work while he is in prison
    D. contract labor in prisons is forbidden
    E. wardens of correctional institutions are required to make weekly reports concerning the condition of their prisons

26. The one of the following which provides SPECIFICALLY for a Commissioner of Correction in the city and assigns duties to that office is the   26._____

    A. State Penal Law
    B. Criminal Procedure Law
    C. Constitution of the State
    D. Charter of the city
    E. Administrative Code of the city

27. The Criminal Procedure Law should be of interest to correction supervisors CHIEFLY because it   27._____

    A. describes unlawful procedures frequently employed by criminals
    B. establishes parole and probation procedures
    C. indicates whether imprisonment should be in a state or local prison
    D. fixes the legal definition of each crime and the appropriate penalty
    E. describes the conditions under which bail may be accepted and the procedures to be followed

28. The one of the following which is considered a court of general jurisdiction rather than a criminal or civil court is the

    A. Appellate Division
    B. Civil Court
    C. Criminal Court
    D. Family Court
    E. Surrogate's Court

29. The one of the following which is a Federal Court is the

    A. Appellate Division
    B. Court of General Sessions
    C. Circuit Court of Appeals
    D. Supreme Court (Criminal Term)
    E. Family Court

30. An order issued by the Supreme Court or Appellate Division to compel a person or body to do or refrain from doing something. This definition applies MOST accurately and completely to

    A. warrant
    B. mandamus
    C. certiorari
    D. writ of habeas corpus
    E. subpoena duces tecum

31. A child less than 16 years of age cannot be convicted of a crime UNLESS

    A. the offense committed is punishable by death or life imprisonment
    B. the offense committed is a felony
    C. negligence was a factor in the crime
    D. violation of a Federal law is involved
    E. it can be demonstrated that the crime was committed with motive and intent

32. A list, prepared by the clerk of the court, of all defendants then at the city prisons whose cases will be heard the following day is called a

    A. court calendar
    B. writ
    C. court probate
    D. daily roster
    E. court recall

33. There is a limitation of time within which prosecution of certain crimes must be commenced. Of the following, the MOST accurate statement is that prosecution for a _____ must be commenced within _____ years.

    A. murder; 5
    B. felony; 5
    C. misdemeanor; 7
    D. felony; 2
    E. murder; 2

34. In order to be adjudged a youthful offender, a defendant MUST be _____ years of age.

    A. under 16
    B. over 16 but under 21
    C. over 16 but under 18
    D. over 15 but under 19
    E. over 18 but under 21

35. The one of the following organizations which publishes the UNIFORM CRIME
REPORTS is the

    A. American Prison Association
    B. New York City Police Department
    C. American Institute of Criminology and Penology
    D. Federal Bureau of Investigation
    E. National Crime Prevention Institute

Questions 36-40.

DIRECTIONS: Column I below lists five books in the field of penology and criminology. In the space at the right, alongside the number of each of the books in Column I, write the letter preceding the author as listed in Column II.

COLUMN I		COLUMN II	
36. Education of Adult Prisoners		A. Sanford Bates	36.___
37. Prisons and Beyond		B. Sheldon & Eleanor Glueck	37.___
38. 500 Criminal Careers		C. Lewis E. Lawes	38.___
39. Criminal Behavior		D. Austin H. MacCormick	39.___
40. Within Prison Walls		E. Thomas M. Osborne	40.___
		F. Leo Palmer	
		G. Walter C. Reckless	

KEY (CORRECT ANSWERS)

1.	B	11.	D	21.	B	31.	A
2.	B	12.	C	22.	E	32.	E
3.	E	13.	D	23.	E	33.	B
4.	B	14.	C	24.	C	34.	D
5.	E	15.	C	25.	E	35.	D
6.	D	16.	E	26.	D	36.	D
7.	A	17.	B	27.	E	37.	A
8.	B	18.	E	28.	A	38.	B
9.	C	19.	D	29.	C	39.	G
10.	E	20.	E	30.	B	40.	E

EXAMINATION SECTION
TEST 1

DIRECTIONS: Each question or incomplete statement is followed by several suggested answers or completions. Select the one that BEST answers the question or completes the statement. *PRINT THE LETTER OF THE CORRECT ANSWER IN THE SPACE AT THE RIGHT.*

1. The MOST accurate statement concerning inmate living quarters is: 1.____
The

   A. open dormitory encourages harmonious group relations and is ordinarily the best approach
   B. open dormitory is usually preferred by inmates who find difficulty in establishing social relationships since it gives them a wider area from which to form close friendships
   C. private room with no window but with a barred cell door facing a corridor is the best approach since the existence of a window fosters unconscious suicidal tendencies
   D. private room with outside window establishes *individuality and territory* and is considered the best approach

2. If a group of rioting inmates demands that they negotiate directly with the Governor of the state, the request should PROBABLY be 2.____

   A. *denied;* leading political figures can always be depended upon to make false or unworkable promises in order to get credit for ending the riot
   B. *denied;* the granting of such a request lends encouragement to other inmates of other institutions to repeat the same show on another stage
   C. *granted;* inmates who do not receive satisfaction will torture hostages and destroy property
   D. *granted;* the public regrettably has a greater confidence in the ability of a governor to handle a riot than in the abilities of correction officials

3. Assume that you are a superior. An inmate comes to you with a request arising out of a grievance he has which he believes to be legitimate. You can see that the inmate is making a request which is important to him. You consider the inmate's request carefully and decide that you cannot grant the inmate's request.
It would be BEST for you to 3.____

   A. give the inmate a firm *no* answer and your reason for doing so
   B. grant the inmate's request because of its importance but point out to him that there were very good reasons for not granting the request
   C. tell the inmate that his request is an important one and you will let him know in the not too distant future whether his request can be granted
   D. tell the inmate that there are two sides to his request and that you will ask the Deputy Warden to frame a written response to the inmate

4. Assume that you are a superior and that the early warning signs of an inmate disturbance are present in your institution. One of the officers you supervise behaves in a very nervous, insecure way in the presence of inmates. You try to encourage the officer to behave in a confident manner but the officer is unable to do so.
In the circumstances, it would probably be BEST to 4.____

A. hold a brief meeting with the other line officers who comprise your staff and ask for suggestions on dealing with the officer
B. order the officer to straighten up or face disciplinary charges
C. recommend that the officer be temporarily assigned to a less sensitive area
D. shock the officer into proper behavior by asking him if he intends to turn *yellow* should trouble break out

5. There is a strong disagreement among correctional administrators concerning the use of inmate councils.
The MOST feasible approach concerning the use of inmate councils is generally the

   A. elimination of inmate advisory groups, since membership in such a group gives the inmate member an opportunity to exploit other inmate members
   B. formation of inmate advisory groups to deal with particular problems, with such groups dissolving as soon as the problem is resolved
   C. popular election by inmates of an inmate advisory group to meet at frequent periodic intervals
   D. taking of formal surveys by supervisory correction personnel to determine inmate attitudes

6. Which of the following may spark a prison riot or major prison disturbance?

   A. Absence of clearly defined and easily understood rules and regulations
   B. Indecisive actions on legitimate inmate grievances
   C. Poor communications
   D. All of the above

7. Which of the following is NOT true?

   A. A disproportionate share of individuals who are prone to violent behavior are to be found in correctional institutions.
   B. Inmates have high self-esteem and are fully committed to the major goal of making large sums of money.
   C. Inmates are more apt to be mentally deficient than persons who are not in correctional institutions.
   D. Inmates are frequently the product of broken homes, are unskilled, and have unstable work records.

8. Of the following, the MOST correct statement is:
Riots

   A. are caused by a conscious desire to bring about revolutionary improvements in the American social system and to put an end to the devaluation of certain elements of the population by those who are in positions of power
   B. come about because institutional life is monotonous and because inmates feel a sense of being hopelessly oppressed and stripped of all human dignity
   C. are complex phenomena for which simple explanations do not in reality exist
   D. are violent acts contrary to law and are proof positive of the moral deterioration of middle-class America

9. Assume that you have made an informal count of a small inmate work crew assigned to a small area on a site that has never known an escape. There is doubt in your mind as to the correctness of your count.
   Your BEST reaction is that

   A. there is no cause for immediate alarm, since only formal crew counts are recorded
   B. you should first count the crew again
   C. you should waste no time in reporting an inmate missing and then, after the report is made, count the crew again
   D. you should ask the crew whether one of the inmates is missing

10. The BASIC function of a correctional institution is

    A. to operate at maximum efficiency
    B. to make certain that every department understands that teamwork is vital and that all departments are important
    C. the protection of society and the rehabilitation of the inmates
    D. the recognition that correctional institutions face a more difficult problem than at any time in the history of our country

11. It is sometimes necessary for a correction officer to order an inmate to do something the officer knows the inmate will not like to do.
    In these circumstances, the following is the recommended BEST procedure:

    A. Convince the inmate of the merit of your order before the inmate carries it out
    B. Do not insist upon immediate compliance with the order but give the inmate time to come to the realization that it is best to comply with an officer's order
    C. If faced with total refusal, restructure the order and emphasize a different aspect of the original order
    D. Make sure that the order is carried out completely

12. The use of food for payment of work or for special privileges has no justification and such practice should never be permitted and will very likely get completely out of control and develop a usage of large amounts of luxury goods.
    Which one of the following would be an EXCEPTION to the preceding passage?

    A. The giving of large portions of meat to those who are given arduous work assignments
    B. An officer who gives extra portions of food to those inmates who have been helpful to the officer during the day
    C. The giving of an extra large piece of pastry by a kitchen helper to an officer while on duty in the dining hall
    D. An officer who allows the kitchen help to keep leftovers which are storable

13. The MAJOR purpose of a perimeter search is to

    A. assure that all cell blocks are secure
    B. discover whether any tools have been taken from the work area
    C. keep illegal items from being passed among the inmates while in open courtyards
    D. make sure contraband doesn't enter from the outside

14. A major point of emphasis in the instruction of a correction officer concerns security and the causes of breach of security.
Experience has shown that MOST escapes are traceable directly to

    A. relatives who smuggle escape instruments to inmates
    B. officers who smuggle contraband to inmates
    C. the haphazard handling of keys and tools
    D. the lack of knowledge among inmates as to the possible consequences of escape

15. Reception centers have been established in several of the larger states.
The BASIC idea behind the reception centers is that

    A. before an offender has been found guilty in court, a sound orientation program should be instituted designed to facilitate good adjustment to healthy social life
    B. before an offender has been found guilty in court, the decision as to the value of lenient treatment should be decided by specialists in the correctional and rehabilitation fields
    C. after an offender has been found guilty in court, the decision as to the place and method of treatment should be decided by specialists in the correction field
    D. after an offender has been found guilty in court, immediate psychiatric examination should determine the inmate's attitude toward work and his future vocational program

16. The key to the successful operation of a classification program in a prison institution is the

    A. professional qualifications of the psychiatrist and social worker
    B. support and leadership given by the head of the institution
    C. careful application of the techniques and purposes of scientific classification
    D. willing participation of the hardened inmates

17. Classification, as the term is generally used in correctional work, is PRIMARILY

    A. a method that will assure coordination in diagnosis, training, and treatment of prison inmates
    B. in itself diagnosis, training, and treatment of prison inmates
    C. integration of like or similar groups of offenders into the general inmate population
    D. the labeling of prison inmates in different mental or attitudinal categories or types and the measurement of willingness to work

18. A study of the Federal prison system has compared the yearly average number of escapes per thousand inmates for the four years BEFORE and AFTER their classification program was established.
This comparison shows that the rate of escapes per year

    A. was much higher before classification
    B. is unknown because no such study has ever been officially approved
    C. was much lower after classification
    D. was about the same before and after classification

19. All studies of parole failures have shown that, of the following, the highest percentage of violations occur after the inmate has been released

    A. six months
    B. one month
    C. one week
    D. 12-14 months

20. Many correctional administrators believe that any institution operating as a single unit becomes increasingly inefficient and unsafe as its inmate population exceeds a critical figure. This critical figure can be enlarged by breaking up the institution into several smaller units, but still operating as a single administrative unit, or by locating two or more separate institutions on the same site.
    In building new facilities or splitting older institutions into more manageable small units, it is considered unwise for the number of inmates to be included in any one unit to exceed

    A. 1200   B. 1000   C. 50   D. 600

21. As a group, youthful offenders are _____ susceptible to positive treatment efforts than juvenile delinquents _____.

    A. *less;* or adult criminals
    B. *more;* or adult criminals
    C. *more;* but they are not as susceptible to positive treatment efforts as adult criminals
    D. *less;* but they are more susceptible to positive treatment efforts than adult criminals

22. Perhaps the young person who becomes legally defined as an offender has developed and become *socialized* in a milieu more characterized by anti-social than social customs and standards. His inability to control himself according to the requirements of the larger social order then signifies commitment to an unacceptable code of conduct rather than psychological aberration.
    An implication of the foregoing is that

    A. a young offender in an institutional setting will accept the guidance of fellow inmates and not that of treatment or custodial personnel
    B. where a youthful offender lacks self-control his behavior toward his associates is bound to be assaultive
    C. the use of narcotics or *hard* drugs may assist the individual to escape from people and problems
    D. the young offender may behave according to the standards of his friends and neighbors

23. There are three major means by which a conviction may be set aside after the ordinary statutory channels of appeal are closed.
    Which one of the following is NOT such a major means?

    A. Parole
    B. Habeas corpus
    C. Pardon
    D. Coram nobis

24. Which of the following types of housing is deemed preferable for female inmates?

    A. Cottage type
    B. Dormitory type
    C. One inmate per cell
    D. Three inmates per cell

25. Regarding library services, which of the following is recommended?

    A. Inmates should be encouraged to ask friends, relatives, and charitable organizations to contribute funds for the operation of the institutional library.
    B. Since most inmates are functional illiterates, at least ten comic books per inmate should be purchased for the institutional library.
    C. The requirement of a male librarian in all-male institutions should be waived since experience has proved that women are highly efficient and effective serving as librarians in all-male institutions.
    D. To discourage the planning of disturbances, inmates should not be permitted to read books in the library.

26. Which of the following measures is deemed to be advisable in establishing property control standards for inmates entering prison?

    A. An inmate's valuables should be itemized and sealed in a clear plastic bag.
    B. Inmates should be permitted to retain on their persons their social security cards, watches, and small quantities of postage stamps.
    C. Inmates who handle inmates' personal property should be carefully selected for their qualities of trustworthiness.
    D. Jewelry taken from inmates at time of incarceration should be carefully described with such words as gold, silver, diamond, or ruby to avoid the possibility of substitution.

27. Emergency doors must be provided into housing and to the areas where prisoners are congregated.
    All housing units should have an emergency entrance door with a lock opening on the _____ only and the door made to swing _____ only.

    A. inside; inward   B. inside; outward
    C. outside; inward   D. outside; outward

28. Which of the following does NOT represent the view of authorities regarding the use of tear gas?

    A. A limitation on using gas inside a building is the danger of getting a concentration which is too dense.
    B. It is economically sound to keep large quantities of gas munitions on hand due to the economies of large scale purchasing.
    C. The threat and availability of gas at the scene of a disturbance has probably halted more incipient disorders than its actual use.
    D. The use of tear gas in suppressing disturbances is more humane than bullets.

29. To schedule an official count at or near the time of officer shift changes is USUALLY found to be a

    A. *bad* practice since officers corning on duty resent being held up while a previous shift makes its count
    B. *bad* practice since officers responsible for the count are too easily distracted
    C. *good* practice since accuracy in the count is assured and interference with inmate activities is avoided
    D. *good* practice since a large number of officers will be on hand if discrepancies in the count are found

30. More disturbances have originated or culminated in the _____ areas than any other area.
    Which of the following words, when inserted in the blank space, would MOST accurately complete the statement?

    A. dining
    B. housing
    C. recreational
    D. work

31. According to a recent handbook on how to recognize and handle abnormal people, the BEST way, generally, to handle a disturbed, potentially violent person is to

    A. display any physical restraint that is readily available and calmly but firmly tell the inmate that the restraint will be employed unless he apologizes for his behavior
    B. try to talk to him and find out what is bothering him, since this tends to gain his confidence
    C. tell him whatever he wants to hear since the deception of an abnormal individual is necessary for his own protection
    D. be as self-confident and assured as possible since an easy approach will appear as a sign of weakness to a deranged mind

32. Assume that you are explaining a procedure to a visitor to an inmate in an institution, but the visitor does not seem to quite understand what you are saying. This lack of understanding has occurred occasionally in the past with other visitors. A language barrier does not appear to be the problem.
    According to a training bulletin issued by the City Department of Correction, the BEST way, generally, to handle this type of situation is to

    A. carefully use appropriately colorful language, since the display of colorful words will likely stimulate the visitor to an understanding of your instructions
    B. gently question the visitor's inborn communications capacity, since a little kidding often goes a long way to bridge a communications gap
    C. slowly increase a show of legitimate authority, since a little authority goes a long way in expediting matters with insecure persons
    D. find out what the visitor does not understand, since this may provide a clue as to improvements in your explanation

Questions 33-42.

DIRECTIONS: Questions 33 through 42 consist of two statements, based on the current Rules and Regulations and Manual of Procedure, Department of Correction.
If BOTH statements are correct, mark your answer A.
If NEITHER statement is correct, mark your answer B.
If Statement I ONLY is correct, but NOT Statement II, mark your answer C.
If Statement II ONLY is correct, but NOT Statement I, mark your answer D.

33. I. In the event of an inmate's death in any institution of the Correction Department, four people only shall be immediately notified in the following order: the institutional physician, the police precinct having jurisdiction, the Commissioner of Correction, and the Director of Operations.
    II. In the event of an attempted suicide by an inmate in his cell, the correction officer who first observes the incident shall immediately administer first aid. In the event that the inmate does not respond to first aid, the correction officer shall notify a superior officer or another correction officer in the vicinity to assist in the administration of first aid.

34. I. Upon the escape of an inmate, if the escapee is a member of a work gang, the officer in charge shall immediately line up all the inmates and, as expeditiously as possible, communicate with his superior officer.
    II. A correction officer shall be constantly alert while on duty, observing everything that takes place on his post within his sight or hearing, and shall periodically patrol his post during his tour of duty.

35. I. Whenever an inmate receives a written communication from a duly accredited reporter requesting permission to interview him, the inmate, if he wishes to be interviewed, shall submit such information in writing to the head of the institution.
    II. The following shall be the only types of punishment administered: reprimand; loss of one or more privileges, temporarily or permanently; loss of part or all good time; punitive segregation; restricted diets.

36. I. A correction officer in charge of any area within an institution shall check all bars, locks, windows, doors, and other security facilities on his post at least twice during his tour of duty for evidence that they are in good condition and have not been tampered with.
    II. When it is deemed necessary at any time to search the person of any employee on duty, such search shall be made by a captain or other superior officer. Refusal of any employee to be searched shall constitute grounds for disciplinary action.

37. I. Whenever prisoners are received from departmental and police vans, they must be searched and counted as soon as possible.
    II. The following categories of inmates shall not be assigned as sentenced help:
        a. Drug Addicts or Drug Offenders
        b. Gambling Law Violators

38. I. A correction officer assigned to court detention pens shall each day check the court calendar with the names of the prisoners sent from the various institutions.
    II. A captain shall call the attention of the assistant deputy warden to all matters of importance within the institution. The assistant deputy warden shall, in turn, call these matters of importance to the attention of the head of institution, the relieving assistant deputy warden, and the relieving captain.

39. I. In the event that any employee is made captive by prisoners, all orders issued by him during his captivity shall have full force and effect, except as pertaining to inmates.
    II. There shall be no restrictions as to correspondents, nor to the number of letters an inmate of any institution may receive as incoming mail or send out as outgoing mail.

40. I.   No cell, tier, floor, or dormitory assignment of inmates, or changes in such assignments, shall be made without the authorization of a captain or superior officer.
     II. Whenever a correction officer receives information from any source which directly or indirectly involves the security of any institution, he shall immediately notify the head of his institution or division.

41. I.   A designated captain shall be responsible for the daily accounting of all firearms and protective equipment assigned to an institution or division.
     II. Whenever an inmate commits an infraction of discipline important enough to necessitate action, the captain or other superior officer on duty in the institution shall, as soon as practicable, but no later than the same day, investigate the complaint and, if in his judgment the facts warrant, he will place the inmate in punishment status.

42. I.   The correction officer assuming the duties of a post requiring the supervision of inmates shall examine the entire area of his post for its security and good order only if the correction officer who was just relieved of this post had not reported all secure and in good order within the previous three hours.
     II. A member of the department shall not indulge in any undue familiarity with inmates nor shall he permit any familiarity, on the part of inmates, toward him.

43. When time is NOT a factor, a supervisor enhances both initiative and cooperation by using which one of the following orders?

    A. Command
    B. Plea
    C. Detailed written instructions
    D. Suggestion

44. The development of a *grapevine* or a *rumor clinic* in an institution is USUALLY the result of

    A. the constant provocation of gossip by a few problem individuals
    B. unofficial approval of this employee activity
    C. lack of adequate communication through official channels
    D. employees' disapproval of the administration

45. Appraisal of an employee during his probationary period by an immediate supervisor who happens to be a personal friend of the employee is

    A. *unacceptable* because familiarity results in favoritism
    B. *unacceptable* because people on probation should not be evaluated by immediate supervisors
    C. *acceptable* because it encourages other employees to perform their duties in a manner satisfactory to the appraiser
    D. *acceptable* because the familiarity of the appraiser helps in a complete evaluation

46. In planning the weekly work routine, it is MOST important for a supervisor to

    A. ask employees which assignments they would prefer
    B. ask for volunteers to perform routine tasks
    C. indicate the daily anticipated attendance
    D. list areas of priority interest

47. Of the following, which is NOT a recommended practice of a supervisor?

    A. Giving reasons for emergency assignments or overtime work
    B. Attempting to detect a deep neurosis by examination of work habits or observation of behavior
    C. Taking corrective disciplinary action when an employee fails to improve his attendance following a corrective interview
    D. Consulting with employees as to the best way of getting a job done

48. If a correction officer attended a preparatory class on supervisory techniques, he would MOST likely be instructed that a good supervisor is one who

    A. believes in strong and centralized administrative control
    B. is extremely ambitious
    C. maintains a favorable attitude towards those he encounters
    D. maintains his own method of handling problems

49. Of the following, the MOST important consideration for recommending a provisional promotion to captain should be the correction officer's

    A. capacity to take disciplinary action
    B. ability to control inmate movement
    C. detailed knowledge of departmental rules and regulations
    D. seniority

50. The parts of the decision-making process are GENERALLY the
    I. research of background material
    II. development of details of alternative plans of action
    III. study and interpretation of collected data
    IV. selection of the best course of action
    V. statement of purpose or need

    The CORRECT answer is:

    A. I, II
    B. I, III, V
    C. I, III, IV, V
    D. All of the above

KEY (CORRECT ANSWERS)

1. D	11. D	21. B	31. B	41. A
2. B	12. A	22. D	32. D	42. C
3. A	13. D	23. A	33. B	43. D
4. C	14. C	24. A	34. C	44. C
5. B	15. C	25. C	35. B	45. A
6. D	16. B	26. A	36. A	46. D
7. B	17. A	27. D	37. D	47. B
8. C	18. C	28. B	38. C	48. C
9. B	19. A	29. D	39. C	49. A
10. C	20. D	30. A	40. D	50. D

TEST 2

DIRECTIONS: Each question or incomplete statement is followed by several suggested answers or completions. Select the one that BEST answers the question or completes the statement. *PRINT THE LETTER OF THE CORRECT ANSWER IN THE SPACE AT THE RIGHT.*

1. A threat to institutional order arises from the behavior of the *resister,* the inmate who flagrantly refuses to cooperate with staff. One study has shown that the *resister* exhibits certain characteristics.
   A characteristic NOT exhibited by *resisters* is

   A. a lower average intelligence than other prisoners
   B. a greater tendency toward sadism
   C. poorer preprison employment records
   D. fewer contacts with families while in prison

   1.____

2. Which of the following is NOT a correct reason for the persistence of the inmate social system?

   A. Conformity with inmate values, beliefs, and behavior provides prestige for the inmate.
   B. Inmates frequently complain of being forced to live with other inmates who are inferior and vicious; consequently, they seek acceptance by like inmates as a way of protection against the physical aggression of inferior inmates.
   C. Confinement threatens the masculinity of the inmate; inmates are motivated to overreact to confinement and loss of the masculine self-image by open support of the masculine values of aggressiveness.
   D. At least one-third of all inmates possess the inborn, hostile instincts of primitive humanity and, since this is a high percentage, inmate social systems tend to reflect the patterns of behavior of this aggressive population.

   2.____

3. According to recognized authorities, the population in a prison is together sufficiently large to create regularities in behavior.
   This means that

   A. the regularities require a de-emphasis of coercion and an emphasis on counseling and psychiatric therapy
   B. confinement is an experience requiring major continuous readjustments
   C. the regularities reflect the efforts of employees and inmates to achieve goals and meet problems
   D. the regularities in a prison imply the systematic lack of concern for the dignity of the individual

   3.____

4. The concept of occupation is useful for differentiating criminal behavior systems according to the degree of commitment to criminal values and to the degree to which it qualifies as a career.
   This statement implies that

   A. a person is less intensively committed to criminality when his feelings about himself and his behavior reflect the criminal group's attitudes toward him
   B. when an individual is strongly committed to a criminal culture, the consistency of his crime-oriented behavior is difficult to redirect through rehabilitative programs

   4.____

C. to *go straight* would cause the inmate to appear *honest* in the sense that his previous personal adjustment to daily recurring events would no longer appear consistent
D. professional career criminals regard violence and use of weapons as a mark of resourcefulness not possessed by ordinary career criminals

5. The statement below which most contemporary criminologists would find MOST accurate is that

   A. criminal behavior is explained by the lack of freedom in a materialistic society
   B. although criminal behavior is learned, it is not learned like most social behavior
   C. the process of becoming a criminal is regarded as the same as all personality development
   D. although criminal techniques are learned, the basic origin of criminality lies in inborn defects

6. Central to the association between urbanization and deviant behavior in American society is the problem neighborhood. Such neighborhoods are generally characterized by all of the following factors EXCEPT

   A. great cultural diversity
   B. total community disorganization
   C. general social instability
   D. high population turnover

7. An authority states that, although urbanization and industrialization have tended to standardize behavior, they have also increased the possibility of deviant behavior.
This means MOST NEARLY that

   A. crime statistics tend to underestimate crimes in rural areas
   B. population density in industrialized cities favors the criminal because sheer numbers, coupled with the close personal relationship characteristic of city life, provides a great many customers for organized crime per 1,000 population
   C. urbanized areas have higher rates for all major crimes because city police systems are understaffed and lack public support
   D. the city-dweller is forced into mechanical conformity but has also been released from traditional constraints

8. Based on authority, the MOST accurate statement concerning the relationship between intelligence and criminality is that

   A. general intelligence as measured by I.Q. tests is unaffected by the individual's cultural background
   B. mental deficiency, by itself, can result in crime
   C. persons at the highest mental levels do not become criminals
   D. mental deficiency may reduce criminality by insulating the individual from frustrations

9. The basic distinction between the professional and non-professional criminal is that the professional criminal

   A. breaks the law more often than the nonprofessional
   B. sees himself as a criminal with a definite means of livelihood, whereas the nonprofessional still retains the basic morals of the dominant society
   C. is part of the larger society, whereas the nonprofessional is isolated from the dominant society
   D. has pride in his criminal techniques, but feels a sense of compassion for his victims, whereas the nonprofessional has neither pride in his techniques nor does he have any sense of guilt

10. Based on objective discussion of the general theory of *white-collar crime*, this type of crime can BEST be defined as any crime committed by a person of respectability and high social _____.

    A. status in the course of his occupation
    B. status in the course of his occupation, excluding crimes of the medical and legal professions, which are generally handled by administrative rather than judicial agencies
    C. status in the course of his occupation, excluding crimes not part of his occupational procedures
    D. status

11. The THREE major ideologies, or systems of belief, affecting law enforcement, court, and correctional activities are the punitive, therapeutic, and preventive ideologies.
    Of the following, the MOST correct statement is that the

    A. therapeutic ideology rather than the punitive or preventive ideology is recognized as offering the ultimate promise for reducing crime
    B. preventive ideology seeks to promote healthy personality development by means of immediate and drastic social changes so that criminals will engage in socially approved conduct
    C. therapeutic ideology considers the criminal to be a victim of defective conditioning of his personality and, consequently, generally seeks a lifetime clinical treatment approach by specially trained psychiatrists
    D. punitive ideology affords the most immediate relief for the requirements of the offended society

12. Group therapy commonly used in the treatment of offenders is intended to have each of the following benefits EXCEPT

    A. creation of a model inmate not demonstrating any potentiality for behavioral change
    B. encouragement of members of the group to see meanings they previously failed to recognize
    C. modification of staff and inmate cultures which are barriers to rehabilitation programs
    D. changing of attitudes in such areas as discipline and authority relationships

13. Crime rates vary with the age of the offender. American data show that the age range which has the highest ARREST RATE is

    A. ages 36 to 45
    B. ages 26 to 35
    C. ages 15 to 25
    D. a figure which cannot be estimated because of the great variations in different kinds of crimes committed by different age groups

14. Prisoners differ in their escape-proneness.
    The following sets of factors are generally associated with the escape behavior of prison inmates EXCEPT set

    A. mental stability and superior intelligence
       cooperative attitude
       mature when first arrested
    B. poor employment record
       uncooperative attitude
       daring and aggressive personality
    C. weak home ties
       habitual offender
       age less than 30 years
    D. poor employment record
       mental instability and inferior intelligence
       served less than 40 percent of his term

15. The correctional agency is an element in the system of criminal justice, which in turn is subject to the social-cultural environment of which it is a product and for which it is a social control instrumentality.
    This statement MOST NEARLY means that

    A. prisons very rarely change
    B. prisons must change if society is to reform
    C. prisons, courts, and police are part of society
    D. the police and courts have a negative impact on prisons

16. Which one of the following statements regarding probation and parole is MOST correct?

    A. Both probation and parole have similarities in objectives, in the use of casework, and in promotion of rehabilitation.
    B. Both probation and parole have similarities in the use of casework and in promotion of rehabilitation, but are dissimilar in their social objectives.
    C. Parole tries to promote change within the offender, whereas probation stresses that punishments should be standardized on the basis of the crime.
    D. Probation generally involves the more serious, criminalistic offender.

17. Walled prisons have been criticized for depriving inmates of normal contact with the outside community and for imposing a daily regime of frustration and aimlessness. The *open institution* has been advocated as an answer to such criticism.
Of the following pairs of statements, the pair which is TRUE is:

   A. I. Penologists generally agree that the open institution will replace the closed prison.
      II. To obtain properly selected inmates, the open institution requires the outside community as the source of its population.
   B. I. Penologists generally agree that the open institution requires the closed prison as the source of its population.
      II. To obtain properly selected inmates, the open institution requires the closed prison as the source of its population.
   C. I. Penologists generally agree that the open institution will replace the closed prison.
      II. Psychological controls are substituted for physical barriers against escape from the open institution.
   D. I. Penologists generally agree that the open institution will not replace the closed prison.
      II. The open institution is far less expensive to construct and to operate than the closed prison.

18. Prison industrial supervisors in this country have generally been accustomed to using excessive numbers of prisoners because

   A. the inmates' qualities as workers usually depress productivity
   B. it is difficult to strike a proper balance between vocational training for prisoner rehabilitation and the achievement of high production for its own sake
   C. prison industrial work is a real asset to vocational training
   D. of the stigma attached to prison-made goods

19. Increases in recidivist rates can result from

   A. more liberal enforcement of parole supervision
   B. increased use of probation by the courts
   C. stricter enforcement of probation supervision
   D. more liberal law enforcement

20. In recent developments in crime prevention, a basic theme has been *reaching the unreached.*
A disproportionate share of the *unreached* consists of

   A. college students arrested for campus demonstrations
   B. multi-problem families
   C. children of affluent suburbia who have been arrested for marijuana possession
   D. highly literate individuals who have been sentenced to correctional institutions for violation of the draft laws

21. Which one of the following statements is correct according to William D. Teeke's article, *Collective Violence in Correctional Institutions,* in a memorable issue of the AMERICAN JOURNAL OF CORRECTION?
Riots are MORE likely to occur in the

   A. January-June period; the beginning of a new calendar year brings hope for a change in the correctional system in general
   B. January-June period; the densely populated Eastern coastal region is usually in the grip of a cold wave and this, coupled with defective heating systems in old institutions, creates many grievances
   C. July-December period; there is no definite evidence as to why this is the most probable time
   D. July-December period; people are hot and most troubled, and, living in dirty and cramped quarters, under close restraint, seek to rebel

21.____

Questions 22-26.

DIRECTIONS: Questions 22 through 26 consist of passages of one or more sentences. Each of the passages contains an incorrectly used word. First, decide which is the incorrectly used word. Then, from among the options given, decide which word, when substituted for the incorrectly used word, makes the meaning of the passage clear.

SAMPLE QUESTION

Prisoners frequently bring hazards to compel prison officials to allow them more medical care of different medical care than has been provided by the prison physician.
They rarely succeed.
   A. negligence
   B. mistreatment
   C. actions
   D. evaluations

The word *hazards* in the passage does not convey the meaning the passage is evidently intended to convey. The word *actions* (answer C), when substituted for the word *hazards,* makes the meaning of the passage clear. Accordingly, the answer to the question is C.

22. In the years since passage of the Harrison Narcotic Act of 1914, making the possession of opium amphetamines illegal in most circumstances, drug use has become a subject of considerable scientific interest and investigation.
There is at present a voluminous literature on drug use of various kinds.

   A. Ingestion
   B. Derivatives
   C. Addiction
   D. Opiates

22.____

23. Of course, the fact that criminal laws are extremely patterned in definition does not mean that the majority of persons who violate them are dealt with as criminals. Quite the contrary, for a great many forbidden acts are voluntarily engaged in within situations of privacy and go unobserved and unreported.

   A. Symbolic
   B. Casual
   C. Scientific
   D. Broad-gauged

23.____

24. The most punitive way to study punishment is to focus attention on the pattern of punitive action: to study how a penalty is applied, to study what is done to or taken from an offender.

   A. Characteristic
   B. Degrading
   C. Objective
   D. Distinguished

24.____

25. The most common forms of punishment in times past have been death, physical torture, mutilation, branding, public humiliation, fines, forfeits of property, banishment, transportation, and imprisonment.
Although this list is by no means differentiated, practically every form of punishment has had several variations and applications.

    A. Specific
    B. Simple
    C. Exhaustive
    D. Characteristic

26. There is another important line of inference between ordinary and professional criminals, and that is the source from which they are recruited.
The professional criminal seems to be drawn from legitimate employment and, in many instances, from parallel vocations or pursuits.

    A. Demarcation
    B. Justification
    C. Superiority
    D. Reference

27. Of the following, what should generally be the MAJOR objective of the institution in dealing with a prisoner?
Focus on

    A. helping him adjust to institutional life
    B. helping him develop his latent talents
    C. helping him prepare for a new career once out of prison
    D. his adjustment to freedom in the community

28. Of the following, the reason which BEST explains why outstanding authorities on penology believe that one city prison may not always be the BEST location for all inmates is that

    A. incarcerating second time offenders in city institutions increases their exposure to the bad influences of their criminal acquaintances
    B. some offenders may have problems which require treatment away from their local environment
    C. incarcerated individuals would be less prone to recidivism in a rural environment
    D. penal institutions on islands have a tendency to increase inmate tensions

29. Under the criminal treatment system, the justification for treating the condition of the individual is the fact that he has engaged in criminal conduct.
In the civil treatment system, the justification for treating the condition is

    A. always related to the crime
    B. given by the courts
    C. never related to the crime
    D. may or may not be related to the crime

30. On the basis of recent trends, which of the following statements would be INCORRECT?

    A. Less than one-quarter of the sentenced prisoners incarcerated in locally operated institutions can be considered civil prisoners.
    B. Many of the persons sentenced to local institutions have either been incarcerated in, or are destined to be incarcerated in, institutions administered by the state.
    C. Most of the persons incarcerated under sentence throughout the state today are first offenders.
    D. There is no reliable evidence to show that education or vocational training applied on a general basis has any effect in reducing recidivism.

31. There are two basic rationales for subjecting persons to treatment: one is called the *civil* system; and the other is called the *criminal* system.
    Of the following, the BASIC difference between these two systems is

    A. that the civil system is used to administer justice to those first time offenders who have committed a mild crime
    B. that the civil system usually requires facilities or institutions separate from those of the criminal system
    C. the criminal institution's employment of more highly skilled personnel
    D. the degree of exposure to community life

    31.____

32. The MAJOR purpose of the recreational facilities located atop a major house of detention for men is to

    A. allow inmates a greater opportunity to socialize and expose themselves to sunshine
    B. enable fewer guards to watch inmates so the cost of institutional operations can be decreased
    C. allow greater freedom of movement of inmates within the confines of the institution
    D. provide relaxing and exhausting activities which will remove tension

    32.____

33. A group of 50 youths is currently commuting from a local prison to an experimental training program in group counseling.
    The purpose of this program is

    A. basically to enable the inmates to serve as counselors for their fellow inmates
    B. chiefly to stimulate inmates and prepare them for future college training
    C. to expose inmates who have almost completed their sentence to civilian community life
    D. chiefly to prepare them for employment at the completion of their incarceration

    33.____

34. A recent ruling by the courts held that no citizen awaiting trial be held in detention for more than _____ days.

    A. 90   B. 60   C. 30   D. 120

    34.____

Questions 35-39.

DIRECTIONS: Questions 35 through 39 are based on the following tables.

Forest City, an imaginary jurisdiction, classifies its offenders as juvenile delinquents, youthful offenders, or adult offenders. There are two institutions for female offenders and five institutions for male offenders. Table A shows the average daily number of inmates for the years shown. Table B shows what percentage of average daily number of male inmates for the years shown were juvenile delinquents, youthful offenders, or adult offenders.

TABLE A - FOREST CITY INMATES

	1990	2000	2001 (estimate)
Institutions for Female Offenders:			
(1) Pleasantdale	70	105	120
(2) Shady Valley	W	190	210
TOTAL	195	295	330
Institutions for Male Offenders:			
(1) Leadurney	260	320	310
(2) Sherman	110	130	Y
(3) Riveredge	1700	1800	1850
(4) Thompson	650	800	Z
(5) Maxim	1200	1625	1700
TOTAL	3920	4675	5030
TOTAL MALE & FEMALE	X	4970	5360

TABLE B - FOREST CITY OFFENDERS
PERCENTAGE OF AVERAGE DAILY NUMBER OF INMATES CLASSIFIED AS JUVENILE DELINQUENTS, YOUTHFUL OFFENDERS, OR ADULT OFFENDERS
(See Code Below)

	1990 A	B	C	2000 A	B	C
Institutions for Female Offenders:						
(1) Pleasantdale	20%	60%	20%	25%	75%	-
(2) Shady Valley	15%	30%	55%	-	35%	65%
Institutions for Male Offenders:						
(1) Leadurney	5%	95%	-	80%	20%	-
(2) Sherman	10%	35%	55%	10%	35%	55%
(3) Riveredge	90%	10%	-	85%	15%	-
(4) Thompson	-	40%	60%	-	35%	65%
(5) Maxim	-	20%	80%	-	5%	95%

CODE
A - JUVENILE OFFENDERS
B - YOUTHFUL OFFENDERS
C - ADULT OFFENDERS

35. From 1990 to 2000, the average daily number of female youthful offenders in the Pleasantdale institution increased MOST NEARLY by

   A. 20
   B. 29
   C. 37
   D. a figure greater than 40

36. One of the following sets of figures belongs in the circled spaces marked Y and Z. Which one of the following sets of figures LOGICALLY belongs in these spaces?

   A. 115 and 990
   B. 115 and 1050
   C. 120 and 990
   D. 120 and 1050

37. The figures which LOGICALLY belong in the circled spaces marked W and X are

   A. 125 and 4115
   B. 125 and 4215
   C. 175 and 4115
   D. 175 and 4215

38. In 2000, of the average daily number of Forest City male and female inmates, the percentage to be found in Maxim was MOST NEARLY

   A. 27%   B. 30%   C. 33%   D. 36%

39. In 1990, the average daily number of adult male offenders was MOST NEARLY 39.____

    A. 60 in Sherman and 390 in Thompson
    B. 110 in Sherman and 650 in Thompson
    C. 390 in Thompson and 1300 in Maxim
    D. 800 in Thompson and 1625 in Maxim

Questions 40-43.

DIRECTIONS: Questions 40 through 43 are based on the following passage.

Female criminality is very much under-reported, especially if one considers offenses such as shoplifting, thefts by prostitutes, offenses against children, and homicide. There are even certain offenses such as homosexuality and exhibitionism that go practically unprosecuted if committed by women. Female offenders are really protected by men, even by victims, who are usually disinclined to complain to authorities. Since women play much less active roles in society than men do, one must be prepared for the fact that women are often the instigators of crimes committed by men and, as instigators, they are hard to detect. There are several crimes that are ordinarily highly detectable in men but have very low detectability in women. Her roles as homemaker, mother, nurse, wife, and so forth, permit the female to commit a crime and yet screen that crime from public view—for example, slowly poisoning her husband or treating her children abusively. In addition, law enforcement officers, judges, and juries are much more lenient toward women than toward men. Such considerations lead to the conclusion that criminality of women is largely masked criminality. Consequently, official statistics and records of criminality should be expected to under-report female offenses. The true measure of female crime must be sought from unofficial sources. The masked character of female crime and its gross under-reporting are consistent with the official view that the female is a very low risk for crime.

40. What has the writer inferred about the incidence of female offenses? 40.____

    A. It gives an adequate representation of the number of crimes committed by men but instigated by women.
    B. It is not to be considered an important area of criminality.
    C. It is understated because the classic female role makes her less visible to social scrutiny.
    D. In every crime the incidence of male offenses is more difficult to detect than that of women.

41. Judges are inclined to be lenient toward female offenders because 41.____

    A. the role of the woman in society has stereotyped her as maternal and non-hostile
    B. the majority of their crimes do not physically harm others
    C. they commit crimes which are difficult to detect
    D. official statistics report them as less likely to commit crimes

42. Of the following, the title MOST suitable for this passage is 42.____

    A. Male Criminality
    B. The Petty Offender
    C. The Female Murderer
    D. Exposing Female Criminality

43. According to the passage, which of the following crimes is LEAST likely to be prosecuted against a woman?

   A. Child abuse
   B. Exhibitionism
   C. Homicide
   D. Prostitution

Questions 44-47.

DIRECTIONS: Questions 44 through 47 are based on the following passage.

The usual explanation for drunken behavior is that alcohol, which is a physiological depressant impairs reasoning and inhibition powers before it depresses the ability to act and to express emotion.

The purely physiological effects of alcohol are very much like those of fatigue. Individual personality and social and cultural influences apparently greatly determine how these effects are reflected in changed behavior as alcohol is consumed. Therefore, one can assert that alcohol alone does not cause drunken behavior; rather, drunken behavior expresses personal character, cultural traditions, and social circumstances, as they influence a person's reactions to the physiological effects of alcohol on his body.

For some people, and in some circumstances, these personal, cultural, and social factors may readily express themselves as criminal behavior. The most obvious case, of course, is public drunkenness.

The exact relationship between various crimes and various stages of intoxication is not completely known. G.M. Scott believes that the moderate stages of intoxication are the ones usually associated with crime, since the latter states of intoxication make performance of crime impossible. Dr. Banay found that many drunks are drawn into crime not only by the need of money to replace wages that drinking prevents them from earning, but also by their increased irritability and pugnacity.... He discovered that most of the sex offenses for which offenders are committed to state prisons show a relation between alcohol and the crime and that the average sex case is a clear-cut illustration of the hypothesis that alcohol covers up an underlying condition and that some dormant tendency is either brought to the surface or aggravated by alcohol.

In addition to drunken behavior resulting in criminal acts, it is also connected to several other important social problems. Reference can be made particularly to dependency, unemployment, desertion, divorce, vagrancy, and suicide. For all of these social ills, alcohol acts as the physiological depressing agent which influences one's deviation from normative behavior.

44. Discussions of intoxication customarily state that alcohol

   A. initially affects the analytic faculty
   B. initially affects the ability to express feelings
   C. reduces the desire for money
   D. stimulates perception of the true nature of one's condition

45. Which one of the following hypotheses would Dr. Banay MOST likely support?

    A. The casual drinker is less likely to commit a crime than the chronic drinker.
    B. An aggressive drunk is likely to have aggressive tendencies when not under the influence of alcohol.
    C. The underlying cause of most sex offenses is excessive drinking.
    D. There is no connection between cultural background and drunken behavior.

46. The title BEST suited for this passage is:

    A. How Alcohol Influences Potential Sexual Offenders
    B. Stages of Intoxication
    C. The Role of Alcoholic Consumption in Human Behavior
    D. The Relationship Between Alcohol and Emotion

47. The writer implies that

    A. a desire to destroy oneself is a frequent side effect of drinking intoxicating liquors
    B. a person who is drunk may find it easier to kill himself
    C. there is a pattern of drinking behavior in the background of most suicides
    D. there is no relationship between the problems of drinking and suicide

Questions 48-50.

DIRECTIONS: Questions 48 through 50 are based on the following passage.

A survey of the drinking behavior of 1,185 persons representing the adult population of Iowa in 2008 aged 21 years and older revealed that approximately 40 percent were abstainers. Of the nearly 1 million drinkers in the State, 47 percent were classed as light drinkers, 37 percent as moderate, and 16 percent as heavy drinkers. Twenty-two percent of the men drinkers were classed as heavy drinkers but only 8 percent of the women drinkers. The proportion of heavy drinkers increased with level of education among drinkers residing in the city –from 15 percent of the least educated to 22 percent of the most educated but decreased among farm residents from 17 percent of the least educated to 4 percent of the most educated. Age differences in the extent of drinking were not pronounced. The age class of 36-45 had the lowest proportions of light drinkers while the age class 61 and over had the lowest proportion of heavy drinkers.

48. Of the total drinking population in Iowa, how many were moderate drinkers?

    A. 370,000　　B. 438　　C. 370　　D. 438,150

49. What percent of the men drinkers surveyed were NOT heavy drinkers?

    A. 60%
    C. 78%
    B. 84%
    D. Cannot be determined

50. According to the passage, which one of the following statements concerning heavy drinking would be CORRECT?

    A. Experts are in sharp conflict regarding the reason for heavy drinking.
    B. The amount of heavy drinking in the city is directly proportional to the amount of education.
    C. The degree of heavy drinking is directly proportional to the age class of the drinkers.
    D. The degree of heavy drinking is inversely to the number of light drinkers.

KEY (CORRECT ANSWERS)

1. A	11. D	21. C	31. B	41. A
2. D	12. A	22. B	32. D	42. D
3. C	13. C	23. D	33. D	43. B
4. B	14. A	24. C	34. A	44. A
5. C	15. C	25. C	35. C	45. B
6. B	16. A	26. A	36. D	46. C
7. D	17. B	27. D	37. A	47. B
8. D	18. A	28. B	38. C	48. A
9. B	19. C	29. D	39. A	49. C
10. C	20. B	30. C	40. C	50. B

EXAMINATION SECTION
TEST 1

DIRECTIONS: Each question or incomplete statement is followed by several suggested answers or completions. Select the one that BEST answers the question or completes the statement. *PRINT THE LETTER OF THE CORRECT ANSWER IN THE SPACE AT THE RIGHT.*

1. Of the following, the CORRECT statement describing the rule regarding visits to institutions by employees of central office is that

    A. employees are not subject to the rules and regulations of the institutions they visit
    B. none of the rules and regulations of an institution are intended to apply to an employee of central office in such a manner as to interfere with the efficient performance of the employee's proper duties while within the institution
    C. the rules and regulations of an institution are intended to apply in all cases to central office employees
    D. the head of the institution determines what institutional rules and regulations apply to central office employees

1.____

2. The one of the following which should NOT be included in a report of an investigation is

    A. information which tells what was done, and who did it
    B. a conclusion regarding the subject of the investigation
    C. an introductory paragraph identifying the subject of the investigation
    D. a recommendation concerned with matters unrelated to the conclusion noted in the report

2.____

3. Whenever a wire tapping or *bugging* device is to be used in an institution, the head of the institution must

    A. ask the proper district attorney for permission
    B. apply to the proper court for authorization
    C. obtain direct authorization of the commissioner of correction
    D. take no other action than to have the device installed

3.____

4. When an employee of the department is given permission to peruse his personal history folder on file at his institution, it is required that

    A. a representative of the employee's collective bargaining unit be present
    B. a superior officer be present
    C. the central personnel office approve his request
    D. the employee submit the proper forms giving the reasons for his request

4.____

5. Assume that an inmate is being held in a court detention pen following transfer from an institution. The captain in charge of the pen receives an order of discharge from the court. The correct action for the captain to take is to

    A. call the institution from which the inmate was transferred to determine what course of action to take
    B. inquire of the court whether the inmate may be discharged from the court detention pen

5.____

C. release the inmate directly from the court detention pen, provided there are no other commitments, warrants, or other detainers in his case
D. return the inmate to his institution for discharge

6. Assume that an employee of an institution has been served with a subpoena to appear in a legal proceeding regarding the official business of the department. Under such circumstances, the head of the institution concerned must

   A. contact the corporation counsel's office
   B. notify the department of investigation
   C. request all pertinent facts from the appropriate district attorney if the matter involves a criminal action
   D. submit without delay to the commissioner an oral and written report of the matter

Questions 7-13.

DIRECTIONS: Questions 7 through 13 consist of two statements. Choose answer
   A. if both statements are correct;
   B. if neither statement is correct;
   C. if statement I only is correct but not statement II;
   D. if statement II only is correct but not statement I

7. I. No manuscript shall be written for publication by any employee of the department which in any way refers to departmental business or individual inmates without first obtaining authorization from the head of his institution.
   II. No research project involving inmates or departmental business shall be undertaken without the written authorization of the commissioner of correction.

8. I. The assistant deputy warden shall serve as the principal assistant to the deputy warden and, in such capacity, he will investigate complaints, unusual occurrences, inmate infractions, and perform such other duties as directed.
   II. A member of the police department shall not be granted an interview with a prisoner unless he receives permission from the district attorney who has jurisdiction of the case.

9. I. Inmates shall be permitted to receive directly from the publisher any publication requested by them, except one which is inflammatory in nature or violates United States postal regulations.
   II. When an employee absents himself without leave and fails to communicate with his institution or division for a period of twenty work days, such absence shall be deemed to constitute a resignation effective on the date of its commencement unless the commissioner, in his discretion, sees fit to accept an explanation, for such unauthorized absence.

10. I. Although a head of an institution shall exercise the right of search of any employee or visitor, an employee who refuses to be searched may not be forceably searched.
    II. An employee of any institution, except a superior officer, may not make a complaint against any other employee of the department.

11.   I. When contraband is found on prisoners who are received from the police, the contraband must be taken from the prisoners by the police officer before they are confined in detention pens or hospital prison wards.
      II. In an emergency an inmate may be transferred to a hospital for treatment upon authorization of the superior officer in charge of the institution at the time.

12.   I. No employee of the department shall, without prior notification to the commissioner of correction, personally or otherwise file any charge against any inmate or employee for any offense or criminal act which occurs in any institution of the department.
      II. Disciplinary charges may be preferred against any employee of the department who fails to pay his financial obligations.

13.   I. Whenever any memorandum, communication or other matter of a derogatory nature is to be placed in an employee's personal history folder, the employee concerned will be notified in writing in all cases.
      II. Unexcused latenesses not exceeding four (4) in number, or not exceeding a total of one (1) hour in one (1) month, shall be deducted from annual leave on an equal time basis.

14. Correctional organizations did not make use of the findings of social science researchers as a basis for program formulation and policy decisions MAINLY because

    A. many administrators were not sincere about rehabilitation but merely wished to manipulate staff and social science consultants for their own professional advancement
    B. the research was not integrated with a knowledge of operational problems, and correctional administrators did not understand the social science approach
    C. rivalry existed among the various disciplines represented by the social science researchers, making it difficult to incorporate their findings into feasible programs
    D. the research did not provide basic information about offenders such as numbers, rates, trends, and individual characteristics

15. The contemporary trend in corrections is toward the integration of research and action. Researchers are becoming increasingly acquainted with correctional organizations, while correctional managers are becoming aware of the uses of social science research in the development of action programs. The one of the following which has been found to be a MAJOR reason for this trend is that

    A. correctional managers now realize that researchers can contribute information on research findings important for correctional program development
    B. correction officers now receive better training
    C. crime has increased rapidly and, therefore, there is a great need for research to determine causes, treatment, and prevention
    D. researchers have become interested in correctional matters today because of their desire to contribute to the development of possible control programs

16. A significant feature of the trend toward an atmosphere of partnership between inmates and staff members in the process of rehabilitation has been the growth of custodial staff communication with both inmates and treatment personnel. As institution staff have been encouraged to be more relaxed about maintaining custody and discipline, they have been able to

A. direct inmates to become more aware of society's need for retribution
B. obtain better opportunities for promotion to higher positions since they get to know inmates better
C. eliminate the need for *stool pigeons* to learn what is going on in the institution
D. rely more on inmate morale and cooperation than on repression for maintaining order

17. Opposition of most prison officials to advisory or governing functions by inmate groups stems from scattered episodes of abuses by such groups. The one of the following that is an abuse is that

    A. inmate cliques have sometimes controlled elections to councils
    B. inmates tend to lose interest in rehabilitation efforts because they can become more manipulative with staff
    C. institution staff resent being told what to do by inmates
    D. the effects of group counseling are minimized as inmate councils manipulate the other inmates

Questions 18-22.

DIRECTIONS: Questions 18 through 22 consist of two statements. Choose answer
   A. if both statements are correct
   B. if neither statement is correct
   C. if statement I only is correct but not statement II
   D. if statement II only is correct but not statement I

18. I. Slightly more than half of the offenders sentenced to correctional treatment in 1965 were placed on probation.
    II. Probation is the correctional treatment used for most offenders today and is likely to be used increasingly in the future.

19. I. There are many offenders for whom incarceration is the appropriate sanction either because of their dangerousness or the seriousness of their offense, or both.
    II. The simple expedient of reducing probation and parole case loads will assure a reduction in recidivism.

20. I. Today, the halfway house is not viewed as a potential alternative to institutionalization since it is a form of institutionalization.
    II. When an individual returns from a temporary release to home, work, or school, his experience can be discussed with him by staff, to try to assess his probable adjustment and to note incipient problems.

21. I. Parole has, on occasion, been attacked as *leniency* because it rarely, if ever, serves as a means of public protection.
    II. The legal framework within which parole decisions are made does not vary widely from one jurisdiction to another.

22. I. The present range of discretion following conviction, which allows judges and correctional authorities to consider individual characteristics before determining sentence, is to a great extent the result of developments in penology which emphasize differential treatment and rehabilitation.
II. There is some danger that if prisoners are conceded certain legal rights they will devote their energies to fighting legal battles rather than accepting the correctional regimen and devoting themselves to more productive activities, and that, therefore, rehabilitation will be impeded.

23. Institutions where there is good morale generally have fewer escapes and escape attempts than do institutions where morale is poor. Morale can be controlled by the manner in which the jail is administered. Of the following, the MOST important element in the control of morale is

    A. elimination of mail censorship
    B. improvements in jail sanitation
    C. liberal visiting provisions with emphasis on open visits
    D. well-trained and capable jail personnel

24. The one of the following that is NOT predicted for the future of corrections is that

    A. empirical research methods will be employed to assess the effectiveness of programs
    B. institutional programs will place greater emphasis on preparation for release and less on escapes and economic production
    C. new correctional institutions will be smaller
    D. parole boards will continue to function at the present level

25. Which of the following is the MOST valid statement concerning female prisoners?

    A. Women have more intense homosexual relationships in prison than men prisoners do.
    B. In their attitudes towards the law and legal institutions, women prisoners appear to be more positive than male prisoners.
    C. Despite the fact that the worst type of female offender is sent to prison, women prisoners cause fewer problems than men when they are actually in prison.
    D. Because the families of women prisoners are less apt to be disrupted, women need less parole assistance than men do.

26. Recidivists outnumber the first-termers in the prison population at any given time. Of this group, it has been found that

    A. low intelligence is the most important cause of recidivism
    B. the percentage of recidivists under twenty years of age is lower than the average
    C. the crime of auto theft has the highest percentage of recidivists
    D. of all the prison admissions in one year, less than half have been there before

27. In the study of the relationship of biological factors to crime, it has been found that epilepsy

    A. occurs more frequently in prison populations than in the general population
    B. is the cause of most cases of arrest for assault
    C. is a factor in the majority of sex crimes
    D. is not a bar to social adjustment, as its side effects are controlled with relative ease

28. With regard to the correctional client, it has been found that

    A. his experience with authority has been aggressive and harsh
    B. he is repressed and introspective rather than an acting-out person
    C. his natural athletic ability is not up to that of the non-offender
    D. he accepts the blame for his anti-social acts but feels no guilt about them

29. Many correctional programs include cosmetic surgery for selected prisoners mainly because

    A. it improves the inmate's physical health and allows him to learn new activities
    B. cosmetic surgery should be available to inmates if it is available to the free community
    C. deviant behavior may be a social reaction to a disfigurement
    D. such treatment is mandated by federal mental health programs

30. Private organizations also serve as watchdogs over the governmental function in corrections and criminal justice. They bring political weight to move agencies of government in desired directions.
    Which of the following statements about a private agency is NOT correct?

    A. The Salvation Army provides material assistance in the form of residential homes, food, and clothing for discharged prisoners.
    B. The American Correctional Association functions as the federal government's coordinating agency for state, municipal, and county institutions.
    C. The Correctional Association of New York includes among its objectives the improvement of conditions existing within prisons.
    D. The Fortune Society supplies speakers on first-hand experience with prison life.

Questions 31-34.

DIRECTIONS: Questions 31 through 34 consist of two statements. Choose answer
    A. if both statements are correct
    B. if neither statement is correct
    C. if statement I only is correct but not statement II
    D. if statement II only is correct but not statement I

31. I. Therapeutic care does not see the client as the victim of forces outside his immediate control which must be counteracted.
    II. Criminals are interesting to the social scientist because their deviant behavior and the societal response to their deviation raise major questions.

32. I. The classical theory of crime assumed that punishment did not serve as a deterrent to crime.
    II. The positivist theory of crime shifted emphasis from penology to criminology.

33. I. The adjustment of the releasee is influenced strongly by the characteristic patterns of the social institutions of his particular postprison milieu.
    II. Success in functional adjustment does not depend upon the degree of deviation between the release prisoner's own norms and those of the group to which he is expected to adjust.

34. I. In most prisons, psychiatrists have little time or hospital space to conduct a program of individual or group therapy, which should be their major function.
    II. Personality characteristics are not indicators of which prisoners are more likely to escape since freedom is the primary goal of all prisoners.

34.____

35. Which of the following statements regarding the drug addict is NOT in accordance with accepted authority?

35.____

   A. Psychologists have emphasized the strong dependency needs and feelings of inadequacy of the addict.
   B. The addict may be comfortable and function well as long as he receives the quantities of drugs he requires.
   C. The cure from physiological dependence on opiates may be secured in a relatively short time.
   D. Under the influence of heroin, the sex drive of the addict is greatly increased.

36. The one of the following which has been a MAJOR obstacle to effective rehabilitation of prison inmates is the fact that

36.____

   A. inmates have not been able to handle the permissiveness of the group approach to treatment
   B. most correctional staff members are not interested in assuming new roles and in communicating constructively with inmates
   C. the inconclusive results of treatment programs have reinforced doubts that prison inmates are capable of behavioral change
   D. the inmate culture itself raises barriers against genuine participation of prisoners in treatment programs

37. While conducting a training session for correction officers, of the following, the MOST valid point that you can make on the subject of suicide is that

37.____

   A. prisoners who are observed talking to themselves in a halting manner are suicidal and must be reported to the psychiatrist
   B. those who try to commit suicide and fail often try again
   C. the prisoner who tells a member of the staff that he is going to commit suicide should be ignored as he is engaging in a manipulative device
   D. minor attempts at suicide, such as injuring the arm with shallow cuts, should be reported to the captain for disciplinary action rather than to a psychiatrist

38. A superior officer brings to your attention the matter of an inmate who continually states that there are people in the jail who are out to get him. He is very agitated about it and fears for his life. The BEST action for you to take is to

38.____

   A. talk to the inmate and try to convince him that his fears are unfounded
   B. assign another inmate to the same cell with instructions to watch him
   C. refer the matter to a superior for possible referral for treatment
   D. reprimand the inmate for causing trouble by this behavior

39. A recent report listed 14 characteristics present in certain individuals in a criminal population. One of these characteristics is *immaturity*. Which one of the following is NOT listed as a characteristic of the immature personality?

    A. Lack of ability to articulate feelings and ideas
    B. Inability to postpone gratification
    C. An orientation of the individual as receiver and a tendency to view others as givers
    D. Preoccupation with concrete and immediate objects, wishes, and needs

40. The custodial aspect of the treatment system presently consists of a trichotomy composed of probation, incarceration, and parole - rather than a single unified operation. The reason for this division is the fact that, historically, incarceration was viewed as a method which

    A. is an inexpensive but slow means of inmate rehabilitation, while probation and parole developed as a means of leading the public to believe that rehabilitation was taking place
    B. emphasizes punishment; probation developed as a means of becoming accustomed to punishment, while parole developed as a primary method for insuring the effectiveness of incarceration
    C. focuses upon punishment; probation developed as a method of avoiding the infliction of punishment, while parole developed as a method of relieving punishment
    D. stresses adjustment to society and thus redemption; probation developed as a method of avoiding the infliction of punishment, while parole developed as a means of relieving punishment

41. The single MOST important factor to bear in mind when considering the problems involved in changing an offender is that the ultimate change sought

    A. depends upon the inmate becoming a self-disciplined person
    B. is a harmonious adjustment to institutional life
    C. is adjustment to freedom in the community
    D. is making the offender aware that institutional life is not a penalty but an opportunity

42. The term *sanction* largely comprises formal community condemnation, deprivation of rights or privileges, and forfeiture of property. All sanctions tend to be characterized as punishment. Punishment is an operational term and requires two additional factors to be effective, as follows:

    A. A high degree of certainty that the commission of the crime will result in sanctions and a belief on the part of the wrongdoer that sanctions are essential for his well-being
    B. An attitude on the part of the general community that punishment is necessary and fair, simultaneously accompanied by an inmate attitude that institutional life is, in most respects, neither better nor worse than life on the *outside*
    C. An intention to make the sanction unpleasant for the individual offender, and a recognition on the part of the individual offender that the sanction is unpleasant
    D. Conversion of institutions from *hotels* to training centers and a recognition that budgetary problems are not nearly as important as the firmness of correctional personnel

43. Rational and efficient utilization of custody requires rational and efficient utilization of incarceration and field supervision, which are the instrumentalities of custody.
The BEST way to accomplish this purpose is to

    A. identify the purpose or purposes to be served, the requirements of same, and the appropriate instrumentality to fulfill these requirements
    B. select field supervision as an instrumentality where there is a clear need for severity as a general deterrent
    C. select incarceration as an instrumentality only when there is assurance that incarceration would last for a minimum of five years
    D. use these instrumentalities, as needed, for the prevention of recidivism

44. The one of the following which authorities, in discussing treatment and rehabilitation of criminal offenders, do NOT suggest is that

    A. treatment that seems most likely to help individuals to overcome problems that seem to impede adjustment to the community must be applied
    B. the treatment system must continue to function as it has in the past since its effectiveness has been demonstrated
    C. treatment should be directed at those characteristics of the offender which are inconsistent with the basic characteristics needed to function acceptably in society
    D. the difficulty in performing at a generally accepted level in basic social areas significantly contributes to criminal conduct

45. The most understandable mood into which many Americans have been plunged by crime is one of frustration and bewilderment.
The BEST explanation for this nood of frustration and bewilderment is tha

    A. an examination of crime in America raises a myriad of issues of the utmost complexity
    B. crimes occur in urban areas where populations are large and there is much conflict between people
    C. successful criminals have many of the attributes of respected members of society
    D. the fight against organized crime involves many segments of business enterprise

46. Crimes can no more be lumped together for purposes of analysis than can measles and schizophrenia, or lung cancer and a broken ankle.
The one of the following which BEST explains the meaning of the foregoing statement is that

    A. controlling violent crime presents a number of distinct problems
    B. crime is a social problem because society makes the laws
    C. individuals who are prone to crime present pathological conditions because of poor mental health
    D. thinking of crimes as a whole is futile because there are so many different kinds of criminal acts

47. The most serious crimes are the ones that consist of or employ physical aggression. The one of the following which is the main reason for this conclusion is that

    A. a small number of murders are cleared by arrest and a small proportion of those arrested are convicted
    B. most of these crimes are committed by drug addicts
    C. such crimes are less susceptible to deterrence by police patrol
    D. the injuries such crimes inflict are grievous and frequently irreparable

47.____

48. America must translate its well-founded alarm about crime into social action that will prevent crime.
The MOST significant of the following actions that can be taken against crime is to

    A. make sure every American is given the opportunities and the freedom that will enable him to assume his responsibilities
    B. enlarge the size of police and correctional forces
    C. require in-service training in human relations to be given to all personnel having contact with any segment of the criminal underwork.
    D. remove the police from confinement in radio motor patrol cars and reassign *them* to foot patrol

48.____

49. Methadone maintenance has gained prominence in programs for the treatment of drug addiction. The viewpoint of the sponsors of this experimental method of treatment is that

    A. medical cure of the addict must be accomplished before his social rehabilitation is attempted
    B. medical cure of the addic and social rehabilitation should be handled simultaneously
    C. methadone maintenance is more realistic than medical cure, because methadone can be given to addicts who are not highly motivated
    D. social rehabilitation of the addict is more important than the medical cure of addiction itself

49.____

50. The American Correctional Association is working towards the accreditation of prisons and other correctional programs. Such accreditation would PRIMARILY involve

    A. federal intervention to ensure that the civil rights of inmates are fully protected
    B. careful evaluation of reports on institutional conditions prepared by state officials
    C. institutional self-evaluation for the elimination of sub-standard practices based on the *Manual of Correctional Standards*
    D. eliminating any existing stresses between professional and custodial personnel

50.____

KEY (CORRECT ANSWERS)

1. B	11. C	21. B	31. D	41. C
2. D	12. A	22. A	32. D	42. C
3. C	13. D	23. D	33. C	43. A
4. B	14. B	24. D	34. C	44. B
5. C	15. A	25. A	35. D	45. A
6. D	16. D	26. C	36. D	46. D
7. D	17. A	27. A	37. B	47. D
8. C	18. A	28. A	38. C	48. A
9. A	19. C	29. C	39. A	49. D
10. B	20. D	30. B	40. C	50. C

TEST 2

DIRECTIONS: Each question or incomplete statement is followed by several suggested answers or completions. Select the one that BEST answers the question or completes the statement. *PRINT THE LETTER OF THE CORRECT ANSWER IN THE SPACE AT THE RIGHT.*

1. No program of rehabilitation can be effective on a prisoner who is convinced in his own mind that he is in prison because he is a victim of a mindless, undirected, and corrupt system of justice. There are numerous reasons for prisoners feeling this way.
Which of the following choices usually has the LEAST validity?

   A. Unequal sentences are received for the same conduct as a result of plea bargaining.
   B. The prisoner was unjustly convicted of a crime committed by someone else.
   C. Money is of considerable assistance in helping an accused person to stay out of jail or prison.
   D. Disparities in sentences are caused by the geographical areas in which the cases are adjudicated.

1.___

2. An integral part of an institutional work program is the matter of wages paid to prisoners. With regard to work programs, *The Official Report of the New York State Special Commission on Attica* advocated the following, with the EXCEPTION of

   A. payment of salaries to inmates in order to help provide them with a sense of self-worth
   B. payment to inmates for their work in accordance with the reasonable value of their services
   C. work assignments as part of the punishment-reward system
   D. payment of inmates while they are being trained

2.___

3. According to *The Official Report of the New york State Special Commission on Attica,* in 1971, prior to the uprising at the Attica Correctional Facility, the GREATEST source of inmate anxiety and frustration was the

   A. remoteness of the institution from the homes of its prisoners
   B. inability of the inmate group to participate in the decision-making processes of the institution
   C. calibre of the correction officers
   D. operation of the conditional release and parole systems

3.___

4. The Special Commission on Attica investigated and commented on the parole system. Which of the following statements on the parole system is NOT correct, on the basis of the *Official Report?*

   A. In practice, the Parole Board, not the judge, decides how long an inmate will serve time.
   B. The grant of parole often depends on factors over which the inmate no longer has control once he is in prison.
   C. Approximately 80 percent of the inmates appearing before the Parole Board were granted parole on their initial appearance during the eight months prior to the uprising at Attica.
   D. Inmates, including those receiving favorable decisions, believe that the parole system is capricious and demeaning.

4.___

5. It must be ironic to a prisoner to recall that society spared no expense to afford him three, four or five trials and appeals, at enormous costs, but then proceeds to forget his plight. This statement IMPLIES that

   A. more money should be spent for the treatment of prisoners and less for the adjudication of criminal cases
   B. substantial sums of money are justifiably required to ensure that the innocent are not wrongly convicted
   C. less money should be spent on the judicial process as it has not helped to reduce the rate of recidivism
   D. more money should be spent for a prisoner's treatment, in order to be consistent with the investment in convicting him

6. Critics of the methadone detoxification program base their opposition on the fact that it

   A. is available to all drug abusers who ask for it
   B. has the effect of bringing the addict's emotional problems to the surface
   C. discourages constructive research for a cure for drug abuse
   D. substitutes one form of addiction for another

7. The theory that some persons adopt illegitimate means of achieving their goals because society has placed obstacles in the way of fulfillment of these goals by legitimate means is known as the

   A. Cloward and Ohlin theory of differential opportunity
   B. Sutherland theory of differential association
   C. Glaser theory of differential identification
   D. Turner theory of differential response to the reference group

8. The percentage of mentally disturbed prisoners of the average population of inmates is approximately

   A. 5% B. 15% C. 35% D. 55%

9. Under which of the following conditions may inmates of jails and detainees register and vote by absentee ballot? The person must

   A. previously have voted In his community
   B. not have been convicted of a Class C felony
   C. not have been convicted of an indictable offense
   D. be a pre-trial prisoner who is eligible to vote

10. Riots in correctional institutions are attributed to a multiplicity of causes. However, the cause which has been singled out as the MOST critical is:

    A. Inadequacies of the bail system, which discriminates against those who would otherwise be eligible for bail except for lack of funds
    B. Overcrowding, which curtails the processing of cases in the courts and interferes with the provision of necessary services to prison inmates
    C. Lack of communication between custodial staff and inmates, due to language difficulties and the need for sensitivity training
    D. Inadequate medical and mental health services, particularly in the detention institutions

11. The modern penal thinking is that prisoners should be rehabilitated and that the punishment should fit the offender rather than the crime.
    According to the McKay Commission and many authorities in the field of correction, application of this theory has been

    A. *successful,* since a fair percentage of released prisoners do not recidivate
    B. *unsuccessful,* because offenders do not stay in penal institutions long enough for proper rehabilitation
    C. *successful,* because most prisoners participate in treatment and work programs which they continue when returned to society
    D. *unsuccessful,* because efforts at rehabilitation have not really been tried with appropriate and adequate programs

12. The classification process is BEST described as

    A. the method of arriving at the most effective means of making the inmate pay for the crime of which he has been convicted
    B. an organized procedure for establishing a program designed to obtain the maximum contribution of the inmate to institutional training activities
    C. organized procedures by means of which diagnosis, treatment-planning, and the carrying out of the component parts of the general treatment program are focused on the individual in prison and on parole
    D. a system in which a committee participates in the assignment of inmates to those programs the prisoners believe will serve them to best advantage

13. It is wholly logical to integrate institutions and parole since the period spent in the institution and that spent on parole are part of the same sentence. The chief reason according to authorities why parole and institution systems have NOT been more closely coordinated administratively in the past is that

    A. custodial personnel view the parole function as ineffective and occasionally view parole boards as being political in their decisions
    B. institutions focus on custody whereas parole boards tend to downgrade the purposes of custody
    C. parole board members are nearly always professional personnel whereas institutional personnel are largely non-professional
    D. since parole boards make quasi-judicial decisions it was felt that they should have a maximum of independence in granting or revoking paroles

14. Control of prison operations and activities has always been important to insure that the program and policy of the institution are carried out and to avoid mismanagement by unscrupulous or incompetent personnel or by individuals or groups of inmates getting into positions of power. Traditionally, the head of the institution sought to control operations by constant personal inspection of all areas and frequent contact with all personnel and a large number of inmates.
    Of the following, the MOST appropriate reason why the head of an institution who practices modern institutional management does not take the role described in this passage is that

A. inmates of modern institutions are harder to control
B. modern correctional institutions have effective rehabilitation programs
C. the head of an institution now depends more on sound organizational planning
D. there are different types of inmates in institutions today

15. The one of the following that is NOT included as an essential feature of good organizational structure for an institution for adult prisoners is a system for

    A. developing and maintaining constructive community relationships
    B. the development and training of personnel
    C. getting information through the use of an inmate *grapevine*
    D. the coordination of activities of the various specialties in the institution

16. It has been held that the maximum population for a prison for adults should not exceed 1,200. The question then arises, *Why in this country do we have institutions of 5,000 or more?* The one of the following which is best offered as a reason for this is that

    A. analysis of operating costs usually show that large overcrowded institutions are characterized by lower per capita costs
    B. both correctional personnel and inmates prefer large institutions since such institutions give one the feeling of belonging to a community
    C. institutions with large inmate populations tend to bring disturbances under control more quickly than small institutions since problem inmates can more readily be segregated and housed in large institutions
    D. the public likes to see new institutions housing enormous numbers of inmates in out-of-the-way places

17. The existence of a program of inmate activities which includes such things as work, recreation, and education is viewed by prison management as

    A. rather low in the priorities accorded to institutional needs
    B. a sound and safe security measure
    C. a security hazard only in poorly managed institutions of the minimum security type
    D. unnecessary at institutions where efficient operating procedures, modern structures, and well-trained personnel help assure security

18. The fundamental responsibility of prison management is the secure custody and control of prisoners. This is universally prescribed by law, custom, and public opinion. Although at times such a concept may seem at variance with attempts to introduce rehabilitative services, it is doubtful that any correctional program which ignores this reality will long endure. Actually services and facilities for rehabilitative treatment can operate effectively only in a climate where control is constant. Conversely, good control cannot be consistently maintained without energizing it with positive correctional and training resources. Of the following, the MOST appropriate conclusion to be drawn from this statement is that

    A. custody and inmate treatment programs are incompatible because the primary role of a correctional institution is custody
    B. there must be good control in an institution if rehabilitation programs are to be most effective

C. inmate treatment programs must be considered separate and apart from custody requirements
D. rehabilitation is less successful where control is constant because programs have to be geared to custody and security needs

19. Assume that a new warden has been placed in charge of an institution. He is faced with the problem of deciding how strict or how relaxed discipline should be. It would be better for him to begin by setting standards of discipline which are

    A. relaxed rather than strict because discipline should bear a direct relationship to the kind of violations committed and to the manner of their being committed
    B. relaxed rather than strict since the good will of correctional personnel is a primary consideration
    C. strict rather than relaxed because it is easier to relax discipline rather than to tighten discipline
    D. strict rather than relaxed since both inmates and correction officers usually devise all manner of strategems to see how far a new warden can be pushed

20. There has been increasing recognition that a major function of the correctional institution is to influence change in the attitudes and behavior of the offender. Counseling is one of the services which has become a tool in meeting this goal. Of the following, the BEST definition of counseling is that it is

    A. a means of giving advice and admonition
    B. a tool for changing a person's personality which is used without the inmate's knowledge
    C. an activity assigned only to professional caseworkers or psychiatric staff
    D. the personal and group relationships undertaken by staff to help inmates solve their problems of adjustment

21. Women's institutions have made notable contributions to penology and, in fact, several of them are rated as among the best institutions. Of the following, the CHIEF reason for women's institutions having achieved this status is that

    A. female prisoners, with few exceptions, are much more inclined to accept the values of society
    B. personnel in women's institutions understand their charges better than do personnel in institutions for men
    C. public opinion, which is less antagonistic toward women offenders, has not blocked innovations implemented in women's institutions
    D. the funds available for each women's institution is greater than for each male institution because there are fewer of them

22. American detention facilities have, in the main, failed to keep abreast of developments in other areas of correctional practice. Of the following, the BEST explanation for this failure is that

    A. detention facilities have generally held very low status in corrections
    B. most detention facilities receive *unusual prisoners*
    C. nearly all detention facilities operate as independent local units with little or no state supervision or inspection
    D. the detention facility is the oldest of all institutions for the incarceration of law violators

23. The MAIN goal of a community residential facility is to 23.____
    A. aid the re-entry of the offender into a society which has excluded him
    B. enable inmates to earn money through outside employment when they have families to support
    C. enable inmates to obtain a sum of money before release from custody
    D. reward inmates for good behavior and proper attitudes while in custody

24. Rotating employees on various job assignments is a practice that is generally 24.____
    A. *desirable,* chiefly because employees and inmates may become too friendly
    B. *undesirable,* chiefly because employees are unable to learn a specific job thoroughly
    C. *desirable,* chiefly because employees can develop greater versatility and teamwork
    D. *undesirable,* chiefly because employees who gain a little knowledge believe they have all the answers

25. Assume that a decision has been made to create a center in a community to meet the needs of released inmates. It can be anticipated that the community will fear the presence of released inmates. An effective way for dealing with community fear is to 25.____
    A. devise programs so that released inmates and members of the community will get to know each other
    B. make sure that the centers are used exclusively by one-time offenders who have no history of addiction to hard drugs
    C. see that extra police patrol the area surrounding the center, particularly during hours of darkness
    D. set up information booths in the center and in the vicinity of the center so that members of the public are given to understand the need for rehabilitative efforts

26. The one of the following which is the CHIEF reason for the difference between administration of justice agencies and that of other units in public administration is that 26.____
    A. correctional institutions are concerned with security
    B. some defendants are proven to be innocent after trial
    C. the administration of justice is much more complicated than other aspects of public administration
    D. correctional institutions produce services their *clients* or *customers* fail to understand or ask for

27. Of the following, the MOST important reason why employees resist change is that 27.____
    A. they have not received adequate training in preparation for the change
    B. experience has shown that when new ideas don't work, employees get blamed and not the individuals responsible for the new ideas
    C. new ideas and methods almost always represent a threat to the security of the individuals involved
    D. new ideas often are not practical and disrupt operations unnecessarily

28. Stress situations are ideal for building up a backlog of knowledge about an employee's behavior. Not only does it inform the supervisor of many aspects of a person's behavior patterns, but it is also vitally important to have fore-knowledge of how people behave under stress in occupations concerned with law enforcement, corrections, and the courts.
The one of the following which is NOT implied by the author of this passage is that

   A. a person under stress may give some indication of his unsuitability for work in a correctional institution
   B. putting people under stress is the best means of determining their usual patterns of behavior
   C. stress situations may give important clues about performance in the correctional service
   D. there is a need to know about a person's reaction to situations *when the chips are down*

29. There are situations requiring a supervisor to give direct orders to subordinates assigned to work under the direct control of other supervisors. Under which of the following conditions would this shift of command responsibility be MOST appropriate?

   A. Emergency operations require the cooperative action of two or more organizational units.
   B. One of the other supervisors is not doing his job, thus defeating the goals of the organization.
   C. The subordinates are performing their assigned tasks in the absence of their own supervisor.
   D. The subordinates ask a superior officer who is not their own supervisor how to perform an assignment given them by their supervisor.

30. The one of the following which BEST differentiates staff supervision from line supervision is that

   A. staff supervision has the authority to immediately correct a line subordinate's action
   B. staff supervision is an advisory relationship
   C. line supervision goes beyond the normal boundaries of direct supervision within a *command*
   D. line supervision does not report findings and make recommendations

31. Decision-making is a rational process calling for a *suspended judgment* by the supervisor until all the facts have been ascertained and analyzed, and the consequences of alternative courses of action studied; then the decision maker

   A. acts as both judge and jury and selects what he believes to be the best of the alternative plans
   B. consults with those who will be most directly involved to obtain a recommendation as to the most appropriate course of action
   C. reviews the facts which he has already analyzed, reduces his thoughts to writing, and selects that course of action which can have the fewest negative consequences if his thinking contains an error
   D. stops, considers the matter for at least a 24-hour period, before referring it to a superior for evaluation

32. Decision-making can be defined as the

   A. delegation of authority and responsibility to persons capable of performing their assigned duties with moderate or little supervision
   B. imposition of a supervisor's decision upon a work group
   C. technique of selecting the course of action with the most desired consequences and the least undesired or unexpected consequences
   D. process principally concerned with improvement of procedures

33. A supervisor who is not well-motivated and has no desire to accept basic responsibilities will

   A. compromise to the extent of permitting poor performance for lengthy periods without correction
   B. get good performance from his work group if the employees are satisfied with their pay and other working conditions
   C. not have marginal workers in his work group if the work is interesting
   D. perform adequately as long as the work of his group consists of routine operations

34. A supervisor is more than a bond or connecting link between two levels of employees. He has joint responsibility which must be shared with both management and with the work group.
    Of the following, the statement which BEST expresses the meaning of this statement is:

   A. A supervisor works with both management and the work group and must reconcile the differences between them
   B. In management, the supervisor is solely concerned with efforts directing the work of his subordinates
   C. The supervisory role is basically that of a liaison man between management and the work force
   D. What a supervisor says and does when confronted with day-to-day problems depends upon his level in the organization

35. Operations research is the observation of operations in business or government, and it utilizes both hypotheses and controlled experiments to determine the outcome of decisions. In effect, it reproduces the future impact on the decision in a clinical environment suited to intensive study. Operations research has

   A. been more promising than applied research in the ascertaining of knowledge for the purpose of decision-making
   B. never been amenable to fact analysis on the grand scale
   C. not been used extensively in government
   D. proven to be the only rational and logical approach to decision-making on long-range problems

36. Assume that a civilian makes a complaint regarding the behavior of a certain correction officer to the supervisor of the correction officer. The supervisor regards the complaint as unjustified and unreasonable. In these circumstances, the supervisor

   A. must make a written note of the complaint and forward it through channels to tte unit or individual responsible for complaint investigations
   B. should assure the complainant that disciplinary action will be appropriate to tte seriousness of the alleged offense
   C. should immediately summer the correction officer, if he is available, so that the correction officer may attempt to straighten out the difficulty
   D. should inform the complainant that his complaint appears to be unjustified, and unreasonable

37. Modern management usually establishes a personal history folder for an employee at the time of hiring. Disciplinary matters appear in such personal history folders. Employees do not like the idea of disciplinary actions appearing in their permanent personal folders. Authorities believe that

   A. after a few years have passed since the commission of the infraction, disciplirary actions should be removed from folders
   B. disciplinary actions should remain in folders; it is not the records but the use of records that requires detailed study
   C. most personnel have not had disciplinary action taken against them and would resent the removal of disciplinary actions from such, folders
   D. there is no point in removing disciplinary actions from personal history fo]ders since employees who have been guilty of infractions should not be allowed to forget their infractions

38. While supervisors should not fear the acceptance of responsibility, they

   A. generally seek out responsibility that subordinates should exercise, particularly when the supervisors do not have sufficient work to do
   B. must be on guard against the abuse of authority that often accompanies the acceptance of total responsibility
   C. should avoid responsibility that is customarily exercised by their superiors
   D. who are anxious for promotions accept responsibility but do not exercise the authority warranted by the responsibility

39. While in the field of corrections the opportunities for work improvement are tremendous, work improvement has been neglected because

   A. custody and treatment have been regarded as more important than on-the-job efficiency
   B. goals in correction are well defined but are not fully understood
   C. the work is not repetitious and productivity cannot be measured easily
   D. there is little hope of rehabilitating the heroin addict until he reaches middle age

40. Planning is part of the decision-making process. By planning is meant the development of details of alternative plans of action. The key to effective planning is

   A. careful research to determine whether a tentative plan has been tried at some time in the past
   B. participation by employees in planning, preferably those employees who will be involved in putting the selected plan into action
   C. speed; poor plans can be discarded after they are put into effect while good plans usually are not put into effect because of delays
   D. writing the plan up in considerable detail and then forwarding the plan, through channels, to the executive officer having final approval of the plan

40.____

41. Correctional institution riots are too complex and varied to be attributed to any one cause. The FIRST cause of riots is the

   A. deprivation of liberty as a result of incarceration
   B. indifferent attitude of the public toward correctional institutions
   C. lack of adequate culinary services
   D. presence in correctional institutions of some inmates with behavior problems

41.____

42. Equating strict discipline with punitive measures and lax discipline with rehabilitation creates a false dichotomy.
The one of the statements given below that would BEST follow from the belief expressed in this statement is that discipline

   A. is important for treatment
   B. militates against inmate treatment programs
   C. is not an important consideration in institutions where effective rehabilitation programs prevail
   D. minimizes the need for punitive measures if it is strict

42.____

43. The form that a riot takes determines what measure will be used to suppress it. New forms of rebellion will require good judgment and great restraint by staff since a standard revolutionary technique is to provoke authorities into over-reacting.
Of the statements given below, the one which follows BEST from the foregoing paragraph is that

   A. most riot situations can be readily controlled when personnel are adequately trained
   B. a large percentage of offenders ordinarily take part in serious riots and, therefore, immediate suppression is sometimes difficult
   C. control must be regained very quickly in situations where power has already been assumed by inmates
   D. it is wise to take an estimate of the situation during riot situations before determining a course of action

43.____

44. The MOST effective agitators are the most difficult to identify. The reason for this is that such agitators

   A. conform both to the expectations of prison management and to the expectations of disgruntled inmates
   B. do not associate with known troublemakers and rarely, if ever, have a history of being placed in segregation

44.____

C. ordinarily have psychotic personalities, which makes it difficult, even for psychiatrists, to determine whether their behavior is aberrant or disturbance provoking
D. pretend to have a much lower degree of intelligence than they actually possess

45. A disturbance which has as its aim a pre-planned bid for control and publicity is likely to be more intensive and dangerous than a spontaneous disturbance because

   A. force is always needed to bring such situations under control
   B. news media generally support inmate grievances
   C. the public demands immediate action in such situations
   D. there are elements of deliberate inmate manipulation, strategic planning, and intent to prolong the disorder

46. If training starts at the lower level of command, it is like planting a seed in tilled ground but removing the sun and the rain. Seeds cannot grow unless they have help from above.
Of the following, the MOST appropriate conclusion to be drawn from this statement is that

   A. the head of an institution may not delegate authority for the planning of an institutional training program for the staff
   B. on-the-job training is better than formalized training courses
   C. regularly scheduled training courses must be planned in advance
   D. staff training is the responsibility of higher levels of command

47. The one of the following that BEST describes the meaning of *in-service staff training* is

   A. the training of personnel who are below average in performance
   B. the training given to each employee throughout his employment
   C. the training of staff only in their own specialized fields
   D. classroom training where the instructor and employees develop a positive and productive relationship leading to improved efficiency on the job

48. The determination of whether and when formal disciplinary charges are to be made against an inmate is usually a matter of concern to the officer. The good officer will usually find it is possible to use the more subtle methods of controlling inmate behavior before finding it necessary to use direct measures. He will know everything humanly possible about what is taking place in his post or area and what types of inmates are in his charge. He will thus be able to anticipate and prevent actions requiring disciplinary measures. If he also has the ability to inspire confidence, he seldom will have serious violations.
The one of the following that BEST describes the belief expressed in this paragraph is that the good officer

   A. always avoids trouble by using subtle methods
   B. has the trait of inspiring confidence in inmates
   C. finds it is never necessary to use more direct measures in disciplining inmates
   D. realizes that the use of direct measures is unfair to inmates

49. All correctional personnel should be concerned about, and involved in, public relations. Of the following, the MOST important reason for this statement is that

   A. a correctional institution is an agency of the government supported by public funds and responsible to the public
   B. correctional institutions are places where law violators are incarcerated and, therefore, the public is interested in them
   C. some inmates need publicity in order to prove their guilt or innocence
   D. personnel sometimes need publicity in order to ensure that their grievances are acted upon by higher authority

50. Which of the following terms BEST describes a *court order* issued after a judgment has become final in order to correct an error of fact which, if presented at the trial, would have been sufficient to cause a different judgment? Writ of

   A. Assistance
   B. Certiorari
   C. Coram Nobis
   D. Mandamus

KEY (CORRECT ANSWERS)

1. B	11. D	21. C	31. A	41. B
2. C	12. C	22. C	32. C	42. A
3. D	13. D	23. A	33. A	43. D
4. C	14. C	24. C	34. A	44. A
5. D	15. C	25. A	35. C	45. D
6. D	16. A	26. D	36. D	46. D
7. A	17. B	27. C	37. A	47. B
8. B	18. B	28. B	38. B	48. B
9. D	19. C	29. A	39. C	49. A
10. B	20. D	30. B	40. B	50. C

EXAMINATION SECTION
TEST 1

DIRECTIONS: Each question or incomplete statement is followed by several suggested answers or completions. Select the one that BEST answers the question or completes the statement. *PRINT THE LETTER OF THE CORRECT ANSWER IN THE SPACE AT THE RIGHT.*

Questions 1-3.

DIRECTIONS: Questions 1 through 3 are based on the following example of a correction officer's report. The report consists of sixteen numbered sentences, some of which are not consistent with the principles of good report writing in correctional matters.

1. On January 5, I was assigned as the *A* officer on the third floor of Institution *Y* during the 12 midnight to 8 A.M. tour of duty. *2.* At about 1:30 A.M. on said date, I heard a cry for help coming from the lower *A* section of the floor. *3.* I immediately ran into the section and found inmate John Doe in cell number 5 holding up inmate Robert James who was hanging from the light fixture of the cell by a bedsheet. *4.* One end of the bedsheet was tied to the outer frame of the light fixture, and the other end was tied around the neck of inmate James. *5.* I immediately ran to the telephone to notify the control room for assistance. *6.* While waiting for assistance, I notified Correction Officer Harold Smith who was assigned as the *B* officer on the floor, and instructed inmate Doe to keep holding the hanging inmate in an upward position. *7.* Correction Officer Thomas Jones arrived at the scene together with Dr. Walter Frazer, who was the physician on duty in the institution at the time. *8.* Correction Officer Smith and I then ran to cell number 5, while Correction Officer Jones operated the *A* section locking mechanism to open the door to cell number 5. *9.* When the cell door was opened, I, together with Correction Officer Smith and Dr. Frazer, entered the cell where I cut the bedsheet with my pen knife to let the hanging inmate down. *10.* I found no suicide note in the cell. *11.* Dr. Frazer ordered the inmate to be placed on the floor outside of the cell so that he could inject emergency medication into the inmate's chest and administer artificial respiration. *12.* Both Correction Officer Smith and I assisted in administering artificial respiration under the physician's supervision. *13.* After the administration of artificial respiration for a period of approximately one-half hour, Dr. Frazer pronounced inmate James dead. *14.* The dead inmate's cell partner, inmate John Doe, stated that he awoke from his sleep and saw his cell partner hanging from the ceiling with a sheet tied around his neck. *15.* There were no pictures anywhere in the cell which would give information as to the deceased's family ties. *16.* It is believed that inmate James committed suicide because of his concern about the sentence he would receive when he appeared in court for sentencing on January 6.

1. A good report should be arranged in logical order. Which of the following sentences from the report does NOT appear in its proper sequence in the report?
Sentence

   A. 2   B. 3   C. 10   D. 13

   1._____

2. Only material that is relevant to the main thought of a report should be included. Which of the following sentences from the report contains material which is LEAST relevant to this report?
Sentence

   A. 8   B. 11   C. 14   D. 15

   2._____

3. Good reports should contain accurate statements based upon definite information. Which of the following sentences from the report contains material which is NOT based on definite information?
Sentence

  A. 5   B. 6   C. 9   D. 16

4. Failure to choose words in written reports that exactly express the thought the writer has in mind results in many a minor mystery for the reader.
Of the following, the MOST important idea in this statement is that

  A. good reports do not contain ambiguous statements
  B. poor report writers do not have sufficient experience for clear writing
  C. some individuals are poor readers and cannot comprehend even the most simple report
  D. good reports do not contain difficult words

5. Unless a report writer uses care, he cannot effectively communicate his thoughts to those receiving and reading his report. Clear thinking must precede clear writing. In accordance with this statement, it is good practice for report writers to

  A. write the report quickly before the details are forgotten
  B. use concrete words to communicate effectively
  C. plan the report before writing it
  D. prepare the report with as many facts as possible

Questions 6-8.

DIRECTIONS: Questions 6 through 8 contain two statements. Each statement may contain one or more sentences. Choose answer
  A. if both statements are correct
  B. if neither statement is correct
  C. if statement I only is correct but not statement II
  D. if statement II only is correct but not statement I

6. I. There is a definite relationship between the length of a report and its clarity. Many report writers who have difficulty conveying their ideas clearly to their readers find upon examination that their reports are very long and that the reader is confused because the ideas are hidden in a profusion of words.
  II. Good report writers know that deciding what to leave out is almost as important as deciding what goes into their report. Words, ideas, or facts that are not essential to the understanding or acceptance of their reports can only obscure and weaken them.

7. I. An extensive vocabulary is a fine asset. It enables you to grasp quickly the ideas tossed at you and it may help you to put your ideas across to someone with a smaller or different stock of words because he will eventually come to understand your style of writing.
  II. It is seldom necessary to make an outline for your written report because the statement of witnesses and other individuals involved in the subject matter of your report provides sufficient data.

8. I. The need to write with an air of professionalism does not make the job of a report   8.____
       writer any easier or more secure because it gives the indication of a pedantic person
       who is only interested in creating an impression.
    II. The conclusion of a written report should contain the writer's evaluation or opinion of
        the occurrence and any suggestions or recommendations with reference to the incident.

Questions 9-13.

DIRECTIONS: Questions 9 through 13 consist of passages of two or more sentences. Each of the passages contains an incorrectly used word. First decide which is the incorrectly used word. Then, from among the options given, decide which word, when substituted for the incorrectly used word, makes the meaning of the passage clear.

Study the following example:

Like the monastery, mental hospital, school youth camp, and military base, the correctional institution is a people-changing organization. All these organizations work with concrete material.
   A. human   B. criminal   C. woven   D. religious

The word *concrete* in the passage does not convey the meaning the passage is evidently intended to convey - that all these organizations share a common characteristic, their work with people. Choices B and D do not apply to ALL the organizations listed. Choice C has no relation to the paragraph. Only choice A (*human*), when substituted for the word *concrete*, makes the meaning of the passage clear.
Accordingly, the answer to the question is A.

9. The prison qualifies as a bureaucracy because it has administrative impediments established to maintain its organization, a hierarchy of authority among its employees, and a system of enforcement for its rules.   9.____

    A. inmates   B. machinery   C. purchases   D. democracy

10. In a situation where inmates have minimal recourse to staff, they are also more vulnerable to abuse and exploitation by other inmates. As a consequence, inmates tend to become progressively more trusting of each other as well as of staff.   10.____

    A. wary   B. conspicuous
    C. compliant   D. contrary

11. Obviously no institution can be operated safely and efficiently unless its occupants conform to some standards of improper behavior. Furthermore, a requirement that inmates be peaceable and industrious can be justified as preparing them for a law-abiding life in the free community.   11.____

    A. resentful   B. orderly
    C. unconcerned   D. difficult

12. Caseloads of different types of offenders should vary in size and in type and intensity of _____ mitigation. Classification and assignment of offenders should be made according to their needs and problems.

    A. treatment
    B. approximation
    C. population
    D. emancipation

13. Strong and informed administrative support in State correctional programs will be required to upgrade services and to adopt the practices of private industry. Labor organizations and business firms could be of inestimable help in advising and digressing the development of new programs, and in neutralizing opposition to them.

    A. grafting
    B. guiding
    C. prohibiting
    D. consuming

Questions 14-15.

DIRECTIONS: Answer Questions 14 and 15 SOLELY on the basis of the following passage.

The public has become increasingly aware that rehabilitation—that great battle cry of prison reform—is one of the great myths of 20th-century penology. The hard truth is that punishment and retribution are the primary, if not the only, functions served by most correctional institutions. Courts can provide enlightened rule-making to assist prison reform and ombudsmen can give prisoners a forum to consider their complaints but the results would be limited. The corrections system will never run with any real efficiency until: (a) prisoners want to be reformed; (b) prison administrators want to help them reform; (c) courts want to help both toward a system of reform; and (d) they all define reform in the same way. If this is not done, the criminal justice system will continue to operate on the model of concentric layers of coercion, a grossly inefficient model.

14. According to the above selection, all of the following will be required in order to improve the corrections system EXCEPT

    A. commitment to reform by prison administrators
    B. development by penal experts of criteria for meaningful rehabilitation
    C. acceptance by prisoners of the need for their cooperation
    D. assistance by the courts in providing a system where reform is possible

15. According to the above selection, meaningful prison reform is MOST likely to result from

    A. the appointment of ombudsmen to replace the courts in ruling on prisoners' complaints
    B. coordination by sociologists of efforts to improve prison conditions
    C. a realization by society that rehabilitation of prisoners is no longer a realistic objective
    D. the joint efforts of those directly concerned and a common understanding of the goals to be achieved

Questions 16-19.

DIRECTIONS: Questions 16 through 19 are to be answered SOLELY on the basis of the following passage.

Morally, there is no basis for the assertion that the commission of a social offense allows society to strip a human being of all his rights except those which, through some sort of *natural law* concept, he needs to survive. Rather, society is justified in punishing offenders only to the extent that it needs to protect itself; excessive retribution is *immoral.* Thus, unless society can demonstrate that a specific deprivation is necessary to its self-preservation, or to its reassertion of authority over the individual offender, it should not be entitled to enforce the deprivation. To place the burden on the prisoner to demonstrate that he should not be deprived of a particular right appears to be unfair and unjustified for two reasons: (1) the resources and skills are unequally distributed in society's favor; (2) the concept of *proportionality* as a rudimentary value is rejected by such an approach, which even theories of retribution and vengeance do not support.

Pragmatically, too, prisoners should be viewed and treated as human beings. Ninety-five percent of all those incarcerated in prisons are returned to the free world. It violates common sense to expect a man who has been treated at best as a cipher while in prison to be enamored of a society which has not only enchained him but also has increased his torment while he is confined. When he is released, his action is likely to be antisocial rather than social. Additionally, the imposition of excessive suffering on offenders permeates society's attitudes toward others in its midst. Just as we are now realizing that violence abroad erodes the barriers against domestic violence, official hostility toward some human beings tends to add an aura of authority to hostility toward and among others. Disinclination to cherish humanity at one point in society leads to total abdication of humanity at another.

16. In the above passage, it is pointed out that

    A. it is a practical approach to treatment to take away all but the basic rights of a prisoner
    B. it is proper to remove an inmate's rights within a system of rewards and punishments
    C. incarceration should not be used for revenge against one who has offended society
    D. the inmate ought to play a primary role in determining treatment methods

17. According to the above passage,

    A. inmates who are treated badly are apt to resort to antisocial behavior when they are returned to society
    B. there is a tendency among inmates to join organizations dedicated to achieving civil rights for the victims of society
    C. society generally sees all inmates as being equal despite inconsistent observation of prisoners' rights
    D. recidivism is a serious problem for the majority of prisoners who are released on parole

18. While criticizing the kind of treatment prisoners receive in our institutions, the passage implies that

    A. the mistreatment of prisoners is an outcome of society's benign attitude toward the law-abiding citizen
    B. cruelty begets cruelty, and that humane treatment will make better citizens of those entrusted to our care
    C. when violence in this country spreads, it increases all over the world
    D. an aura of authority has replaced official hostility in correctional institutions

19. According to the above passage, penal authorities are justified in depriving prisoners of rights

    A. in order to satisfy society's desire for retribution against criminal offenders
    B. until prisoners can demonstrate that particular deprivations are unjustified
    C. whenever the preservation of order within the institution will be facilitated
    D. only when it is necessary to protect society or maintain control over the inmate

Questions 20-25.

DIRECTIONS: Questions 20 through 25 are to be answered on the basis of the following notes and tables.
1. Assume that a certain imaginary jurisdiction, Perryville, contains five correctional institutions. These facilities are named Howe, Jackson, Grant, Pershing, and Marshall.
2. Assume that there are 365 days in each year.
3. Assume that the number of inmates at each institution listed above does not change during 1995 or 2000.

TABLE A

Some Characteristics of Perryville's Correctional Facilities - 1995

Facility	Inmate Population (No. of Inmates)	Yearly Budget	Daily Cost Per Inmate	Total Personnel (staff)	Ratio of Staff to Inmate Population
Howe	75	$1,916,250	$70.00	25	1:3
Jackson	100	$1,825,000		25	1:4
Grant	125	$2,007,500	$44.00	25	1:5
Pershing		$2,427,250	$35.00		1:5
Marshall	375		$52.50	125	1:3

TABLE B

Some Characteristics of Perryville's Correctional Facilities - 2000

Facility	Inmate Population (No. of Inmates)	Yearly Budget	Daily Cost Per Inmate	Total Personnel (staff)	Ratio of Staff to Inmate Population
Howe	90	$2,299,500	$70.00	30	1:3
Jackson	140	$2,810,500	$55.00	20	1:7
Grant	150	$2,737,500	$50.00	25	1:6
Pershing	200	$2,920,000	$40.00	50	1:4
Marshall	300	$6,022,500	$55.00	60	1:5

20. In 1995, the daily cost per inmate at the Jackson Correctional Facility was

    A. $41.00   B. $50.00   C. $62.50   D. $65.00

21. If the total number of inmates at all five of Perryville's correctional institutions was 865 in 1995, the total number of personnel at the Pershing Correctional Institution during the same year was

    A. 28 B. 32 C. 36 D. 38

22. In 2000, the percentage of the total inmate population of Perryville's correctional facilities held at the Grant Facility was MOST NEARLY

    A. 14% B. 17% C. 23% D. 32%

23. The average number of personnel at Perryville's correctional institutions in 2000 was MOST NEARLY

    A. 28 B. 38 C. 47 D. 168

24. Of the following, the facility which showed the greatest percent increase in number of inmates in 2000 as compared to 1995 was

    A. Marshall B. Grant C. Jackson D. Howe

25. If, for 2001, the total inmate population of Perryville's five correctional institutions increased by 200 inmates, the percentage increase over the total 2000 population was MOST NEARLY

    A. 18% B. 23% C. 31% D. 33%

KEY (CORRECT ANSWERS)

1. C		11. B	
2. D		12. A	
3. D		13. B	
4. A		14. B	
5. C		15. D	
6. A		16. C	
7. B		17. A	
8. D		18. B	
9. B		19. D	
10. A		20. B	

21. D
22. B
23. B
24. C
25. B

READING COMPREHENSION
UNDERSTANDING AND INTERPRETING WRITTEN MATERIAL
EXAMINATION SECTION
TEST 1

DIRECTIONS: Each question or incomplete statement is followed by several suggested answers or completions. Select the one that BEST answers the question or completes the statement. *PRINT THE LETTER OF THE CORRECT ANSWER IN THE SPACE AT THE RIGHT.*

Questions 1-3.

DIRECTIONS: Questions 1 through 3 are to be answered SOLELY on the basis of the following passage.

The basic disparity between punitive and correctional crime control should be noted. The first explicitly or implicitly assumes the availability of choice or freedom of the will and asserts the responsibility of the individual for what he does. Thus, the concept of punishment has both a moral and practical justification. However, correctional crime control, though also deterministic in outlook, either explicitly or implicitly considers criminal behavior as the result of conditions and factors present in the individual or his environment; it does not think in terms of free choices available to the individual and his resultant responsibility, but rather in terms of the removal of the criminogenic conditions for which the individual may not be responsible and over which he may not have any control. Some efforts have been made to achieve a theoretical reconciliation of these two rather diametrically opposed approaches but this has not been accomplished, and their coexistence in practice remains an unresolved contradiction.

1. According to the *correctional* view of crime control mentioned in the above passage, criminal behavior is the result of
    A. environmental factors for which individuals should be held responsible
    B. harmful environmental factors which should be eliminated
    C. an individual's choice for which he should be held responsible and punished
    D. an individual's choice and can be corrected in a therapeutic environment

2. According to the above passage, the one of the following which is a problem in correctional practice is
    A. identifying emotionally disturbed individuals
    B. determining effective punishment for criminal behavior
    C. reconciling the punitive and correctional views of crime control
    D. assuming that a criminal is the product of his environment and has no free will

3. According to the above passage, the one of the following which is an ASSUMPTION underlying the punitive crime control viewpoint rather than the correctional viewpoint is that crime is caused by

A. inherited personality traits
B. poor socio-economic background
C. lack of parental guidance
D. irresponsibility on the part of the individual

Questions 4-9.

DIRECTIONS: Questions 4 through 9 are to be answered SOLELY on the basis of the following passage.

Man's historical approach to criminals can be conveniently summarized as a succession of three R's: Revenge, Restraint, and Reformation. Revenge was the primary response prior to the first revolution in penology in the 18th and 19th centuries. It was replaced during that revolution by an emphasis upon restraint. When the second revolution occurred in the late 19th and 20th centuries, reformation became an important objective. Attention was focused upon the mental and emotional makeup of the offender and efforts were made to alter these as the primary sources of difficulty.

We have now entered yet another revolution in which a fourth concept has been added to the list of R's: Reintegration. This has come about because students of corrections feel that a singular focus upon reforming the offender is inadequate. Successful rehabilitation is a two-sided coin, including reformation on one side and reintegration on the other.

It can be argued that the third revolution is premature. Society itself is still very ambivalent about the offender. It has never really replaced all vestiges of revenge or restraint, simply supplemented them. Thus, while it is unwilling to kill or lock up all offenders permanently, it is also unwilling to give full support to the search for alternatives.

4. According to the above passage, revolutions against accepted treatment of criminals have resulted in all of the following approaches to handling criminals EXCEPT
   A. revenge   B. restraint   C. reformation   D. reintegration

5. According to the above passage, society NOW views the offender with
   A. uncertainty   B. hatred   C. sympathy   D. acceptance

6. According to the above passage, the second revolution directed PARTICULAR attention to
   A. preparing the offender for his return to society
   B. making the pain of punishment exceed the pleasure of crime
   C. exploring the inner feelings of the offender
   D. restraining the offender from continuing his life of crime

7. According to the above passage, students of corrections feel that the lack of success of rehabilitation programs is due to
   A. the mental and emotional makeup of the offender
   B. vestiges of revenge and restraint which linger in correction programs
   C. failure to achieve reintegration together with reformation
   D. premature planning of the third revolution

8. The above passage suggests that the latest revolution will 8.____
   A. fail and the cycle will begin again with revenge or restraint
   B. be the last revolution
   C. not work unless correctional goals can be defined
   D. succumb to political and economic pressures

9. The one of the following titles which BEST expresses the main idea of the above passage is 9.____
   A. IS CRIMINAL JUSTICE ENOUGH?
   B. APPROACHES IN THE TREATMENT OF THE CRIMINAL OFFENDER
   C. THE THREE R'S IN CRIMINAL REFORMATION
   D. MENTAL DISEASE FACTORS IN THE CRIMINAL CORRECTION SYSTEM

Questions 10-15.

DIRECTIONS: Questions 10 through 15 are to be answered SOLELY on the basis of the following passage.

In a study by J.E. Cowden, an attempt was made to determine which variables would best predict institutional adjustment and recidivism in recently committed delinquent boys. The results suggested in particular that older boys, when first institutionalized, who are initially rated as being more mature and more amenable to change, will most likely adjust better than the average boy adjusts to the institution. Prediction of institutional adjustment was rendered slightly more accurate by using the variables of age and personality prognosis in combined form.

With reference to the prediction of recidivism, boys who committed more serious offenses showed less recidivism than average. These boys were also older than average when first committed. The variable of age accounts in part for both their more serious offenses and for their lower subsequent rate of recidivism.

The results also showed some trends suggesting that boys from higher socio-economic b backgrounds tended to commit more serious offenses leading to their institutionalization as delinquents. However, neither the ratings of socio-economic status nor *home-environment* appeared to be significantly related to recidivism in this study.

Cowden also found an essentially linear relationship between personality prognosis and recidivism, and between institutional adjustment and recidivism. When these variables were used jointly to predict recidivism, accuracy of prediction was increased only slightly, but in general the ability to predict recidivism fell far below the ability to predict institutional adjustment.

10. According to the above passage, which one of the following was NOT found to be a significant factor in predicting recidivism? 10.____
    A. Age
    B. Personality
    C. Socio-economic background
    D. Institutional adjustment

11. According to the above passage, institutional adjustment was MORE accurately predicted when the variables used were 11.____
    A. socio-economic background and recidivism
    B. recidivism and personality
    C. personality and age
    D. age and socio-economic background

12. According to the above passage, which of the following were variables in   12.____
    predicting both recidivism and institutional adjustment?
    A. Age and personality   B. Family background and age
    C. Nature of offense and age   D. Personality

13. Which one of the following conclusions is MOST justified by the above passage?   13.____
    A. Institutional adjustment had a lower level of predictability and recidivism.
    B. Recidivism and seriousness of offense are negatively correlated to some degree.
    C. Institutional adjustment and personality prognosis, when considered together, are significantly better predictors of recidivism than either one alone.
    D. A delinquent boy from a lower class family background is more likely to have committed a serious first offense than a delinquent boy from a higher socio-economic background.

14. The study discussed in the above passage found that delinquent boys from a   14.____
    higher socio-economic background tended to
    A. commit more serious crimes
    B. commit less serious crimes
    C. show more recidivism than average
    D. show less recidivism than average

15. The MOST appropriate conclusion to be drawn from the study discussed above   15.____
    is that
    A. delinquent boys from higher socio-economic backgrounds show less institutional adjustment than average
    B. a high positive correlation was found between recidivism and institutional adjustment
    C. home environment, although not significantly related to recidivism, did influence institutional adjustment
    D. older boys are more likely to commit more serious first offenses and show less recidivism than younger boys

Questions 16-18.

DIRECTIONS: Questions 16 through 18 are to be answered SOLELY on the basis of the following passage.

Educational programming of the offender has become part of the dominant philosophy in the correctional community. Due to the recent increase in national funding for demonstration prison education projects, future research endeavors may well be facilitated so that we can better evaluate the effectiveness of specific educational approaches. Research on past programs has resulted in various conclusions as to their effectiveness in the reduction of recidivism. Even though some programs have seemed promising, when they are properly evaluated, the initial results have been found to be spurious. Invalidity stemmed, by and large, from the fact that inmates shown to be *successful* in such educational programs may have *had it made* anyway, particularly when those selected for the program were the best risks. Success of the program was judged on the basis of a study of recidivism which, due to lack of funds, was of insufficient duration.

Research is the bookkeeping of corrections. Unfortunately, many correctional enterprises operate without such bookkeeping. When this happens, like businesses without bookkeeping, they may soon be bankrupt. However, unlike business, corrections can provide a steady salary for its employees even when it is bankrupt.

Despite these sad conclusions, effective program implementation can become a reality through continued experimentation and evaluation, utilizing acceptable methodological procedures and specially trained personnel, as well as having the necessary total institutional support.

16. According to the above passage, the apparent success of past correctional educational programs was due in LARGE part to
    A. biased samples
    B. competent trainers
    C. societal acceptance
    D. inferior goals

    16.____

17. The second paragraph in the above passage states that *Research is the bookkeeping of corrections*.
    Which of the following MOST accurately describes what is meant by this statement?
    A. Since correctional facilities are government institutions, only records of government research grants and the use of those grants can indicate when the institution is in financial difficulty.
    B. Research provides to correctional institutions information which is essential for their decision-making.
    C. Without grants for research, correctional institutions will become financially bankrupt even though they are still able to pay employee salaries.
    D. Correctional institutions must keep abreast of research or they will find themselves educationally bankrupt.

    17.____

18. According to the above passage, the future of educational programming is brighter than its past because of
    A. social awareness
    B. longer programs
    C. increased national funding
    D. more highly qualified administrators

    18.____

Questions 19-23.

DIRECTIONS: Questions 19 through 23 are to be answered SOLELY on the basis of the following passage.

The social problems created by the urban delinquent gang member require the attention and resources of the entire community. Recent studies have shown that we are dealing with a boy who early in life has his first official contact with the police and who, shortly afterwards, is bound for juvenile court. The gang member commits several delinquencies before reaching adult status and the earlier his onset of delinquency, the more serious become his violations of the law. There is also evidence of increasingly serious delinquency involvement of a substantial proportion of the gang members. Of major significance are the shorter periods of time between each succeeding offense and the delinquents; employment or threat to employ force and violence.

All of these findings testify to the urgent need for prevention and treatment to be directed at pre- and early adolescence and to be sensitive to the importance of the first signs of youthful disregard for society's legal norms. Follow-up studies on delinquent gang members revealed that forty percent of the gang members continued into adult crime. For several reasons, this is a minimal figure and should probably be twenty percent higher. It is reasonable to infer that, given more thorough follow-up techniques and a longer follow-up period, an appreciable number of those for whom no criminal records were located will acquire them. In any event, these studies have revealed a strong linkage between delinquency and crime. This linkage has been established by following up a group of gang members into adulthood rather than by tracing back a group of adult offenders into delinquency, and by utilizing a sample of juveniles dealt with by the police rather than those appearing before a juvenile court, or in a clinic.

19. According to the above passage, as delinquents get older, their crimes GENERALLY become _____ serious _____ frequent.
    A. more; and more
    B. more; but less
    C. less; but more
    D. less; and less

20. The above passage SUGGESTS that delinquents should receive
    A. severe punishment at the time of their first offense
    B. institutional care until such time that they may prove themselves capable of functioning in a free society
    C. treatment at pre- and early adolescence at the first signs of disregard for societal norms
    D. continuous psychological counseling from the time of their first offense until the delinquent reaches legal age

21. According to the above passage, delinquent gang members pose a problem which should be the responsibility of the
    A. community
    B. police
    C. courts
    D. social worker

22. According to the above passage, follow-up studies on delinquent gang members have underestimated the percent of gang members who continued to adult crime because
    A. their sample was biased as it only involved urban gang members
    B. the studies did not follow the *career* of the sample group for a long enough period of time
    C. the studies concerned only those juveniles who, as adults, were dealt with by the police and not those who appeared in court or were referred to a clinic
    D. the method used, that of following up a group of gang members rather than tracing back a group of adult offenders, was invalid

23. According to the above passage, the actual percent of delinquent gang members who continue into adult crime is MOST NEARLY
    A. 20%
    B. 40%
    C. 50%
    D. 60%

Questions 24-25.

DIRECTIONS: Questions 24 through 25 are to be answered SOLELY on the basis of the following passage.

The criminal justice system is generally regarded as having the basic objective of reducing crime. However, one must also consider its larger objective of minimizing the total social costs associated with crime and crime control. Both of these components are complex and difficult to measure completely. The social costs associated with crime come from the long- and short-term physical damage, psychological harm, and property losses to victims as a result of crimes committed. Crime also creates serious indirect effects. It can induce a feeling of insecurity that is only partially reflected in business losses and economic disruption due to anxiety about venturing into high crime rate areas.

Balanced against these costs associated with crime must be the consequences of actions taken to reduce them. Money spent on developing, maintaining, and operating criminal justice agencies is part of the cost of the crime control system. But there are also indirect costs, such as welfare payments to prisoners' families, income lost by offenders who are denied good jobs, legal fees, and wages lost by witnesses. In addition, there are penalties suffered by suspects erroneously arrested or sentenced, the limitation on personal liability resulting from police surveillance, and the invasion of privacy in maintaining criminal records.

24. According to the above passage, all of the following are indirect costs of the crime control system EXCEPT
    A. wages lost by witnesses
    B. money spent for legal services
    C. payments made to the families of prisoners
    D. money spent on operating criminal justice agencies

25. According to the above passage, actions taken to reduce crime
    A. will reduce the indirect costs of the crime control system
    B. may result in a decrease of personal liberty
    C. may cause psychological harm to victims of crime
    D. should immediately start improving the criminal justice system

KEY (CORRECT ANSWERS)

1.	B		11.	C
2.	C		12.	A
3.	D		13.	B
4.	A		14.	A
5.	A		15.	D
6.	C		16.	A
7.	C		17.	B
8.	C		18.	C
9.	B		19.	A
10.	C		20.	C

21. A
22. B
23. D
24. D
25. B

TEST 2

DIRECTIONS: Each question or incomplete statement is followed by several suggested answers or completions. Select the one that BEST answers the question or completes the statement. *PRINT THE LETTER OF THE CORRECT ANSWER IN THE SPACE AT THE RIGHT.*

Questions 1-4.

DIRECTIONS: Questions 1 through 4 are to be answered SOLELY on the basis of the following passage.

The initial contact between the offender and the correctional social worker frequently occurs at the point of extreme crisis, when the usual adaptive mechanisms have been broken down. In many areas of correctional practice, such as probation and parole, this contact is often followed by long periods during which limited freedom is officially imposed. It is at such points that response to the offer of hope for restoring equilibrium may mean most, and that new coping capacities and new person-environment relationships develop. As a result, many correctional social workers have become skilled in strategies of crisis intervention. What they learn from such endeavors does not generally find its way into the professional literature; thus, the correctional social worker has contributed little to developing and testing practice theory. However, beginning efforts are being made to remedy this situation, and it is probable that corrections may provide an important laboratory from which tomorrow's understanding of the theory and strategies of crisis intervention will emerge.

1. Which of the following is the MOST appropriate title for the above passage? 1.____
   A. CORRECTIONAL SOCIAL WORK IN CRISIS
   B. CRISIS INTERVENTION AND CORRECTIONAL SOCIAL WORK
   C. COPING CAPACITIES OF PROBATIONERS AND PAROLEES
   D. THE THEORY AND PRACTICE OF CRISIS INTERVENTION

2. It can be concluded from the above passage that crisis intervention as a method of treatment and rehabilitation in correctional social work is based on the premise that a(n) 2.____
   A. offender may be more likely to respond to help and change his lifestyle a a time of crisis, such as being on probation or parole, when incarceration is the only other alternative
   B. person is not likely to respond to help and change his lifestyle unless he is in a crisis situation, such as being on probation or parole, when he is threatened by imprisonment
   C. offender sentenced to probation or parole is likely to respond to help and change his lifestyle, because his freedom is limited and supervision is imposed on him
   D. situation such as probation or parole, in which an offender is supervised and his freedom is limited, presents ideal conditions for constructive personality change

3. On the basis of the above passage, it would be VALID to assume that
   A. offenders sentenced to probation and parole usually develop coping capacities which would not emerge during imprisonment
   B. offenders who are rehabilitated as a result of probation and parole have greater coping capacities in crisis situations
   C. a life crisis situation such as being sentenced to probation or parole may become a positive force toward an offender's rehabilitation
   D. an offender's ability to develop new coping capacities in times of crisis should be a decisive factor in determining the recommended sentence

4. According to the above passage, correctional social workers' experiences in crisis intervention have
   A. encouraged use of crisis intervention strategy
   B. contributed to theory rather than practice
   C. not resulted in further learning
   D. not generally been reported in print

Questions 5-9.

DIRECTIONS: Questions 5 through 9 are to be answered SOLELY on the basis of the following passage.

The group worker must be concerned with two major goals in correctional treatment of juvenile offenders: (a) sustaining and reinforcing conventional value systems, and (b) enhancing the youth's positive self-image and general feeling of worthiness. The group processes involved in working toward these ends are so interrelated that treatment can meet both goals by improving interpersonal skills and experiences. As an initial concept, it is important to recognize that, in spite of delinquent behavior, adolescents usually do exhibit conscience formation, as may be seen in their support of conformity values, evidence of guilt and conventional behavior, and rationalization of delinquent behavior. It is this very ambivalence toward the conventional order that can be the basis for rehabilitation. On the basis of the distinction between real guilt and guilt reflecting emotional problems, an ideal therapeutic objective is to reach the point at which the internal and external controls are in general harmony and agency expectations are closely allied to and consistent with group and individual expectations.

5. Which of the following is the BEST title for the above passage?
   A. GROUP TREATMENT OF JUVENILE OFFENDERS
   B. THE GROUP WORKER AND CORRECTIONAL TREATMENT
   C. THE JUVENILE OFFENDER
   D. CONSCIENCE FORMATION IN JUVENILE OFFENDERS

6. On the basis of the above passage, it would be VALID to assume that group treatment of the juvenile offender can result in the development of
   A. greater self-confidence
   B. rationalization of delinquent behavior
   C. guilt and conscience formation
   D. increased conscientiousness

7. On the basis of the above statement, it would be VALID to conclude that juvenile offenders
   A. are anxious for rehabilitation
   B. have no internal or external controls
   C. are deficient in interpersonal skills and experiences
   D. feel more guilt because of emotional problems than because of offenses committed

7._____

8. According to the above passage, a characteristic of juvenile offenders which makes them amenable to correctional treatment is that they
   A. can be reached by group processes
   B. have a general feeling of worthiness
   C. show signs of conscience formation
   D. are ambivalent toward rehabilitation

8._____

9. According to the above passage, an IDEAL therapeutic objective in the group treatment of juvenile offenders would be based on
   A. agency expectations
   B. group expectations
   C. the distinction between real guilt and irrational guilt
   D. the harmony between external and internal controls

9._____

Questions 10-14.

DIRECTIONS: Questions 10 through 14 are to be answered SOLELY on the basis of the following passage.

Mental disorders are found in a fairly large number of the inmates in correctional institutions. There are no exact figures as to the number of inmates who are mentally disturbed—partly because it is hard to draw a precise line between *mental disturbance* and *normality*—but experts find that somewhere between 15% and 25% of inmates are suffering from disorders that are obvious enough to show up in routine psychiatric examinations. Society has not yet really come to grips with the problem of what to do with mentally disturbed offenders. There is not enough money available to set up treatment programs for all the people identified as mentally disturbed; and there would probably not be enough qualified psychiatric personnel available to run such programs even if they could be set up. Most mentally disturbed offenders are, therefore, left to serve out their time in correctional institutions, and the burden of dealing with them falls on correction officers. This means that a correction officer must be sensitive enough to human behavior to know when he is dealing with a person who is not mentally normal, and that the officer must be imaginative enough to be able to sense how an abnormal individual might react under certain circumstances.

10. According to the above passage, mentally disturbed inmates in correctional institutions
    A. are usually transferred to mental hospitals when their condition is noticed
    B. cannot be told from other inmates because tests cannot distinguish between sane people and normal people
    C. may constitute as much as 25% of the total inmate population
    D. should be regarded as no different from all the other inmates

10._____

11. The above passage says that today the job of handling mentally disturbed inmates is MAINLY up to
    A. psychiatric personnel
    B. other inmates
    C. correction officers
    D. administrative officials

11.____

12. Of the following, which is a reason given in the passage for society's failure to provide adequate treatment programs for mentally disturbed inmates?
    A. Law-abiding citizens should not have to pay for fancy treatment programs for criminals.
    B. A person who breaks the law should not expect society to give him special help.
    C. It is impossible to tell whether an inmate is mentally disturbed.
    D. There are not enough trained people to provide the kind of treatment needed.

12.____

13. The expression *abnormal individual*, as used in the last sentence of the passage, refers to an individual who is
    A. of average intelligence
    B. of superior intelligence
    C. completely normal
    D. mentally disturbed

13.____

14. The reader of the passage would MOST likely agree that
    A. correction officers should not expect mentally disturbed persons to behave the same way a normal person would behave
    B. correction officers should not report infractions of the rules committed by mentally disturbed persons
    C. mentally disturbed persons who break the law should be treated exactly the same way as anyone else
    D. mentally disturbed persons who have broken the law should not be imprisoned

14.____

Questions 15-19.

DIRECTIONS: Questions 15 through 19 are to be answered SOLELY on the basis of the following passage.

When a young boy or girl is released from one of the various facilities operated by the Division for Youth, supportive services to help the youth face community, group, and family pressures are needed as much as, if not more than, at any other time. These services are the responsibility of two units of the Division for Youth, the Aftercare Unit, which serves youths discharged from the urban homes, camps, and START Centers, and the Community Service Bureaus, which serve youths released from the division's school and center programs. To assure that supportive services for released youths are easily identifiable and accessible, the division has developed the *store-front* services center, located in the heart of those areas to which many of the youngsters are returning. The storefront concept and structure is able to coordinate more closely services to the particular needs and situation of the youths and to draw on the feeling of community participation and achievement by persuading the community to join in helping them.

5 (#2)

15. Of the following, the BEST description of the storefront services center's relationship to neighborhood residents is that it
    A. actively encourages their participation
    B. accepts their help when offered
    C. asks neighborhood residents to develop rehabilitation programs
    D. limits participation to qualified neighborhood professional youth workers

    15.____

16. On the basis of the paragraph, which of the following statements is CORRECT?
    A. Supportive services are not needed as much after a youth is released from a facility as during his stay.
    B. Storefront services centers are located near the facilities operated by the Division for Youth
    C. The Community Service Bureaus serve youths released from urban homes.
    D. Youths are given supportive services in their communities after release from facilities operated by the Division for Youth

    16.____

17. Of the following, the MOST suitable title for the above paragraph would be
    A. PROBLEMS OF YOUTHS RETURNING TO SOCIETY
    B. COMMUNITY, GROUP, AND FAMILY PRESSURES ON RELEASED YOUTHS
    C. NEIGHBORHOOD SUPPORTIVE SERVICES FOR RELEASED YOUTHS
    D. A SURVEY OF FACILITIES OPERATED BY THE DIVISION FOR YOUTH

    17.____

18. Which of the following characteristics of the storefront services is mentioned in the above paragraph?
    A. Cost   B. Availability   C. Size   D. Complexity

    18.____

19. On the basis of the paragraph, which of the following statements about the Aftercare Unit is INCORRECT?
    It
    A. is a part of the Division for Youth
    B. serves youths released from school programs
    C. is similar in function to the Community Service Bureaus
    D. was partly responsible for the development of storefront centers

    19.____

20. The intended purposes of imprisonment are to punish, to correct through fear of repeated punishment, to provide opportunity for penitence, and to protect society by isolating the criminal. In point of fact, other emotions—notably hate for and a desire for revenge against those responsible for their imprisonment—are a greater product of imprisonment than is fear.
    On the basis of this paragraph alone, the MOST accurate of the following conclusions is that
    A. a basis for further criminality is established by emotional factors resulting from previous imprisonment
    B. imprisonment will achieve its intended purpose only to the extent that it substitutes emotional reactions for logical thought

    20.____

C. opportunities for penitence are made more necessary by the growth of a desire for revenge
D. society's protection is necessarily limited to the time an individual is imprisoned

21. The misconduct of juveniles is a symptom of some inner or outer disturbance, usually both. To the casual observer, his behavior may seem naughty or vicious, or both. To the delinquent himself, it has as much meaning as socially approved activity has for the well-behaved.
Misconduct, according to this statement,
A. has meaning to the delinquent only if it carries with it strong social disapproval
B. is resorted to in many cases as an attention-getter device to impress the casual observer
C. may result from personal maladjustments and is meaningful to the delinquent
D. stems from a juvenile's rejection of social approval for his normal activities

21.____

Questions 22-25.

DIRECTIONS: Questions 22 through 25 are to be answered SOLELY on the basis of the following passage.

There is controversy and misunderstanding about the proper function of juvenile courts and their probation departments. There are cries that the whole process produces delinquents rather than rehabilitates them. There are speeches by the score about *getting tough* with the kids. Another large group thinks we should be more understanding and gentle with delinquents. This distrust of the services offered can be attributed in large part to the confusion in the use of these services throughout the country.
On the one hand, the juvenile courts are tied to the criminal court system, with an obligation to decide guilt and innocence for offenses specifically stated and formally charged. On the other hand, they have the obligation to provide treatment, supervision, and guidance to youngsters in trouble, without respect to the crimes of which they are accused. These two conflicting assignments must be carried out—quite properly—in an informal, private way, which will not stigmatize a youngster during his formative years.
And, as the courts' preoccupation with the latter task has increased, the former (that of dispensing justice) has retreated, with the result that grave injustices are bound to occur.

22. The title below that BEST expresses the ideas of this passage is
A. A PROBLEM FOR TODAY'S TEENAGERS
B. REHABILITATING YOUTHFUL CRIMINALS
C. FITTING THE PUNISHMENT TO THE CRIME
D. JUSTICE FOR JUVENILE OFFENDERS

22.____

23. The author contends that public distrust of juvenile courts is PRIMARILY the result of
    A. the dual function of these courts
    B. lack of a sufficient number of probation officers
    C. injustices done by the courts
    D. the cost of keeping up the courts

23.____

24. The above passage suggests that the author
    A. is familiar with the problem
    B. is impatient with justice
    C. sides with those who favor leniency for juvenile offenders
    D. regards all offenses as equally important

24.____

25. The tone of the above passage is
    A. highly emotional
    B. highly personal
    C. optimistic
    D. calm

25.____

KEY (CORRECT ANSWERS)

1.	B		11.	C
2.	A		12.	D
3.	C		13.	D
4.	D		14.	A
5.	A		15.	A
6.	A		16.	D
7.	C		17.	C
8.	C		18.	B
9.	C		19.	B
10.	C		20.	A

21. C
22. D
23. A
24. A
25. D

REPORT WRITING

EXAMINATION SECTION

TEST 1

DIRECTIONS: Each question or incomplete statement is followed by several suggested answers or completions. Select the one that BEST answers the question or completes the statement. *PRINT THE LETTER OF THE CORRECT ANSWER IN THE SPACE AT THE RIGHT.*

Questions 1-5.

DIRECTIONS: Questions 1 through 5 are to be answered on the basis of the Report of Offense that appears below.'

REPORT OF OFFENSE	Report No. 26743
	Date of Report 10-12
Inmate *Joseph Brown*	
Age 27	Number *61274*
Sentence *90 days*	Assignment *KU-187*
Place of offense *R.P.W. 4-1*	Date of offense *10/11/*
Offense Assaulting inmate	
Details *During 9:00 P.M., cellblock cleanup, inmate John Jones asked for pail being used by* Brown. Brown refused. Correction officer requested that Brown comply. Brown then threw *pail at Jones with intent to injure him and said he would "get" Jones. Jones not hurt.*	
Force used by officer *None*	
Name of reporting officer *R. Rodriguez*	No. *C-2056*
Name of superior officer *P. Ferguson*	

1. The person who made out this report is
   A. Joseph Brown B. John Jones
   C. R. Rodriguez D. P. Ferguson

2. Disregarding the details, the specific offense reported was
   A. insulting a fellow inmate
   B. assaulting a fellow inmate
   C. injuring a fellow inmate
   D. disobeying a correct officer

3. The number of the inmate who committed the offense is
   A. 26743 B. 61274 C. KU-187 D. CJ-2056

4. The offense took place on
   A. October 11 B. June 12 C. December 10 D. November 13

5. The place where the offense occurred is identified in the report as
   A. Brown's cell B. Jones' cell C. KU-187 D. R.P.W., 4-1

Questions 6-10.

DIRECTIONS: Questions 6 through 10 are to be answered on the basis of the Report of Loss or Theft that appears below.

REPORT OF LOSS OR THEFT	Date: *12/4*	Time: *9:15 A.M.*
Complaint made by: *Richard Aldridge*		☐ Owner
306 S. Walter St.		☒ Other – explain:
		Head of Acctg. Dept.
Type of Property: *Computer*		Value: *$450.00*
Description: *Dell Inspiron laptop*		
Location: *768 N. Margin Ave., Accounting Dept. 3rd Floor*		
Time: *Overnight 12/3 – 12/4*		
Circumstances: *Mr. Aldridge reports he arrived at work 8:45 A.M., found office door open and machine missing. Nothing else reported missing. I investigated and found signs of forced entry; door lock was broken.*		
	Signature of Reporting Officer: *B.L. Ramirez*	
Notify:		
☐ Q Building & Grounds Office, 768 N. Margin Ave.		
☐ Q Lost Property Office, 110 Brand Ave. 0		
☒ Security Office, 703 N. Wide Street		

6. The person who made this complaint is
   A. a secretary
   B. a security officer
   C. Richard Aldridge
   D. B.L. Ramirez

6._____

7. The report concerns a computer that has been
   A. lost   B. damaged   C. stolen   D. sold

7._____

8. The person who took the computer PROBABLY entered the office through
   A. a door
   B. a window
   C. the roof
   D. the basement

8._____

9. When did the head of the Accounting Department FIRST notice that the computer was missing?
   A. December 4 at 9:15 A.M.
   B. December 4 at 8:45 A.M.
   C. The night of December 3
   D. The night of December 4

9._____

10. The event described in the report took place at
    A. 306 South Walter Street
    B. 768 North Margin Avenue
    C. 110 Brand Avenue
    D. 703 North Wide Street

10._____

Questions 11-15.

DIRECTIONS: Questions 11 through 15 are to be answered on the basis of the following excerpt from a recorded Annual Report of the Police Department. This material should be read first and then referred to in answering these questions, which are to be answered SOLELY on the basis of the material herein contained.

LEGAL BUREAU

One of the more important functions of this bureau is to analyze and furnish the department with pertinent information concerning Federal and State statutes and local laws which affect the department, law enforcement or crime prevention. In addition, all measures introduced in the State Legislature and the City Council, which may affect this department, are carefully reviewed by members of the Legal Bureau and, where necessary, opinions and recommendations thereon are prepared.

Another important function of this office is the prosecution of cases in the Magistrate's Courts. This is accomplished by assignment of attorneys who are members of the Legal Bureau to appear in those cases which are deemed to raise issues of importance to the department or questions of law which require technical presentation to facilitate proper determination; and also in those cases where request is made for such appearance by a magistrate, some other official of the city, or a member of the force. Attorneys are regularly assigned to prosecute all cases in the Family Court.

Proposed legislation was prepared and sponsored for introduction in the State Legislature and, at this writing, one of these proposals has already been enacted into law and five others are presently on the Governor's desk awaiting executive action. The new law prohibits the sale or possession of a hypodermic syringe or needle by an unauthorized person. The bureau's proposals awaiting executive action pertain to: an amendment to the Code of Criminal Procedure prohibiting desk officers from taking bail in gambling cases or in cases mentioned in Section 552, Code of Criminal Procedure, including confidence men and swindlers as jostlers in the Penal Law; prohibiting the sale of switch-blade knives of any size to children under 16 and bills extending the licensing period of gunsmiths.

The Legal Bureau has regularly cooperated with the Corporation Counsel and the District attorneys in respect to matters affecting this department, and has continued to advise and represent the Police Athletic League, the Police Sports Association, the Police Relief Fund, and the Police Pension Fund.

The following is a statistical report of the activities of the bureau during the current year as compared with the previous year:

	Current Year	Previous Year
Memoranda of law prepared	68	83
Legal matters forwarded to Corporation Counsel	122	144
Letters requesting legal information	756	807
Letters requesting departmental records	139	111
Matters for publication	17	26
Court appearances of members of bureau	4,678	4,621
Conferences	94	103
Lectures at Police Academy	30	33
Reports on proposed legislation	194	255
Deciphering of codes	79	27
Expert testimony	31	16
Notices to court witnesses	55	81
Briefs prepared	22	18
Court papers prepared	258	—

11. One of the functions of the Legal Bureau is to
    A. review and make recommendations on proposed federal laws affecting law enforcement
    B. prepare opinions on all measures introduced in the state legislature and the City Council
    C. furnish the Police Department with pertinent information concerning all new federal and state laws
    D. analyze all laws affecting the work of the Police Department

12. The Legal Bureau sponsored a bill that would
    A. extend the licenses of gunsmiths
    B. prohibit the sale of switch-blade knives to children of any size
    C. place confidence men and swindlers in the same category as jostlers in the Penal Law
    D. prohibit desk officers from admitting gamblers, confidence men, and swindlers to bail

13. From the report, it is NOT reasonable to infer that
    A. fewer bills affecting the Police Department were introduced in the current year
    B. the preparation of court papers was a new activity assumed in the current year
    C. the Code of Criminal Procedure authorizes desk officers to accept bail in certain cases
    D. the penalty for jostling and swindling is the same

14. According to the statistical report, the activity showing the GREATEST percentage of decrease in the current year compared with the previous year was
    A. matters for publication
    B. reports on proposed legislation
    C. notices to court witnesses
    D. memoranda of law prepared

15. According to the report, the percentage of bills prepared and sponsored by the Legal Bureau, which were passed by the State Legislature and sent to the Governor for approval, was
    A. approximately 3.2%
    B. approximately 2.6%
    C. approximately .5%
    D. not capable of determination from the data given

KEY (CORRECT ANSWERS)

1.	C	6.	C	11.	D
2.	B	7.	C	12.	C
3.	B	8.	A	13.	D
4.	A	9.	B	14.	A
5.	D	10.	B	15.	D

TEST 2

DIRECTIONS: Each question or incomplete statement is followed by several suggested answers or completions. Select the one that BEST answers the question or completes the statement. *PRINT THE LETTER OF THE CORRECT ANSWER IN THE SPACE AT THE RIGHT.*

Questions 1-2.

DIRECTIONS: Questions 1 and 2 are to be answered on the basis of the Instructions, the Bridge and Tunnel Officer's Toll Report form, and the situation given below. The questions ask how the report form should be filled in based on the Instructions and the information given in the situation.

INSTRUCTIONS

Assume that a Bridge and Tunnel Officer on duty in a toll booth must make an entry on the following report form immediately after each incident in which a vehicle driver does not pay the correct toll.

BRIDGE AND TUNNEL OFFICER'S TOLL REPORT			
Officer_____		Date_____	
Time	Type of Vehicle	Toll Collected	Explanation of Entry
1._____	_____	_____	_____
2._____	_____	_____	_____

SITUATION

John McDonald is a Bridge and Tunnel Officer assigned to toll booth 4, between the hours of 11 P.M. and 1 A.M.. On this particular tour, two incidents occurred. At 11:43 P.M., a five-axle truck stopped at the toll booth and Officer McDonald collected a $2.50 toll from the driver. As the truck passed, he realized the toll should have been $3.30, and he quickly copied the vehicle's license plate number as M724HJ. At 12:35 A.M., a motorcycle went through toll lane 4 without paying the toll. The motorcycle did not have any license plate.

1. The entry which should be made on line1 in the second column is   1._____
    A. 11:43 P.M.
    B. 12:34 A.M.
    C. five-axle truck
    D. motorcycle

2. The above passage does NOT provide the information necessary to fill in which   2._____
   of the following items?
    A. Officer
    B. Date
    C. Line 1, Toll Collected
    D. Line 2, Time

2 (#2)

FACT SITUATION

Peter Miller is a Correction Officer assigned to duty in Cell-block A. His superior officer is John Doakes. Miller was on duty at 1:30 P.M. on March 21 when he heard a scream for help from Cell 12. He hurried to Cell 12 and found inmate Richard Rogers stamping out a flaming book of matches. Inmate John Jones was screaming. It seems that Jones had accidentally set fire to the entire book of matches while lighting a cigarette, and he had burned his left hand. Smoking was permitted at this hour. Miller reported the incident by phone, and Jones was escorted to the dispensary where his hand was treated at 2:00 P.M. by Dr. Albert Lorillo. Dr. Lorillo determined that Jones could return to his cellblock, but that he should be released from work for four days. The doctor scheduled a re-examination for March 22. A routine investigation of the incident was made by James Lopez. Jones confirmed to this officer that the above statement of the situation was correct,

REPORT OF INMATE INJURY	
(1) Name of Inmate	(2) Assignment
(3) Number	(4) Location
(5) Nature of Injury	(6) Date
(7) Details (how, when, where injury was incurred)	
(8) Received medical attention: date _____ time _____	
(9) Treatment	
(10) Disposition (check one or more): _____ (10-1) Return to housing area ___(10-2) Return to duty _____ (10-3) Work release _____ days _____ (10-4) Re-examine in _____ days	
(11) Employee reporting injury_____	
(12) Employee's supervisor or superior officer_____	
(13) Medical officer treating injury_____	
(14) Investigating officer_____	
(15) Head of institution_____	

3. Which of the following should be entered in Item 1?
    A. Peter Miller
    B. John Doakes
    C. Richard Rogers
    D. John Jones

4. Which of the following should be entered in Item 11?
    A. Peter Miller
    C. James Lopez
    C. Richard Rogers
    D. John Jones

5. Which of the following should be entered in Item 8?
    A. 2/21, 1:30 P.M.
    B. 2/21, 2:00 P.M.
    C. 3/21, 1:30 P.M.
    D. 3/21, 2:00 P.M.

6. For Item 10, which of the following should be checked?
    A. 10-4 only
    B. 10-1 and 10-4
    C. 10-1, 10-3, and 10-4
    D. 10-2, 10-4, and 10-4

7. Of the following items, which one CANNOT be filled in on the basis of the information given in the Fact Situation? Item
   A. 12
   B. 13
   C. 14
   D. 15

7._____

Questions 8-11.

DIRECTIONS: Questions 8 through 11 are to be answered on the basis of the Fact Situation and the Traffic Control Report form below. Read the Fact Situation carefully, and examine the blank report form. The questions ask how the report form should be filled in based on the information given in the Fact Situation.

FACT SITUATION

Mary Fields is a Traffic Control Agent. Her City Employee Number is Z90019. She is assigned to duty at the intersection of Silver Street and Amber Avenue. On the morning of May 15, she arrives at this intersection at 9:00 A.M. and sees that there is a new *patch job* on the surface of Amber Avenue in the middle of the pedestrian crosswalk and near the northwest corner of the intersection. They day before, an emergency crew was digging here. The hole is now closed and resurfaced, but the patch job on the surface was not done very well. The patch is nearly an inch higher than the surrounding surface, and it has a sharp edge that pedestrians are likely to trip on. Mary Fields thinks this condition is dangerous, and she reports it on the Traffic Control Report form.

TRAFFIC CONTROL REPORT
DEFECTIVE EQUIPMENT OR UNSAFE CONDITION

1. Date of observation _____ 2. Time_____
3. Exact location_____
4. Type of equipment or condition found to be defective or unsafe_____
5. Type of defect_____
6. Name of reporting Agent_____
7. Employee No._____ 8. Precinct No._____

---

8. Which of the following should be entered in Blank 3?
   A. Silver Street at Amber Avenue, near northwest corner
   B. Silver Street at Amber Avenue, near northwest corner
   C. Amber Avenue at Silver Street, near northeast corner
   D. Amber Avenue at Silver Street, near northwest corner

8._____

9. Which of the following should be entered in Blank 4?
   A. Pedestrian traffic signals
   B. Pedestrian crosswalk markings
   C. Surface patch
   C. Unsafe condition

9._____

10. The information called for in Blank 5 is needed to determine what kind of repairs must be made and what kind of repair crew must be sent.
    Which of the following entries for Blank 5 will be MOST useful to the people who receive this report in deciding what kind of repair crew to assign to the job?
    A. Pedestrians may stumble and fall.
    B. New patch is higher than rest of surface.
    C. Emergency crew dug a hole here.
    D. Street repairs were not done very well.

11. There is one blank on the form for which the Fact Situation does not provide the information needed.
    The blank that CANNOT be filled out on the basis of the information given is Blank
    A. 2   B. 6   C. 7   D. 8

Questions 12-15.

DIRECTIONS: Questions 12 through 15 are to be answered on the basis of the Fact Situation and the Report of Arrest form below. Questions ask how the report form should be filled in based on the information given in the Fact Situation.

FACT SITUATION

Jesse Stein is a special officer (security officer) who is assigned to a welfare center at 435 East Smythe Street, Brooklyn. He was on duty there Thursday morning, February 1. At 10:30 A.M., a client named Jo Ann Jones, 40 years old, arrived with her 10-year-old son Peter. Another client, Mary Alice Wiell, 45 years old, immediately began to insult Mrs Jones. When Mrs. Jones told her to go away, Mrs. Wiell pulled out a long knife. The special officer (security officer) intervened and requested Mrs. Wiell to drop the knife. She would not, and he had to use necessary force to disarm her. He arrested her on charges of disorderly conduct, harassment, and possession of a dangerous weapon. Mrs. Wiell lives at 118 Healy Street, Brooklyn, Apartment 4F, and she is unemployed. The reason for her aggressive behavior is not known.

REPORT OF ARREST	
(01) (Prisoner's surname)(first)(initial)	(08) (Precinct)
(02) (Address)	(09) (Date of Arrest – Month, Day)
(03) (Date of Birth) (04) (Age) (05) (Sex)	(10) (Time of arrest)
(06) (Occupation) (07) (Where employed)	(11) (Place of arrest)
(12) (Specific offenses)	
(13) (Arresting officer)	(14) (14) Officer's No.)

12. What entry should be made in Blank 01?
    A. Jo Ann Jones
    B. Jones, Jo Ann
    C. Mary Wiell
    D. Wiell, Mary A.

13. Which of the following should be entered in Blank 04?
    A. 40
    B. 40's
    C. 45
    D. Middle-aged

14. Which of the following should be entered in Blank 09?
    A. Wednesday, February 1, 10:30 A.M.
    B. February 1
    C. Thursday morning, February 2
    D. Morning, February 4

15. Of the following, which would be the BEST entry to make in Blank 11?
    A. Really Street Welfare Center
    B. Brooklyn
    C. 435 e. Smythe St., Brooklyn
    D. 118 Heally St., Apt. 4F

KEY (CORRECT ANSWERS)

1.	C	6.	C	11.	D
2.	B	7.	D	12.	D
3.	D	8.	D	13.	C
4.	A	9.	C	14.	B
5.	D	10.	B	15.	C

PREPARING WRITTEN MATERIAL
EXAMINATION SECTION
TEST 1

Questions 1-15.

DIRECTIONS: For each of Questions 1 through 15, select from the options given below the MOST applicable choice, and mark your answer accordingly.
    A. The sentence is correct.
    B. The sentence contains a spelling error only.
    C. The sentence contains an English grammar error only.
    D. The sentence contains both a spelling error and an English grammar error.

1. He is a very dependible person whom we expect will be an asset to this division.   1.____

2. An investigator often finds it necessary to be very diplomatic when conducting an interview.   2.____

3. Accurate detail is especially important if court action results from an investigation.   3.____

4. The report was signed by him and I since we conducted the investigation jointly.   4.____

5. Upon receipt of the complaint, an inquiry was begun.   5.____

6. An employee has to organize his time so that he can handle his workload efficiantly.   6.____

7. It was not apparent that anyone was living at the address given by the client.   7.____

8. According to regulations, there is to be at least three attempts made to locate the client.   8.____

9. Neither the inmate nor the correction officer was willing to sign a formal statement.   9.____

10. It is our opinion that one of the persons interviewed were lying.   10.____

11. We interviewed both clients and departmental personel in the course of this investigation.   11.____

12. It is concievable that further research might produce additional evidence.   12.____

13. There are too many occurences of this nature to ignore.   13.____

14. We cannot accede to the candidate's request. 14.____

15. The submission of overdue reports is the reason that there was a delay in completion of this investigation. 15.____

Questions 16-25.

DIRECTIONS: Each of Questions 16 through 25 may be classified under one of the following four categories:
    A. Faulty because of incorrect grammar or sentence structure.
    B. Faulty because of incorrect punctuation.
    C. Faulty because of incorrect spelling.
    D. Correct

Examine each sentence carefully to determine under which of the above four options it is best classified. Then, in the space at the right, write the letter preceding the option which is the BEST of the four suggested above. Each incorrect sentence contains but one type of error. Consider a sentence to be correct if it contains none of the types of errors mentioned, even though there may be other correct ways of expressing the same thought.

16. Although the department's supply of scratch pads and stationary have diminished considerably, the allotment for our division has not been reduced. 16.____

17. You have not told us whom you wish to designate as your secretary. 17.____

18. Upon reading the minutes of the last meeting, the new proposal was taken up for consideration. 18.____

19. Before beginning the discussion, we locked the door as a precautionery measure. 19.____

20. The supervisor remarked, "Only those clerks, who perform routine work, are permitted to take a rest period." 20.____

21. Not only will this duplicating machine make accurate copies, but it will also produce a quantity of work equal to fifteen transcribing typists. 21.____

22. "Mr. Jones," said the supervisor, "we regret our inability to grant you an extention of your leave of absence. 22.____

23. Although the employees find the work monotonous and fatigueing, they rarely complain. 23.____

24. We completed the tabulation of the receipts on time despite the fact that Miss Smith our fastest operator was absent for over a week. 24.____

25. The reaction of the employees who attended the meeting, as well as the reaction of those who did not attend, indicates clearly that the schedule is satisfactory to everyone concerned. 25.____

KEY (CORRECT ANSWERS)

1. D
2. A
3. A
4. C
5. A

6. B
7. B
8. C
9. A
10. C

11. B
12. B
13. B
14. A
15. C

16. A
17. D
18. A
19. C
20. B

21. A
22. C
23. C
24. B
25. D

TEST 2

Questions 1-15.

DIRECTIONS: Questions 1 through 15 consist of two sentences. Some are correct according to ordinary formal English usage. Others are incorrect because they contain errors in English usage, spelling, or punctuation. Consider a sentence correct if it contains no errors in English usage, spelling, or punctuation, even if there may be other ways of writing the sentence correctly. Mark your answer:
    A. If only sentence I is correct.
    B. If only sentence II is correct.
    C. If sentences 1 and II are correct.
    D. If neither sentence I nor II is correct.

1. I. The influence of recruitment efficiency upon administrative standards is readily apparant.
   II. Rapid and accurate thinking are an essential quality of the police officer.

2. I. The administrator of a police department is constantly confronted by the demands of subordinates for increased personnel in their respective units.
   II. Since a chief executive must work within well-defined fiscal limits, he must weigh the relative importance of various requests.

3. I. The two men whom the police arrested for a parking violation were wanted for robbery in three states.
   II. Strong executive control from the top to the bottom of the enterprise is one of the basic principals of police administration.

4. I. When he gave testimony unfavorable to the defendant loyalty seemed to mean very little.
   II. Having run off the road while passing a car, the patrolman gave the driver a traffic ticket.

5. I. The judge ruled that the defendant's conversation with his doctor was a privileged communication.
   II. The importance of our training program is widely recognized; however, fiscal difficulties limit the program's effectiveness.

6. I. Despite an increase in patrol coverage, there were less arrests for crimes against property this year.
   II. The investigators could hardly have expected greater cooperation from the public.

7. I. Neither the patrolman nor the witness could identify the defendant as the driver of the car.
   II. Each of the officers in the class received their certificates at the completion of the course.

8. I. The new commander made it clear that those kind of procedures would no longer be permitted.
    II. Giving some weight to performance records is more advisable than making promotions solely on the basis of test scores.

9. I. A deputy sheriff must ascertain whether the debtor, has any property.
    II. A good deputy sheriff does not cause histerical excitement when he executes a process.

10. I. Having learned that he has been assigned a judgment debtor, the deputy sheriff should call upon him.
    II. The deputy sheriff may seize and remove property without requiring a bond.

11. I. If legal procedures are not observed, the resulting contract is not enforseable.
    II. If the directions from the creditor's attorney are not in writing, the deputy sheriff should request a letter of instructions from the attorney.

12. I. The deputy sheriff may confer with the defendant and enter this defendants' place of business.
    II. A deputy sheriff must ascertain from the creditor's attorney whether the debtor has any property against which he may proceede.

13. I. The sheriff has a right to do whatever is necessary for the purpose of executing the order of the court.
    II. The written order of the court gives the sheriff general authority and he is governed in his acts by a very simple principal.

14. I. Either the patrolman or his sergeant are always ready to help the public.
    II. The sergeant asked the patrolman when he would finish the report.

15. I. The injured man could not hardly talk.
    II. Every officer had ought to had in their reports on time.

Questions 16-26.

DIRECTIONS: For each of the sentences given below, numbered 16 through 25, select from the following choices the MOST correct choice and print your choice in the space at the right. Select as your answer:
  A. If the statement contains an unnecessary word or expression
  B. If the statement contains a slang term or expression ordinarily not acceptable in government report writing.
  C. If the statement contains an old-fashioned word or expression, where a concrete, plain term would be more useful.
  D. If the statement contains no major faults.

16. Every one of us should try harder.

17. Yours of the first instant has been received.

18. We will have to do a real snow job on him.   18.____

19. I shall contact him next Thursday.   19.____

20. None of us were invited to the meeting with the community.   20.____

21. We got this here job to do.   21.____

22. She could not help but see the mistake in the checkbook.   22.____

23. Don't bug the Director about the report.   23.____

24. I beg to inform you that your letter has been received.   24.____

25. This project is all screwed up.   25.____

KEY (CORRECT ANSWERS)

1.	D		11.	B
2.	C		12.	D
3.	A		13.	A
4.	D		14.	D
5.	B		15.	D
6.	B		16.	D
7.	A		17.	C
8.	D		18.	B
9.	D		19.	D
10.	C		20.	D

21.	B
22.	D
23.	B
24.	C
25.	B

TEST 3

DIRECTIONS: Questions 1 through 25 are sentences taken from reports. Some are correct according to ordinary English usage. Others are incorrect because they contain errors in English usage, spelling, or punctuation. Consider a sentence correct if it contains no errors in English usage, spelling, or punctuation, even if there may be other ways of writing the sentence correctly. Mark your answer:
- A. If only sentence I is correct
- B. If only sentence II is correct
- C. If sentences I and II are correct
- D. If neither sentence I nor II is correct

1.
   I. The Neighborhood Police Team Commander and Team Patrolmen are encouraged to give to the public the widest possible verbal and written disemination of information regarding the existence and purposes of the program.
   II. The police must be vitally interelated with every segment of the public they serve.

2.
   I. If social gambling, prostitution, and other vices are to be prohibited, the law makers should provide the manpower and method for enforcement.
   II. In addition to checking on possible crime locations such as hallways, roofs yards and other similar locations, Team Patrolmen are encouraged to make known their presence to members of the community.

3.
   I. The Neighborhood Police Team Commander is authorized to secure, the cooperation of local publications, as well as public and private agencies, to further the goals of the program.
   II. Recruitment from social minorities is essential to effective police work among minorities and meaningful relations with them.

4.
   I. The Neighborhood Police Team Commander and his men have the responsibility for providing patrol service within the sector territory on a twenty-four hour basis.
   II. While the patrolman was walking his beat at midnight he noticed that the clothing stores' door was partly open.

5.
   I. Authority is granted to the Neighborhood Police Team to device tactics for coping with the crime in the sector.
   II. Before leaving the scene of the accident, the patrolman drew a map showing the positions of the automobiles and indicated the time of the accident as 10 M. in the morning.

6.
   I. The Neighborhood Police Team Commander and his men must be kept apprised of conditions effecting their sector.
   II. Clear, continuous communication with every segment of the public served based on the realization of mutual need and founded on trust and confidence is the basis for effective law enforcement.

7. I. The irony is that the police are blamed for the laws they enforce when they are doing their duty.
   II. The Neighborhood Police Team Commander is authorized to prepare and distribute literature with pertinent information telling the public whom to contact for assistance.

8. I. The day is not far distant when major parts of the entire police compliment will need extensive college training or degrees.
   II. Although driving under the influence of alcohol is a specific charge in making arrests, drunkenness is basically a health and social problem.

9. I. If a deputy sheriff finds that property he has to attach is located on a ship, he should notify his supervisor.
   II. Any contract that tends to interfere with the administration of justice is illegal.

10. I. A mandate or official order of the court to the sheriff or other officer directs it to take into possession property of the judgment debtor.
    II. Tenancies from month-to-month, week-to-week, and sometimes year-to-year are termenable.

11. I. A civil arrest is an arrest pursuant to an order issued by a court in civil litigation.
    II. In a criminal arrest, a defendant is arrested for a crime he is alleged to have committed.

12. I. Having taken a defendant into custody, there is a complete restraint of personal liberty.
    II. Actual force is unnecessary when a deputy sheriff makes an arrest.

13. I. When a husband breaches a separation agreement by failing to supply to the wife the amount of money to be paid to her periodically under the agreement, the same legal steps may be taken to enforce his compliance as in any other breach of contract.
    II. Having obtained the writ of attachment, the plaintiff is then in the advantageous position of selling the very property that has been held for him by the sheriff while he was obtaining a judgment.

14. I. Being locked in his desk, the investigator felt sure that the records would be safe.
    II. The reason why the witness changed his statement was because he had been threatened.

15. I. The investigation had just began then an important witness disappeared.
    II. The check that had been missing was located and returned to its owner, Harry Morgan, a resident of Suffolk County, New York.

16. I. A supervisor will find that the establishment of standard procedures enables his staff to work more efficiently.
    II. An investigator hadn't ought to give any recommendations in his report if he is in doubt.

    16._____

17. I. Neither the investigator nor his supervisor is ready to interview the witness.
    II. Interviewing has been and always will be an important asset in investigation.

    17._____

18. I. One of the investigator's reports has been forwarded to the wrong person.
    II. The investigator stated that he was not familiar with those kind of cases.

    18._____

19. I. Approaching the victim of the assault, two large bruises were noticed by me.
    II. The prisoner was arrested for assault, resisting arrest, and use of a deadly weapon.

    19._____

20. I. A copy of the orders, which had been prepared by the captain, was given to each patrolman.
    II. It's always necessary to inform an arrested person of his constitutional rights before asking him any questions.

    20._____

21. I. To prevent further bleeding, I applied a tourniquet to the wound.
    II. John Rano a senior officer was on duty at the time of the accident.

    21._____

22. I. Limiting the term "property" to tangible property, in the criminal mischief setting, accords with prior case law holding that only tangible property came within the purview of the offense of malicious mischief.
    II. Thus, a person who intentionally destroys the property of another, but under an honest belief that he has title to such property, cannot be convicted of criminal mischief under the Revised Penal Law.

    22._____

23. I. Very early in it's history, New York enacted statutes from time to time punishing, either as a felony or as a misdemeanor, malicious injuries to various kinds of property: piers, boos, dams, bridges, etc.
    II. The application of the statute is necessarily restricted to trespassory takings with larcenous intent: namely with intent permanently or virtually permanently to "appropriate" property or "deprive" the owner of its use.

    23._____

24. I. Since the former Penal Law did not define the instruments of forgery in a general fashion, its crime of forgery was held to be narrower than the common law offense in this respect and to embrace only those instruments explicitly specified in the substantive provisions.
    II. After entering the barn through an open door for the purpose of stealing, it was closed by the defendants.

    24._____

25. I. The use of fire or explosives to destroy tangible property is proscribed by the criminal mischief provisions of the Revised Penal Law.
    II. The defendant's taking of a taxicab for the immediate purpose of affecting his escape did not constitute grand larceny.

25.____

KEY (CORRECT ANSWERS)

1.	D		11.	C
2.	D		12.	B
3.	B		13.	C
4.	A		14.	D
5.	D		15.	B
6.	D		16.	A
7.	C		17.	C
8.	D		18.	A
9.	C		19.	B
10.	D		20.	C

21.	A
22.	C
23.	B
24.	A
25.	A

TEST 4

Questions 1-4.

DIRECTIONS: Each of the two sentences in Questions 1 through 4 may be correct or may contain errors in punctuation, capitalization, or grammar. Mark your answer:
- A. If there is an error only in sentence I
- B. If there is an error only in sentence II
- C. If there is an error in both sentences I and II
- D. If both sentences are correct.

1.
   I. It is very annoying to have a pencil sharpener, which is not in working order.
   II. Patrolman Blake checked the door of Joe's Restaurant and found that the lock has been jammed.

   1.____

2.
   I. When you are studying a good textbook is important.
   II. He said he would divide the money equally between you and me.

   2.____

3.
   I. Since he went on the city council a year ago, one of his primary concerns has been safety in the streets.
   II. After waiting in the doorway for about 15 minutes, a black sedan appeared.

   3.____

Questions 4-8.

DIRECTIONS: Each of the sentences in Questions 4 through 8 may be classified under one of the following four categories:
- A. Faulty because of incorrect grammar
- B. Faulty because of incorrect punctuation
- C. Faulty because of incorrect capitalization or incorrect spelling
- D. Correct

Examine each sentence carefully to determine under which of the above four options it is BEST classified. Then, in the space at the right, print the capitalized letter preceding the option which is the BEST of the four suggested above. Each faulty sentence contains but one type of error. Consider a sentence to be correct if it contains none of the types of errors mentioned, even though there may be other correct ways of expressing the same thought.

4. They told both he and I that the prisoner had escaped.   4.____

5. Any superior officer, who, disregards the just complaints of his subordinates, is remiss in the performance of his duty.   5.____

6. Only those members of the national organization who resided in the Middle west attended the conference in Chicago.   6.____

7. We told him to give the investigation assignment to whoever was available.   7.____

8. Please do not disappoint and embarass us by not appearing in court.   8.____

Questions 9-13

DIRECTIONS: Each of Questions 9 through 13 consists of three sentences lettered A, B, and C. In each of these questions, one of the sentences may contain an error in grammar, sentence structure, or punctuation, or all three sentences may be correct. If one of the sentence in a question contains an error in grammar, sentence structure, or punctuation, print in the space at the right the capital letter preceding the sentence which contains the error. If all three sentences are correct, print the letter D.

9. A. Mr. Smith appears to be less competent than I in performing these duties. 9.____
   B. The supervisor spoke to the employee, who had made the error, but did not reprimand him.
   C. When he found the book lying on the table, he immediately notified the owner.

10. A. Being locked in the desk, we were certain that the papers would not be taken. 10.____
    B. It wasn't I who dictated the telegram; I believe it was Eleanor.
    C. You should interview whoever comes to the office today.

11. A. The clerk was instructed to set the machine on the table before summoning the manager. 11.____
    B. He said that he was not familiar with those kind of activities.
    C. A box of pencils, in addition to erasers and blotters, was included in the shipment of supplies.

12. A. The supervisor remarked, "Assigning an employee to the proper type of work is not always easy." 12.____
    B. The employer found that each of the applicants were qualified to perform the duties of the position.
    C. Any competent student is permitted to take this course if he obtains the consent of the instructor.

13. A. The prize was awarded to the employee whom the judges believed to be most deserving. 13.____
    B. Since the instructor believes his book is the better of the two, he is recommending it for use in the school.
    C. It was obvious to the employees that the completion of the task by the scheduled date would require their working overtime.

Questions 14-20.

DIRECTIONS: In answering Questions 14 through 20, choose the sentence which is BEST from the point of view of English usage suitable for a business report.

14. A. The client's receiving of public assistance checks at two different addresses were disclosed by the investigation.
    B. The investigation disclosed that the client was receiving public assistance checks at two different addresses.
    C. The client was found out by the investigation to be receiving public assistance checks at two different addresses.
    D. The client has been receiving public assistance checks at two different addresses, disclosed the investigation.

    14.____

15. A. The investigation of complaints are usually handled by this unit, which deals with internal security problems in the department.
    B. This unit deals with internal security problems in the department usually investigating complaints.
    C. Investigating complaints is this unit's job, being that it handles internal security problems in the department.
    D. This unit deals with internal security problems in the department and usually investigates complaints.

    15.____

16. A. The delay in completing this investigation was caused by difficulty in obtaining the required documents from the candidate.
    B. Because of difficulty in obtaining the required documents from the candidate is the reason that there was a delay in completing this investigation.
    C. Having had difficulty in obtaining the required documents from the candidate, there was a delay in completing this investigation.
    D. Difficulty in obtaining the required documents from the candidate had the affect of delaying the completion of this investigation.

    16.____

17. A. This report, together with documents supporting our recommendation, are being submitted for your approval.
    B. Documents supporting our recommendation is being submitted with the report for your approval.
    C. This report, together with documents supporting our recommendation, is being submitted for your approval.
    D. The report and documents supporting our recommendation is being submitted for your approval.

    17.____

18. A. The chairman himself, rather than his aides, has reviewed the report.
    B. The chairman himself, rather than his aides, have reviewed the report.
    C. The chairmen, not the aide, has reviewed the report.
    D. The aide, not the chairmen, have reviewed the report.

    18.____

19. A. Various proposals were submitted but the decision is not been made.
    B. Various proposals has been submitted but the decision has not been made.
    C. Various proposals were submitted but the decision is not been made.
    D. Various proposals have been submitted but the decision has not been made.

20. A. Everyone were rewarded for his successful attempt.
    B. They were successful in their attempts and each of them was rewarded.
    C. Each of them are rewarded for their successful attempts.
    D. The reward for their successful attempts were made to each of them.

21. The following is a paragraph from a request for departmental recognition consisting of five numbered sentences submitted to a Captain for review. These sentences may or may not have errors in spelling, grammar, and punctuation:
    (1) The officers observed the subject Mills surreptitiously remove a wallet from the woman's handbag and entered his automobile. (2) As they approached Mills, he looked in their direction and drove away. (3) The officers pursued in their car. (4) Mills executed a series of complicated manuvers to evade the pursuing officers. (5) At the corner of Broome and Elizabeth Streets, Mills stopped the car, got out, raised his hands and surrendered to the officers.
    Which one of the following BEST classifies the above with regard to spelling, grammar, and punctuation?
    A. 1, 2, and 3 are correct, but 4 and 5 have errors.
    B. 2, 3, and 5 are correct, but 1 and 4 have errors.
    C. 3, 4, and 5 are correct, but 1 and 2 have errors.
    D. 1, 2, 3, and 5 are correct, but 4 has errors.

22. The one of the following sentences which is grammatically PREFERABLE to the others is:
    A. Our engineers will go over your blueprints so that you may have no problems in construction.
    B. For a long time he had been arguing that we, not he, are to blame for the confusion.
    C. I worked on his automobile for two hours and still cannot find out what is wrong with it.
    D. Accustomed to all kinds of hardships, fatigue seldom bothers veteran policemen.

23. The MOST accurate of the following sentences is:
    A. The commissioner, as well as his deputy and various bureau heads, were present.
    B. A new organization of employers and employees have been formed.
    C. One or the other of these men have been selected.
    D. The number of pages in the book is enough to discourage a reader.

24. The MOST accurate of the following sentences is:
    A. Between you and me, I think he is the better man.
    B. He was believed to be me.
    C. Is it us that you wish to see?
    D. The winners are him and her.

24.____

KEY (CORRECT ANSWERS)

1.	C		11.	B
2.	A		12.	B
3.	C		13.	D
4.	A		14.	B
5.	B		15.	D
6.	C		16.	A
7.	D		17.	C
8.	C		18.	A
9.	B		19.	D
10.	A		20.	B

21.	B
22.	A
23.	D
24.	A

PREPARING WRITTEN MATERIAL

PARAGRAPH REARRANGEMENT
COMMENTARY

The sentences that follow are in scrambled order. You are to rearrange them in proper order and indicate the letter choice containing the correct answer at the space at the right.

Each group of sentences in this section is actually a paragraph presented in scrambled order. Each sentence in the group has a place in that paragraph; no sentence is to be left out. You are to read each group of sentences and decide upon the best order in which to put the sentences so as to form a well-organized paragraph.

The questions in this section measure the ability to solve a problem when all the facts relevant to its solution are not given.

More specifically, certain positions of responsibility and authority require the employee to discover connection between events sometimes, apparently, unrelated. In order to do this, the employee will find it necessary to correctly infer that unspecified events have probably occurred or are likely to occur. This ability becomes especially important when action must be taken on incomplete information.

Accordingly, these questions require competitors to choose among several suggested alternatives, each of which presents a different sequential arrangement of the events. Competitors must choose the MOST logical of the suggested sequences.

In order to do so, they may be required to draw on general knowledge to infer missing concepts or events that are essential to sequencing the given events. Competitors should be careful to infer only what is essential to the sequence. The plausibility of the wrong alternatives will always require the inclusion of unlikely events or of additional chains of events which are NOT essential to sequencing the given events.

It's very important to remember that you are looking for the best of the four possible choices, and that the best choice of all may not even be one of the answers you're given to choose from.

There is no one right way to solve these problems. Many people have found it helpful to first write out the order of the sentences, as they would have arranged them, on their scrap paper before looking at the possible answers. If their optimum answer is there, this can save them some time. If it isn't, this method can still give insight into solving the problem. Others find it most helpful to just go through each of the possible choices, contrasting each as they go along. You should use whatever method feels comfortable and works for you.

While most of these types of questions are not that difficult, we've added a higher percentage of the difficult type, just to give you more practice. Usually there are only one or two questions on this section that contain such subtle distinctions that you're unable to answer confidently. And you then may find yourself stuck deciding between two possible choices, neither of which you're sure about.

PREPARING WRITTEN MATERIAL
PARAGRAPH REARRANGEMENT

EXAMINATION SECTION

TEST 1

DIRECTIONS: The sentences that follow are in scrambled order. You are to rearrange them in proper order and indicate the letter choice containing the CORRECT answer. *PRINT THE LETTER OF THE CORRECT ANSWER IN THE SPACE AT THE RIGHT.*

1. Police Officer Jenner responds to the scene of a burglary at 2106 La Vista Boulevard. He is approached by an elderly man named Richard Jenkins, whose account of the incident includes the following five sentences:
   I. I saw that the lock on my apartment door had been smashed and the door was open.
   II. My apartment was a shambles; my belongings were everywhere and my television set was missing.
   III. As I walked down the hallway toward the bedroom, I heard someone opening a window.
   IV. I left work at 5:30 P.M. and took the bus home.
   V. At that time, I called the police.
   The MOST logical order for the above sentence to appear in the report is
   A. I, V, IV, II, III   B. IV, I, II, III, V   C. I, V, II, III, IV   D. IV, III, II, V, I

1.____

2. Police Officer LaJolla is writing an Incident Report in which back-up assistance was required. The report will contain the following five sentences:
   I. The radio dispatcher asked what my location was and he then dispatched patrol cars for back-up assistance.
   II. At approximately 9:30 P.M., while I was walking my assigned footpost, a gunman fired three shots at me.
   III. I quickly turned around and saw a white male, approximately 5'10", with black hair, wearing blue jeans, a yellow T-shirt, and white sneaker, running across the avenue carrying a handgun.
   IV. When the back-up officers arrived, we searched the area but could not find the suspect.
   V. I advised the radio dispatcher that a gunman had just fired a gun at me, and then I gave the dispatcher a description of the man
   The MOST logical order for the above sentences to appear in the report is:
   A. III, V, II, IV, I   B. II, III, V, I, IV   C. III, II, IV, I, V   D. II, V, I, III, IV

2.____

3. Police Officer Durant is completing a report of a robbery and assault. The report will contain the following five sentences:
   I. I went to Mount Snow Hospital to interview a man who was attacked and robbed of his wallet earlier that night.
   II. An ambulance arrived at 82nd Street and 3rd Avenue and took an intoxicated, wounded man to Mount Snow Hospital
   III. Two youths attacked the man and stole his wallet.

3.____

IV. A well-dressed man left Hanratty's Bar very drunk, with his wallet hanging out of his back pocket.
   V. A passerby dialed 911 and requested police and ambulance assistance.
   The MOST logical order for the above sentences to appear in the report is
      A. I, II, IV, III, V   B. IV, III, V, II, I   C. IV, V, II, III, I   D. V, IV, III, II, I

4. Police Officer Boswell is preparing a report of an armed robbery and assault which will contain the following five sentences:
   I. Both men approached the bartender and one of them drew a gun.
   II. The bartender immediately went to grab the phone at the bar.
   III. One of the men leaped over the counter and smashed a bottle over the bartender's head.
   IV. Two men in a blue Buick drove up to the bar and went inside.
   V. I found the cash register empty and the bartender unconscious on the floor, with the phone still dangling off the hook.
   The MOST logical order for the above sentences to appear in the report is
      A. IV, I, II, II, V   B. V, IV, III, I, II   C. IV, III, II, V, I   D. II, I, III, IV, V

5. Police Officer Mitzler is preparing a report of a bank robbery, which will contain the following five sentences:
   I. The teller complied with the instructions on the note, but also hit the silent alarm.
   II. The perpetrator then fled south on Broadway.
   III. A suspicious male entered the bank at approximately 10:45 A.M.
   IV. At this time, an undetermined amount of money has been taken.
   V. He approached the teller on the far right side and handed her a note.
   The MOST logical order for the above sentences to appear in the report is:
      A. III, V, I, II, IV   B. I, III, V, II, IV   C. III, V, IV, I, II   D. III, V, II, IV, I

6. A Police Officer is preparing an Accident Report for an accident which occurred at the intersection of East 119th Street and Lexington Avenue. The report will include the following five sentences:
   I. On September 18, while driving ten children to school, a school bus driver passed out.
   II. Upon arriving at the scene, I notified the dispatcher to send an ambulance.
   III. I notified the parents of each child once I got to the station house.
   IV. He said the school bus, while traveling west on East 119th Street, struck a parked Ford which was on the southwest corner of East 119th Street.
   V. A witness by the name of John Ramos came up to me to describe what happened.
   The MOST logical order for the above sentences to appear in the Accident Report is:
      A. I, II, V, III, IV   B. I, II, V, IV, III   C. II, V, I, III, IV   D. II, V, I, IV, III

7. A Police Officer is preparing a report concerning a dispute. The report will contain the following five sentences:
   I. The passenger got out of the back of the taxi and leaned through the front window to complain to the driver about the fare.

II. The driver of the taxi caught up with the passenger and knocked him to the ground; the passenger then kicked the driver and a scuffle ensued.
III. The taxi drew up in front of the high-rise building and stopped.
IV. The driver got out of the taxi and followed the passenger into the lobby of the apartment building.
V. The doorman tried but was unable to break up the fight, at which point he called the precinct.

The MOST logical order for the above sentences to appear in the report is
A. III, I, IV, II, V   B. III, IV, I, II, V   C. III, IV, II, V, I   D. V, I, III, IV, II

8. Police Officer Morrow is writing an Incident Report. The report will include the following four sentences:
I. The man reached into his pocket and pulled out a gun.
II. While on foot patrol, I identified a suspect, who was wanted for six robberies in the area, from a wanted picture I was carrying.
III. I drew my weapon and fired six rounds at the suspect, killing him instantly.
IV. I called for back-up assistance and told the man to put his hands up.

The MOST logical order for the above sentences to appear in the report is
A. II, III, IV, I   B. IV, I, III, II   C. IV, I, II, III   D. II, IV, I, III

9. Sergeant Allen responds to a call at 16 Grove Street regarding a missing child. At the scene, the Sergeant is met by Police Officer Samuels, who gives a brief account of the incident consisting of the following five sentences:
I. I transmitted the description and waited for you to arrive before I began searching the area.
II. Mrs. Banks, the mother, reports that she last saw her daughter Julie about 7:30 A.M. when she took her to school.
III. About 6 P.M., my partner and I arrived at this location to investigate a report of a missing 8-year-old girl.
IV. When Mrs. Banks left her, Julie was wearing a red and white striped T-shirt, blue jeans, and white sneakers.
V. Mrs. Banks dropped her off in front of the playground of P.S. 11.

The MOST logical order for the above sentences to appear in the report is
A. III, V, IV, II, I   B. III, II, V, IV, I   C. III, IV, I, II, V   D. III, II, IV, I, V

10. Police Officer Franco is completing a report of an assault. The report will contain the following five sentences:
I. In the park I observed an elderly man lying on the ground, bleeding from a back wound.
II. I applied first aid to control the bleeding and radioed for an ambulance to respond.
III. The elderly man stated that he was sitting on the park bench when he was attacked from behind by two males.
IV. I received a report of a man's screams coming from inside the park, and I went to investigate.
V. The old man could not give a description of his attackers.

The MOST logical order for the above sentences to appear in the report is
A. IV, I, II, III, V   B. V, III, I, IV, II   C. IV, III, V, II, I   D. II, I, V, IV, III

11. Police Officer Williams is completing a Crime Report. The report contains the following five sentences:
    I.   As Police Officer Hanson and I approached the store, we noticed that the front door was broken.
    II. After determining that the burglars had fled, we notified the precinct of the burglary.
    III. I walked through the front door as Police Officer Hanson walked around to the back.
    IV. At approximately midnight, an alarm was heard at the Apex Jewelry Store.
    V.   We searched the store and found no one.
    The MOST logical order for the above sentences to appear in the report is
       A. I, IV, II, III, V   B. I, IV, III, V, II   C. IV, I, III, II, V   D. IV, I, III, V, II

    11.____

12. Police Officer Clay is giving a report to the news media regarding someone who has jumped from the Empire State Building. His report will include the following five sentences:
    I.   I responded to the 86th floor, where I found the person at the edge of the roof.
    II. A security guard at the building had reported that a man was on the roof at the 86th floor.
    III. At 5:30 P.M., the person jumped from the building.
    IV. I received a call from the radio dispatcher at 4:50 P.M. to respond to the Empire State Building.
    V.   I tried to talk to the person and convince him not to jump.
    The MOST logical order for the above sentences to appear in the report is
       A. I, II, IV, III, V   B. III, IV, I, II, V   C. II, IV, I, III, V   D. IV, II, I, V, III

    12.____

13. The following five sentences are part of a report of a burglary written by Police Officer Reed:
    I.   When I arrived at 2400 1st Avenue, I noticed that the door was slightly open.
    II. I yelled out, *Police, don't move!*
    III. As I entered the apartment, I saw a man with a TV set passing through a window to another man standing on a fire escape.
    IV. While on foot patrol, I was informed by the radio dispatcher that a burglary was in progress at 2400 1st Avenue.
    V.   However, the burglars quickly ran down the fire escape.
    The MOST logical order for the above sentences to appear in the report is
       A. I, III, IV, V, II   B. IV, I, III, V, II   C. IV, I, III, II, V   D. I, IV, III, II, V

    13.____

14. Police Officer Jenkins is preparing a report for Lost or Stolen Property. The report will include the following five sentences:
    I.   On the stairs, Mr. Harris slipped on a wet leaf and fell on the landing.
    II. It wasn't until he got to the token booth that Mr. Harris realized his wallet was no longer in his back pants pocket.
    III. A boy wearing a football jersey helped him up and brushed off the back of Mr. Harris' pants.
    IV. Mr. Harris states he was walking up the stairs to the elevated subway at Queensborough Plaza.
    V.   Before Mr. Harris could thank him, the boy was running down the stairs to the street.

    14.____

170

The MOST logical order for the above sentences to appear in the report is
A. IV, III, V, I, II   B. IV, I, III, V, II   C. I, IV, II, III, V   D. I, II, IV, III, V

15. Police Officer Hubbard is completing a report of a missing person. The report will contain the following five sentences:
    I. I visited the store at 7:55 P.M. and asked the employees if they had seen a girl fitting the description I had been given.
    II. She gave me a description and said she had gone into the local grocery store at about 6:15 P.M.
    III. I asked the woman for a description of her daughter.
    IV. The distraught woman called the precinct to report that her daughter, aged 12, had not returned from an errand.
    V. The storekeeper said a girl matching the description had been in the store earlier, but he could not give an exact time.
    The MOST logical order for the above sentences to appear in the report is
    A. I, III, II, V, IV   B. IV, III, II, I, V   C. V, I, II, III, IV   D. III, I, II, IV, V

15.____

16. A police officer is completing an entry in his Daily Activity Log regarding traffic summonses which he issued. The following five sentences will be included in the entry:
    I. I was on routine patrol parked 16 yards west of 170th Street and Clay Avenue.
    II. The summonses were issued for unlicensed operator and disobeying a steady red light.
    III. At 8 A.M. hours, I observed an auto traveling westbound on 170th Street not stop for a steady red light at the intersection of Clay Avenue and 170th Street.
    IV. I stopped the driver of the auto and determined that he did not have a valid driver's license.
    V. After a brief conversation, I informed the motorist that he was receiving two summonses.
    The MOST logical order for the above sentences to appear in the report is
    A. I, III, IV, V, II   B. III, IV, II, V, I   C. V, II, I, III, IV   D. IV, V, II, I, III

16.____

17. The following sentences appeared on an Incident Report:
    I. Three teenagers who had been ejected from the theater were yelling at patrons who were now entering.
    II. Police Officer Dixon told the teenagers to leave the area.
    III. The teenager said that they were told by the manager to leave the theater because they were talking during the movie.
    IV. The theater manager called the precinct at 10:20 P.M. to report a disturbance outside the theater.
    V. A patrol car responded to the theater at 10:42 P.M. and two police officers went over to the teenagers.
    The MOST logical order for the above sentences to appear in the Incident Report is
    A. I, V, IV, III, II   B. IV, I, V, III, II   C. IV, I, III, V, II   D. IV, III, I, V, II

17.____

18. Activity Log entries are completed by police officers. Police Officer Samuels has written an entry concerning vandalism and part of it contains the following five sentences:
    I. The man, in his early twenties, ran down the block and around the corner.
    II. A man passing the store threw a brick through a window of the store.
    III. I arrived on the scene and began to question the witnesses about the incident.
    IV. Malcolm Holmes, the owner of the Fast Service Shoe Repair Store, was working in the back of the store at approximately 3 P.M.
    V. After the man fled, Mr. Holmes called the police.
    The MOST logical order for the above sentences to appear in the Activity Log is
    A. IV, II, I, V, III   B. II, IV, I, III, V   C. II, I, IV, III, V   D. IV, II, V, III, I

18.____

19. Police Officer Buckley is preparing a report concerning a dispute in a restaurant. The report will contain the following five sentences:
    I. The manager, Charles Chin, and a customer, Edward Green, were standing near the register arguing over the bill.
    II. The manager refused to press any charges providing Green pay the check and leave.
    III. While on foot patrol, I was informed by a passerby of a disturbance in the Dragon Flame Restaurant.
    IV. Green paid the $15.00 check and left the restaurant.
    V. According to witnesses, the customer punched the owner in the face when Chin asked him for the amount due.
    The MOST logical order for the above sentences to appear in the report is
    A. III, I, V, II, IV   B. I, II, III, IV, V   C. V, I, III, II, IV   D. III, V, II, IV, I

19.____

20. Police Officer Wilkins is preparing a report for leaving the scene of an accident. The report will include the following five sentences:
    I. The Dodge struck the right rear fender of Mrs. Smith's 2010 Ford and continued on its way.
    II. Mrs. Smith stated she was making a left turn from 40th Street onto Third Avenue.
    III. As the car passed, Mrs. Smith noticed the dangling rear license plate #412AEJ.
    IV. Mrs. Smith complained to police of back pains and was removed by ambulance to Bellevue Hospital.
    V. An old green Dodge traveling up Third Avenue went through the red light at 40th Street and Third Avenue.
    The MOST logical order for the above sentences to appear in the report is
    A. V, III, I, II, IV   B. I, III, II, V, IV   C. IV, V, I, II, III   D. II, V, I, III, IV

20.____

21. Detective Simon is completing a Crime Report. The report contains the following five sentences:
    I. Police Officer Chin, while on foot patrol, heard the yelling and ran in the direction of the man.
    II. The man, carrying a large hunting knife, left the High Sierra Sporting Goods Store at approximately 10:30 A.M.

21.____

III. When the man heard Police Officer Chin, he stopped, dropped the knife, and began to cry.
IV. As Police Officer Chin approached the man, he drew his gun and yelled, *Police, freeze.*
V. After the man left the store, he began yelling, over and over, *I am going to kill myself!*

The MOST logical order for the above sentences to appear in the report is
A. V, II, I, IV, III   B. II, V, I, IV, III   C. II, V, IV, I, III   D. II, I, V, IV, III

22. Police Officer Miller is preparing a Complaint Report which will include the following five sentences:
    I. From across the lot, he yelled to the boys to get away from his car.
    II. When he came out of the store, he noticed two teenage boys trying to break into his car.
    III. The boys fled as Mr. Johnson ran to his car.
    IV. Mr. Johnson stated that he parked his car in the municipal lot behind Tams Department Store.
    V. Mr. Johnson saw that the door lock had been broken, but nothing was missing from inside the auto.

    The MOST logical order for the above sentences to appear in the report is
    A. IV, I, II, V, III   B. II, III, I, V, IV   C. IV, II, I, III, V   D. I, II, III, V, IV

22.____

23. Police Officer O'Hara completes a Universal Summons for a motorist who has just passed a red traffic light. The Universal Summons includes the following five sentences:
    I. As the car passed the light, I followed in the patrol car.
    II. After the driver stopped the car, he stated that the light was yellow, not red.
    III. A blue Cadillac sedan passed the red light on the corner of 79th Street and 3rd Avenue at 11:25 P.M.
    IV. As a result, the driver was informed that he did pass a red light and that his brake lights were not working.
    V. The driver in the Cadillac stopped his car as soon as he saw the patrol car, and I noticed that the brake lights were not working.

    The MOST logical order for the above sentences to appear in the Universal Summons is
    A. I, III, V, II, IV   B. III, I, V, II, IV   C. III, I, V, IV, II   D. I, III, IV, II, V

23.____

24. Detective Egan is preparing a follow-up report regarding a homicide on 170th Street and College Avenue. An unknown male was found at the scene. The report will contain the following five sentences:
    I. Police Officer Gregory wrote down the names, addresses, and phone numbers of the witnesses.
    II. A 911 operator received a call of a man shot and dispatched Police Officers Worth and Gregory to the scene.
    III. They discovered an unidentified male dead on the street.
    IV. Police Officer Worth notified the Precinct Detective Unit immediately.
    V. At approximately 9:00 A.M., an unidentified male shot another male in the chest during an argument.

24.____

The MOST logical order for the above sentences to appear in the report is
A. V, II, III, IV, I   B. II, III, V, IV, I   C. IV, I, V, II, III   D. V, III, II, IV, I

25. Police Officer Tracey is preparing a Robbery Report which will include the following five sentences:
    I. I ran around the corner and observe a man pointing a gun at a taxidriver.
    II. I informed the man I was a police officer and that he should not move.
    III. I was on the corner of 125th Street and Park Avenue when I heard a scream coming from around the corner.
    IV. The man turned around and fired one shot at me.
    V. I fired once, shooting him in the arm and causing him to fall to the ground.

    The MOST logical order for the above sentences to appear in the report is
    A. I, III, IV, II, V   B. IV, V, II, I, III   C. III, I, II, IV, V   D. III, I, V, II, IV

KEY (CORRECT ANSWERS)

1.	B		11.	D
2.	B		12.	D
3.	B		13.	C
4.	A		14.	B
5.	A		15.	B
6.	B		16.	A
7.	A		17.	B
8.	D		18.	A
9.	B		19.	A
10.	A		20.	D

21.	B
22.	C
23.	B
24.	A
25.	C

TEST 2

DIRECTIONS: The sentences that follow are in scrambled order. You are to rearrange them in proper order and indicate the letter choice containing the CORRECT answer. *PRINT THE LETTER OF THE CORRECT ANSWER IN THE SPACE AT THE RIGHT*

1. Police Officer Weiker is completing a Complaint Report which will contain the following five sentences:
    I. Mr. Texlor was informed that the owner of the van would receive a parking ticket and that the van would be towed away.
    II. The police tow truck arrived approximately one half hour after Mr. Texlor complained.
    III. While on foot patrol on West End Avenue, I saw the owner of Rand's Restaurant arrive to open his business.
    IV. Mr. Texlor, the owner, called to me and complained that he could not receive deliveries because a van was blocking his driveway.
    V. The van's owner later reported to the precinct that his van had been stolen, and he was then informed that it had been towed.
    The MOST logical order for the above sentences to appear in the report is
    A. III, V, I, II, IV   B. III, IV, I, II, V   C. IV, III, I, II, V   D. IV, III, II, I, V

    1.____

2. Police Officer Ames is completing an entry in his Activity Log. The entry contains the following five sentences:
    I. Mr. Sands gave me a complete description of the robber.
    II. Alvin Sands, owner of the Star Delicatessen, called the precinct to report he had just been robbed.
    III. I then notified all police patrol vehicles to look for a white male in his early twenties wearing brown pants and shirt, a black leather jacket, and black and white sneakers.
    IV. I arrived on the scene after being notified by the precinct that a robbery had just occurred at the Star Delicatessen.
    V. Twenty minutes later, a man fitting the description was arrested by a police officer on patrol six blocks from the delicatessen.
    The MOST logical order for the above sentences to appear in the Activity Log is
    A. II, I, IV, III, V   B. II IV, III, I, V   C. II, IV, I, III, V   D. II, IV, I, V, III

    2.____

3. Police Officer Benson is completing a Complaint Report concerning a stolen taxicab, which will include the following five sentences:
    I. Police Officer Benson noticed that a cab was parked next to a fire hydrant.
    II. Dawson *borrowed* the cab for transportation purposes since he was in a hurry.
    III. Ed Dawson got into his car and tried to start it, but the battery was dead.
    IV. When he reached his destination, he parked the cab by a fire hydrant and placed the keys under the seat.
    V. He looked around and saw an empty cab with the engine running.
    The MOST logical order for the above sentences to appear in the report is
    A. I, III, II, IV, V   B. III, I, II, V, IV   C. III, V, II, IV, I   D. V, II, IV, III, I

    3.____

175

4. Police Officer Hatfield is reviewing his Activity Log entry prior to completing a report. The entry contains the following five sentences:
   I. When I arrived at Zand's Jewelry Store, I noticed that the door was slightly open.
   II. I told the burglar I was a police officer and that he should stand still or he would be shot.
   III. As I entered the store, I saw a man wearing a ski mask attempting to open the safe in the back of the store.
   IV. On December 16, 2020, at 1:38 A.M., I was informed that a burglary was in progress at Zand's Jewelry Store on East 59th Street.
   V. The burglar quickly pulled a knife from his pocket when he saw me.
   The MOST logical order for the above sentences to appear in the report is
   A. IV, I, III, V, II   B. I, IV, III, V, II   C. IV, III, II, V, I   D. I, III, IV, V, II

4._____

5. Police Officer Lorenz is completing a report of a murder. The report will contain the following five statements made by a witness:
   I. I was awakened by the sound of a gunshot coming from the apartment next door and I decided to check.
   II. I entered the apartment and looked into the kitchen and the bathroom.
   III. I found Mr. Hubbard's body slumped in the bathtub.
   IV. The door to the apartment was open, but I didn't see anyone.
   V. He had been shot in the head.
   The MOST logical order for the above sentences to appear in the report is
   A. I, III, II, IV, V   B. I, IV, II, III, V   C. IV, II, I, III, V   D. III, I, II, IV, V

5._____

6. Police Officer Baldwin is preparing an accident report which will include the following five sentences:
   I. The old man lay on the ground for a few minutes, but was not physically hurt.
   II. Charlie Watson, a construction worker, was repairing some brick work at the top of a building at 54th Street and Madison Avenue.
   III. Steven Green, his partner, warned him that this could be dangerous, but Watson ignored him.
   IV. A few minutes later, one of the bricks thrown by Watson smashed to the ground in front of an old man, who fainted out of fright.
   V. Mr. Watson began throwing some of the bricks over the side of the building.
   The MOST logical order for the above sentences to appear in the report is
   A. II, V, III, IV, I   B. I, IV, II, V, III   C. III, II, IV, V, I   D. II, III, I, IV, V

6._____

7. Police Officer Porter is completing an Incident Report concerning her rescue of a woman being held hostage by a former boyfriend. Her report will contain the following five sentences:
   I. I saw a man holding .25 caliber gun to a woman's head, but he did not see me.
   II. I then broke a window and gained access to the house.
   III. As I approached the house on foot, a gunshot rang out and I heard a woman scream.
   IV. A decoy van brought me as close as possible to the house where the woman was being held hostage.

7._____

V. I ordered the man to drop his gun, and he released the woman and was taken into custody.
The MOST logical order for the above sentences to appear in the report is
A. I, III, II, IV, V B. IV, III, II, I, V C. III, II, I, IV, V D. V, I, II, III, IV

8. Police Officer Byrnes is preparing a crime report concerning a robbery. The report will consist of the following five sentences:
   I. Mr. White, following the man's instructions, opened the car's hood, at which time the man got out of the auto, drew a revolver, and ordered White to give him all the money in his pockets.
   II. Investigation has determined there were no witnesses to this incident.
   III. The man asked White to check the oil and fill the tank.
   IV. Mr. White, a gas attendant, states that he was working alone at the gas station when a black male pulled up to the gas pump in a white Mercury.
   V. White was then bound and gagged by the male and locked in the gas station's rest room.
   The MOST logical order for the above sentences to appear in the report is
   A. IV, I, III, II, V B. III, I, II, V, IV C. IV, III, I, V, II D. I, III, IV, II, V

9. Police Officer Gale is preparing a report of a crime committed against Mr. Weston. The report will consist of the following five sentences:
   I. The man, who had a gun, told Mr. Weston not to scream for help and ordered him back into the apartment.
   II. With Mr. Weston disposed of in this fashion, the man proceeded to ransack the apartment.
   III. Opening the door to see who was there, Mr. Weston was confronted by a tall white male wearing a dark blue jacket and white pants.
   IV. Mr. Weston was at home alone in his living room when the doorbell rang.
   V. Once inside, the man bound and gagged Mr. Weston and locked him in the bathroom.
   The MOST logical order for the above sentences to appear in the report is
   A. III, V, II, I, IV B. IV, III, I, V, II C. III, V, IV, II, I D. IV, III, V, I, II

10. A police officer is completing a report of a robbery, which will contain the following five sentences:
    I. Two police officers were about to enter the Red Rose Coffee Shop on 47th Street and 8th Avenue.
    II. They then noticed a male running up the street carrying a brown paper bag.
    III. They heard a woman standing outside the Broadway Boutique yelling that her store had just been robbed by a young man, and she was pointing up the street.
    IV. They caught up with him and made an arrest.
    V. The police officers pursued the male, who ran past them on 8th Avenue.
    The MOST logical order for the above sentences to appear in the report is
    A. I, III, II, V, IV B. III, I, II, V, IV C. IV, V, I, II, III D. I, V, IV, III, II

11. Police Officer Capalbo is preparing a report of a bank robbery. The report will contain the following five statements made by a witness:
    I. Initialing, all I could see were two men, dressed in maintenance uniforms, sitting in the area reserved for bank officers.
    II. I was passing the bank at 8 P.M. and noticed that all the lights were out, except in the rear section.
    III. Then I noticed two other men in the bank, coming from the direction of the vault, carrying a large metal box.
    IV. At this point, I decided to call the police.
    V. I knocked on the window to get the attention of the men in the maintenance uniforms, and they chased the two men carrying the box down a flight of steps.
    The MOST logical order for the above sentences to appear in the report is
       A. IV, I, II, V, III   B. I, III, II, V, IV   C. II, I, III, V, IV   D. II, III, I, V, IV

11.____

12. Police Officer Roberts is preparing a crime report concerning an assault and a stolen car. The report will contain the following five sentences:
    I. Upon leaving the store to return to his car, Winters noticed that a male unknown to him was sitting in his car.
    II. The man then re-entered Winters' car and drove away, fleeing north on 2nd Avenue.
    III. Mr. Winters stated that he parked his car in front of 235 East 25th Street and left the engine running while he went into the butcher shop at that location.
    IV. Mr. Robert Gering, a witness, stated that the male is known in the neighborhood as Bobby Rae and is believed to reside at 323 East 114th Street.
    V. When Winters approached the car and ordered the man to get out, the man got out of the auto and struck Winters with his fists, knocking him to the ground.
    The MOST logical order for the above sentences to appear in the report is
       A. III, II, V, I, IV   B. III, I, V, II, IV   C. I, IV, V, II, III   D. III, II, I, V, IV

12.____

13. Police Officer Robinson is preparing a crime report concerning the robbery of Mr. Edwards' store. The report will consist of the following five sentences:
    I. When the last customer left the store, the two men drew revolvers and ordered Mr. Edwards to give them all the money in the cash register.
    II. The men proceeded to the back of the store as if they were going to do some shopping.
    III. Janet Morley, a neighborhood resident, later reported that she saw the men enter a green Ford station wagon and flee northbound on Albany Avenue.
    IV. Edwards complied after which the gunmen ran from the store.
    V. Mr. Edwards states that he was stocking merchandise behind the store counter when two white males entered the store.
    The MOST logical order for the above sentences to appear in the report is
       A. V, II, III, I, IV   B. V, II, I, IV, III   C. II, I, V, IV, III   D. III, V, II, I, IV

13.____

14. Police Officer Wendell is preparing an accident report for a 6-car accident that occurred at the intersection of Bath Avenue and Bay Parkway. The report will consist of the following five sentences:
   I. A 2016 Volkswagen Beetle, traveling east on Bath Avenue, swerved to the left to avoid the Impala, and struck a 2014 Ford station wagon which was traveling west on Bath Avenue.
   II. The Seville then mounted the curb on the northeast corner of Bath Avenue and Bay Parkway and struck a light pole.
   III. A 2013 Buick Lesabre, traveling northbound on Bay Parkway directly behind the Impala, struck the Impala, pushing it into the intersection of Bath Avenue and Bay Parkway.
   IV. A 2015 Chevy Impala, traveling northbound on Bay Parkway, had stopped for a red light at Bath Avenue.
   V. A 2017 Toyota, traveling westbound on Bath Avenue, swerved to the right to avoid hitting the Ford station wagon, and struck a 2017 Cadillac Seville double-parked near the corner.
   The MOST logical order for the above sentences to appear in the report is
   A. IV, III, V, II, I   B. III, IV, V, II, I   C. IV, III, I, V, II   D. III, IV, V, I, II

14.____

15. The following five sentences are part of an Activity Log entry Police Officer Rogers made regarding an explosion:
   I. I quickly treated the pedestrian for the injury.
   II. The explosion caused a glass window in an office building to shatter.
   III. After the pedestrian was treated, a call was placed to the precinct requesting additional police officers to evacuate the area.
   IV. After all the glass settled to the ground, I saw a pedestrian who was bleeding from the arm.
   V. While on foot patrol near 5th Avenue and 53rd Street, I heard a loud explosion.
   The MOST logical order for the above sentences to appear in the report is
   A. II, V, IV, I, III   B. V, II, IV, III, I   C. V, II, I, IV, III   D. V, II, IV, I, III

15.____

16. Police Officer David is completing a report regarding illegal activity near the entrance to Madison Square Garden during a recent rock concert. The report will obtain the following five sentences:
   I. As I came closer to the man, he placed what appeared to be tickets in his pocket and began to walk away.
   II. After the man stopped, I questioned him about *scalping* tickets.
   III. While on assignment near the Madison Square Garden entrance, I observed a man apparently selling tickets.
   IV. I stopped the man by stating that I was a police officer.
   V. The man was then given a summons, and he left the area.
   The MOST logical order for the above sentences to appear in the report is
   A. I, III, IV, II, V   B. III, I, IV, V, II   C. III, IV, I, II, V   D. III, I, IV, II, V

16.____

17. Police Officer Sampson is preparing a report containing a dispute in a bar. The report will contain the following five sentences:
   I. John Evans, the bartender, ordered the two men out of the bar.
   II. Two men dressed in dungarees entered the C and D Bar at 5:30 P.M.
   III. The two men refused to leave and began to beat up Evans.
   IV. A customer in the bar saw me on patrol and yelled to me to come separate the three men.
   V. The two men became very drunk and loud within a short time.
   The MOST logical order for the above sentences to appear in the report is
   A. II, I, V, III, IV   B. II, III, IV, V, I   C. III, I, II, V, IV   D. II, V, I, III, IV

17._____

18. A police officer is completing a report concerning the response to a crime in progress. The report will include the following five sentences:
   I. The officers saw two armed men run out of the liquor store and into a waiting car.
   II. Police Officers Lunty and Duren received the call and responded to the liquor store.
   III. The robbers gave up without a struggle.
   IV. Lunty and Duren blocked the getaway car with their patrol car.
   V. A call came into the precinct concerning a robbery in progress at Jane's Liquor Store.
   The MOST logical order for the above sentence to appear in the report is
   A. V, II, I, IV, III   B. II, V, I, III, IV   C. V, I, IV, II, III   D. I, V, II, III, IV

18._____

19. Police Officers Jenkins is preparing a Crime Report which will consist of the following five sentences:
   I. After making inquirie in the vicinity, Smith found out that his next door neighbor, Viola Jones, had seen two local teenagers, Michael Heinz and Vincent Gaynor, smash his car's windshields with a crowbar.
   II. Jones told Smith that the teenagers live at 8700 19th Avenue.
   III. Mr. Smith heard a loud crash at approximately 11:00 P.M., looked out of his apartment window, and saw two white males running away from his car.
   IV. Smith then reported the incident to the precinct, and Heinz and Gaynor were arrested at the address given.
   V. Leaving his apartment to investigate further, Smith discovered that his car's front and rear windshields had been smashed.
   The MOST logical order for the above sentences to appear in the report is
   A. III, IV, V, I, II   B. III, V, I, II, IV   C. III, I, V, II, IV   D. V, III, I, II, IV

19._____

20. Sergeant Nancy Winston is reviewing a Gun Control Report which will contain the following five sentences:
   I. The man fell to the floor when hit in the chest with three bullets from 22 caliber gun.
   II. Merriam's 22 caliber gun was seized, and he was given a summons for not having a pistol permit.
   III. Christopher Merriam, the owner of A-Z Grocery, shot a man who attempted to rob him.
   IV. Police Officer Franks responded and asked Merriam for his pistol permit, which he could not produce.

20._____

V. Merriam phoned the police to report he had just shot a man who had attempted to rob him.

The MOST logical order for the above sentences to appear in the report is
A. III, I, V, IV, II B. I, III, V, IV, II C. III, I, V, II, IV D. I, III, II, V, IV

21. Detective John Manville is completing a report for his superior regarding the murder of an unknown male who was shot in Central Park. The report will contain the following five sentences:
   I. Police Officers Langston and Cavers responded to the scene.
   II. I received the assignment to investigate the murder in Central Park from Detective Sergeant Rogers.
   III. Langston notified the Detective Bureau after questioning Jason.
   IV. An unknown male, apparently murdered, was discovered in Central Park by Howard Jason, a park employee, who immediately called the police.
   V. Langston and Cavers questioned Jason.

   The MOST logical order for the above sentences to appear in the report is
   A. I, IV, V, III, II B. IV, I, V, II, III C. IV, I, V, III, II D. IV, V, I, III, II

21.____

22. A police officer is completing a report concerning the arrest of a juvenile. The report will contain the following five sentences:
   I. Sanders then telephoned Jay's parents from the precinct to inform them of their son's arrest.
   II. The store owner resisted, and Jay then shot him and ran from the store.
   III. Jay was transported directly to the precinct by Officer Sanders.
   IV. James Jay, a juvenile, walked into a candy store and announced a hold-up.
   V. Police Officer Sanders, while on patrol, arrested Jay a block from the candy store.

   The MOST logical order for the above sentences to appear in the report is
   A. IV, V, II, I, III B. IV, II, V, III, I C. II, IV, V, III, I D. V, IV, II, I, III

22.____

23. Police Officer Olsen prepared a crime report for a robbery which contained the following five sentences:
   I. Mr. Gordon was approached by this individual who then produced a gun and demanded the money from the cash register.
   II. The man then fled from the scene on foot, southbound on 5th Avenue.
   III. Mr. Gordon was working at the deli counter when a white male, 5'6", 150-160 lbs., wearing a green jacket and blue pants, entered the store.
   IV. Mr. Gordon complied with the man's demands and handed him the daily receipts.
   V. Further investigation has determined there are no other witnesses to this robbery.

   The MOST logical order for the above sentences to appear in the report is
   A. I, III, IV, V, II B. I, IV, II, III, V C. III, IV, I, V, II D. III, I, IV, II, V

23.____

24. Police Officer Bryant responded to 285 E. 31st Street to take a crime report of a burglary of Mr. Bond's home. The report will contain a brief description of the incident, consisting of the following five sentences:
   I. When Mr. Bond attempted to stop the burglar by grabbing him, he was pushed to the floor.
   II. The burglar had apparently gained access to the home by forcing open the 2nd floor bedroom window facing the fire escape.
   III. Mr. Bond sustained a head injury in the scuffle, and the burglar exited the home through the front door.
   IV. Finding nothing in the dresser, the burglar proceeded downstairs to the first floor, where he was confronted by Mr. Bond who was reading in the dining room.
   V. Once inside, he searched the drawers of the bedroom dresser.
   The MOST logical order for the above sentences to appear in the report is
      A. V, IV, I, II, III   B. II, V, IV, I, III   C. II, IV, V, III, I   D. III, II, I, V, IV

24.____

25. Police Officer Derringer responded to a call of a rape-homicide case in his patrol area and was ordered to prepare an incident report, which will contain the following five sentences:
   I. He pushed Miss Scott to the ground and forcibly raped her.
   II. Mary Scott was approached from behind by a white male, 5'7", 150-160 lbs. wearing dark pants and a white jacket.
   III. As Robinson approached the male, he ordered him to stop.
   IV. Screaming for help, Miss Scott alerted one John Robinson, a local grocer, who chased her assailant as he fled the scene.
   V. The male turned and fired two shots at Robinson, who fell to the ground mortally wounded.
   The MOST logical order for the above sentences to appear in the report is
      A. IV, III, I, II, V   B. II, IV, III, V, I   C. II, IV, I, V, III   D. II, I, IV, III, V

25.____

KEY (CORRECT ANSWERS)

1.	B	11.	C
2.	C	12.	B
3.	C	13.	B
4.	A	14.	C
5.	B	15.	D
6.	A	16.	D
7.	B	17.	D
8.	C	18.	A
9.	B	19.	B
10.	A	20.	A

21. C
22. B
23. D
24. B
25. D

EXAMINATION SECTION
TEST 1

DIRECTIONS: Each question or incomplete statement is followed by several suggested answers or completions. Select the one that BEST answers the question or completes the statement. *PRINT THE LETTER OF THE CORRECT ANSWER IN THE SPACE AT THE RIGHT.*

1. Assume that a supervisor finds that his employees have become fatigued from doing a very long and repetitious job.
   The one of the following which would be the BEST way to relieve this fatigue is to
   A. assign other work so that the employees can switch to different assignments in the middle of the day
   B. let the employees listen to a radio while they work
   C. break the job down into very small parts so that each employee can concentrate on one simple task
   D. allow the employees to take frequent rest periods

   1.____

2. Assume that one of your subordinates is injured and will be out for at least six weeks.
   Of the following, the BEST way to handle the work normally assigned to this person is to
   A. allow the work to remain uncompleted until the injured person returns, since he is the one who can BEST do this work
   B. divide this work equally among the persons under your supervision who can do this work
   C. do all the work yourself
   D. give the injured person's work to the most efficient member of your staff

   2.____

3. Suppose that another supervisor tells you about a new way to organize some of your unit's work. The idea sounds good to you. However, before you were in this unit, a similar plan was tried and it failed.
   The MOST important thing for you to do FIRST is to
   A. find out why the previous attempt failed
   B. suggest that the other supervisor tell his idea to top management
   C. try the plan to see whether it works
   D. find proof that the plan has worked elsewhere

   3.____

4. One of your subordinates comes to you with a grievance. You discuss it with him so that you may fully understand the problem as he sees it. However, since you are uncertain as to the proper answer, you should
   A. tell him that you cannot help him with this problem
   B. tell him that you will have to check further and make an appointment to see him again
   C. send him to see your immediate superior for a solution to the problem
   D. ask him to find out from his co-workers whether this problem has come up before

   4.____

5. A supervisor reprimanded one of his subordinates severely for making a serious error in judgment while performing an assignment for which he had volunteered.
The supervisor's action was
   A. *incorrect*, chiefly because in the future the worker will probably try to avoid taking on responsibility
   B. *correct*, chiefly because this will insure that the worker will not make the same mistake in the future
   C. *correct*, chiefly because the worker should be discouraged from using his own judgment on the job
   D. *incorrect*, chiefly because the reprimand came too late to correct the error that had already been made

6. Of the following, the BEST way for a supervisor to inform all his subordinates of a change in lunch rules is, in MOST cases, to
   A. call a staff meeting
   B. tell each one individually
   C. issue a memorandum
   D. tell one or two employees to pass the word around

7. For a supervisor to assign work giving only general instructions to his subordinate would be advisable when
   A. the supervisor is confident that the worker knows how to do the job
   B. the assignment is a simple one
   C. the subordinate is himself a supervisory employee
   D. errors in the work will not cause serious delay

8. One of the DISADVANTAGES of setting minimum standards of performance for custodial employees is that
   A. such standards eliminate the basis for evaluating employees
   B. the custodial employees may keep their performance at the minimum level
   C. standards are always subject to change
   D. the supervisor may feel that his initiative is being restricted

9. One of your subordinates has been functioning below his usual level. You feel that something of a personal nature may be affecting his work. When you ask him casually whether anything is wrong, he says everything is fine.
As a next step, it would be BEST to
   A. make frequent casual and humorous comments about the poor quality of his work but refrain, at this time, from any serious discussion
   B. warn him that failure to maintain his customary level of performance might result in disciplinary action
   C. express your concern privately and reveal your interest in the reason for his change in work performance
   D. discuss with him the work of another employee, suggesting that the other employee would be a good example to follow

10. Assume you are teaching a new job to one of your subordinates. After you have demonstrated the job, you can BEST maintain the worker's interest by
    A. showing him training films about the job
    B. giving him printed material that explains why the job is important
    C. having him observe other workers do the job
    D. letting him attempt to do the job by himself under supervision

11. *Insubordination is sometimes a protest against inferior or arbitrary leadership.*
    For the supervisor, the MOST basic implication of the above statement is:
    A. Accusations of insubordination are easy to make, but usually difficult to prove.
    B. Insubordination cannot be permitted if an organization wishes to remain effective.
    C. When an employee discusses an order instead of carrying it out, he has not understood it.
    D. When an employee questions an order, review it to make sure it is reasonable.

12. In appraising a subordinate's mistakes, a supervisor should ALWAYS consider the
    A. absolute number of mistakes, without regard to severity
    B. number of mistakes in proportion to the number of decisions made
    C. total number of mistakes made by other, regardless of assignment
    D. number of mistakes which were discovered upon higher review

13. If you are the supervisor of an office in which the work frequently involves lifting heavy boxes, you should instruct your staff in the proper method of lifting to avoid injury.
    In giving these instructions, you should stress that a person lifting heavy objects MUST
    A. keep his feet close together
    B. bend at the waist
    C. keep his back as straight as possible
    D. use his back muscles to straighten up

14. Of the following, the BEST qualified supervisor is one who
    A. knows the basic principles and procedures of all the jobs which he supervises
    B. has detailed working knowledge of all aspects of the job he supervises but knows little about principles of supervision
    C. is able to do exceptionally well at least one of the jobs which he supervises and as some knowledge of the others
    D. knows little or nothing about most of the jobs which he supervises but knows the principles of supervision

15. The rate at which an employee will learn will vary according to a number of considerations.
    Of the following, which is LEAST likely to be controllable by the supervisor or the trainer? The
    A. manner in which the material is presented
    B. state of readiness of the learner
    C. scheduling of practice sessions
    D. nature of the material

15.____

16. When considering whether to use written material rather than oral instructions as a means of giving instructions to employees, the one of the following which should be given GREATEST consideration is the employees'
    A. personal preferences   B. attitude toward supervision
    C. general educational level D. salary level

16.____

17. Assume that one of your subordinates has been assigned to attend job training classes.
    The one of the following which would probably be the BEST evidence of the success of the course is that the employee
    A. feels that he has learned something
    B. continues to study after the course is over
    C. has had a good class record
    D. improves in his work performance

17.____

18. Of the following, the situation LEAST likely to result if a supervisor shows favoritism toward particular employees is
    A. laxity in the work of the favored employees
    B. resentment from the other, less-favored employees
    C. increased ability among the favored employees
    D. lowering of morale among employees

18.____

19. The one of the following reasons for evaluating employees' performance, whether done formally or informally, which is NOT considered to be POSITIVE in nature is to
    A. give individual counsel to employees
    B. motivate employees toward improvement
    C. provide recognition of superior service
    D. set penalties for substandard performance

19.____

20. Assume that, because there has been an unexpected and temporary increase in the short-term work of your unit, you have had temporarily assigned to you several staff members from another agency.
    Of the following, in dealing with these employees, it would be LEAST advisable to
    A. assign them to long-term projects
    B. organize tasks so that they can begin work immediately
    C. set standards, making allowances to give them time to learn your ways
    D. direct them in the same way, in general, as you do your regular staff

20.____

21. It has been suggested that one way to increase employee productivity would be to require employees dealing with the public to have proficiency in a relevant foreign language.
    Of the following, the MAJOR reason for implementing such a proposal, from the viewpoint of effective public administration, would be to
    A. encourage the foreign-born to learn English
    B. exchange information more rapidly and accurately
    C. increase the public prestige of the agency
    D. stimulate ethnic pride among all groups

21.____

22. Assume that the clerk who normally keeps your unit's records will be on vacation for four weeks.
    If other clerks are equally qualified to keep these records, your BEST choice to replace the clerk would be the person who
    A. has skills which are needed least for other duties during this period
    B. volunteers for this work
    C. is next in turn for a special assignment
    D. has handled this task before

22.____

23. Assume that you have under your supervision several young clerical employees who have the bad habit of fooling around when they should be working.
    Of the following, the BEST disciplinary action to take would be to
    A. ignore it; these young people will outgrow it
    B. join in the fun briefly in order to bring it to a quicker end each time it occurs
    C. bring to their attention the fact that this behavior is not acceptable and if it continues shift the make-up of the group to keep these young persons apart
    D. warn them that this type of behavior is reason for dismissal and be quick to make an example of the first one who starts it again

23.____

24. Seeking the advice of community leaders has human relations value for a public agency in planning or executing its programs CHIEFLY because it
    A. allows for the keeping of careful records concerning individual suggestions
    B. lets community leaders know that the agency has regard for their opinions
    C. permits the agency to state in writing which programs seem most appropriate
    D. unifies community leaders against the programs of competing private agencies

24.____

25. Good community relations is often action-oriented.
    Which of the following activities of a public agency is LEAST likely to be considered as action-oriented by the people of a local community?
    A. Conducting a survey to gather information about the local community
    B. Extending the use of a facility to those previously excluded
    C. Providing a service that was formerly non-existent
    D. Removing something considered objectionable by the local community

25.____

KEY (CORRECT ANSWERS)

1.	A		11.	D
2.	B		12.	B
3.	A		13.	C
4.	B		14.	A
5.	A		15.	B
6.	C		16.	C
7.	A		17.	D
8.	B		18.	D
9.	C		19.	D
10.	D		20.	A

21. B
22. A
23. C
24. B
25. A

TEST 2

DIRECTIONS: Each question or incomplete statement is followed by several suggested answers or completions. Select the one that BEST answers the question or completes the statement. *PRINT THE LETTER OF THE CORRECT ANSWER IN THE SPACE AT THE RIGHT.*

1. Methods of communication with employees are of three types: oral, written, and visual.
   A MAJOR advantage of the written word is that it
   A. insures that content will remain unchanged no matter how many persons may be involved in its transmission
   B. facilitates two-way communication in delicate or confidential situations
   C. strengthens chain-of-command procedures in transmission of information and instruction by requiring the use of prescribed channels
   D. encourages the active participation of employees in the solution of complicated problems

   1.____

2. The use of the conference technique in training often requires more preparatory work on the part of the trainer than does a good lecture PRIMARILY because
   A. a conference would cover material of a more technical nature
   B. the trainer will be required to supply more printed material to the participants
   C. a conference usually involves a greater number of trainees
   D. the trainer must be prepared for a wide variety of possible occurrences

   2.____

3. The one of the following which is NOT an advantage of the lecture over most other methods of training is that it can be given
   A. over the radio or on record   B. to large numbers of trainees
   C. without interruptions   D. with little preparation

   3.____

4. Of the following, the one which is LEAST appropriate as a purpose for using an employee attitude survey is to
   A. develop a supervisory training program
   B. learn the identity of dissatisfied employees
   C. re-evaluate employee relations policies
   D. re-orient publications designed for employees

   4.____

5. The competent trainer seeks to become knowledgeable both in the work of the agency and in the duties of the positions for which he is to conduct training. Of the following, the GREATEST practical value that result when the trainer gains such knowledge is that
   A. he will be more likely to instruct employees to perform their work in a manner consistent with actual practice
   B. all levels of staff will be favorably impressed by a display of interest in the agency and its work
   C. employees will become familiar with the trainer and will not consider him an outsider
   D. the trainer will gain an accurate picture of the capacity of each employee for training

   5.____

6. Assume that you, the supervisor of a small office, are involved in planning the reorganization of your bureau's work. Management has decided not to inform your staff of the reorganization until the plans are completed.
   If one of your subordinates tells you that he has heard a rumor about reorganization of the department, you should reply that
   A. the reorganization involves the bureau, not the department
   B. you haven't heard anything about departmental reorganization and that he should stop spreading rumors
   C. you will inform your staff at the appropriate time if any definite plans are made involving a reorganization
   D. you do not know what is being planned but will ask your superior for details

   6._____

7. Of the following training methods, the one in which the trainee's role is usually LEAST active is the _____ method.
   A. case-study   B. conference
   C. group discussion   D. lecture

   7._____

8. Differences in morale between two work groups can sometimes be attributed to differences in the supervision they receive.
   Of the following, the behavior MOST characteristic of a supervisor of a group with high morale is that he
   A. assigns the least difficult tasks to employees with the most seniority
   B. is concerned primarily with his ultimate responsibility, production
   C. delegates authority and responsibility to his staff
   D. is lenient with his workers when they violate rules

   8._____

9. Informal performance evaluations of individual employees, prepared systematically and regularly over a period of several years, are considered to be useful to a supervisor PRIMARILY because
   A. he will be able to assign tasks based only on these records
   B. unlike formal records, since they are fitted to the characteristics of individual employees, they provide for quick comparisons
   C. he need not discuss them with employees, since they are informal
   D. whatever personnel action he recommends can be substantiated by cumulative records

   9._____

10. When instructing first-line supervisors in the proper method of evaluating the performance of probationary employees, it is LEAST important for a higher-level supervisor to
    A. explain in detail the standards to be used
    B. inform them of the possibility of higher management review
    C. caution them concerning common errors of evaluation
    D. mention the purposes of probationary employee evaluation

    10._____

11. Assume that your agency is considering abolishing its official performance rating system but that you, a supervisor of a fairly large office, would like to devise a system for your own use.
    The FIRST step in setting up a system would be to
    A. decide what factors and personal characteristics are important and should be rated
    B. compare several rating methods to see which would be easiest to use
    C. have a private conference with each employee to discuss his performance
    D. set specific standards of employee performance, allowing your workers to make suggestions

12. The basic organizational structure of a municipal agency may have come about for several reasons.
    Of the following, the MOST important influence on the nature of its structure is the agency's
    A. professional attitude
    B. public reputation
    C. overall goal
    D. staff morale

13. The term *formal organization* refers to that organization structure agreed upon by top management whereas the term *informal organization* refers to the more spontaneous and flexible organizational ties developed by subordinates.
    The one of the following which BEST describes the usual *informal organization* is that it represents a(n)
    A. destructive system of relationships which should be eliminated
    B. concealed system of relationships whose goals are the same as management's
    C. actual system of relationships which should be recognized
    D. dysfunctional system of relationships which should be ignored

14. The reluctance of supervisors to delegate work to subordinates when they should is GENERALLY due to the supervisor's
    A. feelings of insecurity in work situations
    B. need to acquire additional experience
    C. inability to exercise control over his subordinates
    D. lack of technical knowledge

15. Assume that you have just been made the supervisor of a group of people you did not know before.
    For you to talk casually with each of your new subordinates with the purpose of getting to know them personally would be
    A. *advisable*, chiefly because subordinates have more confidence in a supervisor who shows personal interest in them
    B. *inadvisable*, chiefly because subordinates resent having their supervisor ask about their outside interests
    C. *advisable*, chiefly because one of the supervisor's main concerns should be to help his subordinates with their personal problems
    D. *inadvisable*, chiefly because a supervisor should not allow his relations with his subordinates to be influenced by their personalities

16. It has been found that high-producing subdivisions of organizations usually have supervisors whose behavior is employee-centered, whereas low-producing units usually have supervisors whose behavior is work-centered.
    Therefore, it could be concluded from these findings that
    A. a high-producing unit may cause a supervisor to be authoritarian
    B. a low-producing unit may cause a supervisor to be work-centered
    C. close supervision usually increases production
    D. employee-centered leadership may reduce production

17. A recent study in managerial science showed that, as the amount of praise increased and amount of criticism decreased, the supervisor was more likely to be perceived by his subordinates as being
    A. concerned with their career advancement
    B. production oriented, through subtle intimidation
    C. seeking personal satisfaction, irrespective of production
    D. uncertain of the subordinates' reliability

18. The power to issue directives or instructions to employees is derived from employees as much as from management.
    It follows MOST logically from this statement that
    A. attitudes toward management can be changed
    B. emphasis on discipline is needed
    C. authority is dependent upon acceptance
    D. employees should be properly supervised for work to be done

19. "In the decision-making process, it is a rare problem that has only one possible solution. Such a solution should be suspected of being nothing but a plausible argument for a preconceived idea."
    The author of the foregoing quotation apparently does NOT believe that
    A. there is usually only one possible solution to a problem
    B. the risks involved in any solution should be weighed against expected gains
    C. each alternative should be evaluated to determine the effort needed
    D. actions should be based on the urgency of problems

20. The supervisor who relies on punitive discipline to enforce his authority is putting limits on the potential of his leadership. Fear of punishment may secure obedience, but it destroys initiative. Such a supervisor's autocratic methods have cut off upward communications.
    Of the following, the major DISADVANTAGE of such autocratic behavior is that
    A. difficulties in the supervision of his subordinates will arise if limits are placed on the supervisor's responsibility
    B. policies that affect the public will be changed too frequently
    C. the supervisor will apply punishment subjectively rather than objectively
    D. instructions will be obeyed to the letter, regardless of changing circumstances

5 (#2)

21. The need for a supervisor to carefully coordinate and direct the work of his unit increases as the work becomes   21.____
    A. more routine
    B. more specialized
    C. less complex
    D. less technical

22. The MAIN goal of discipline as used by a supervisor should be to   22.____
    A. keep the employees' respect
    B. influence behavior, so that work will be completed properly
    C. encourage the employees to work faster
    D. set an example for others

23. One of your subordinates has exhibited discourtesy and non-cooperation on several occasions.   23.____
    Of the following, the MOST appropriate attitude for you to adopt in dealing with this problem is that
    A. disciplinary measures for such an individual generally creates additional problems
    B. failure to correct such behavior may lead to worse offenses
    C. it is a mistake to make an issue out of minor infractions
    D. the harsher the medicine, the faster the cure

24. Assume that an employee has complained to you, his supervisor, that he cannot concentrate on his work because two of his co-workers make too much noise. You pay particular attention to these employees for several days and do not find them making excessive noise.   24.____
    The NEXT step you should take in handling this grievance is to
    A. have a talk with all three employees, urging them to cooperate and be considerate of one another
    B. arrange for the complainant to change his work location to a place away from the two co-workers
    C. talk to the complainant to find out if the complaint he made to you is the real cause of his dissatisfaction
    D. tell the complainant that you have found his grievance to be unfounded

25. In planning the application of an existing agency program to a local community, it is generally necessary to discover relevant problems and possibilities for service.   25.____
    Of the following, the BEST way to learn about such problems and possibilities for service would usually be to
    A. begin the program on a full-scale basis and await reactions
    B. seek opinions and advice from community residents and leaders
    C. hold staff meetings with agency employees who have worked in similar communities
    D. study official federal reports about already completed programs of the same kind

KEY (CORRECT ANSWERS)

1. A
2. D
3. D
4. B
5. A

6. C
7. D
8. C
9. D
10. B

11. A
12. C
13. C
14. A
15. A

16. B
17. A
18. C
19. A
20. D

21. B
22. B
23. B
24. C
25. B

TEST 3

DIRECTIONS: Each question or incomplete statement is followed by several suggested answers or completions. Select the one that BEST answers the question or completes the statement. *PRINT THE LETTER OF THE CORRECT ANSWER IN THE SPACE AT THE RIGHT.*

1. Which of the following characteristics would be LEAST detrimental to a supervisor in his efforts to set up and maintain good relations with other supervisors with whom he must deal in the course of his duties?
   A. Not getting involved in consultation on any supervisory problems they might have
   B. Indicating that they should improve their supervising methods and offering suggestions on how to do so
   C. Emphasizing his own role as a member of management
   D. Sharing information which has proved useful in his unit

1.____

2. Both trainers and supervisors might agree that there is usually a best way to do a particular job. Yet a supervisor or instructor sometimes does not teach a new employee the best way, the most efficient way, to do a complex job.
Sometimes, in such cases, the supervisor temporarily changes the sequence of operations, increases the number of steps needed to do a job, or makes other changes in the method, which then deviates from the one considered most efficient.
When is such a difference in approach MOST justified when teaching a new employee a complex job?
   A. When the changes in approach correspond to the learning ability of the new employee
   B. When the new employee's performance on the job is closely supervised to compensate for a change in approach
   C. Where the steps in performing the task have not been defined in a manual of procedures
   D. When the instructor has ideas of improving upon the methods for doing the job

2.____

3. Considerable thought in the field of management is directed toward the advantages and disadvantages of authoritarian methods of influencing behavior, and, in the so-called authoritarian model, a nucleus of rather consistent ideas prevail.
Which of the following is LEAST characteristic of an administrative system based on the authoritarian model?
   A. A conviction of a need for order and efficiency in a world consisting mainly of people who lack direction and incentive
   B. Rules and contracts are the basis for action, and decisions are made on an impersonal basis
   C. The right to give orders and instructions is inherent in the hierarchical arrangement of an organizational structure
   D. Realization that subordinates' needs for affiliation and recognition can contribute to management's objectives

3.____

4. Of the following, the FIRST step in planning an operation is to
   A. obtain relevant information
   B. identify the goal to be achieved
   C. consider possible alternatives
   D. make necessary assignments

5. A supervisor who is extremely busy performing routine tasks is MOST likely making incorrect use of what basis principle of supervision?
   A. Homogeneous Assignment
   B. Span of Control
   C. Work Distribution
   D. Delegation of Authority

6. Controls help supervisors to obtain information from which they can determine whether their staffs are achieving planned goals.
   Which one of the following would be LEAST useful as a control device?
   A. Employee diaries
   B. Organization charts
   C. Periodic inspections
   D. Progress charts

7. A certain employee has difficulty in effectively performing a particular portion of his routine assignments, but his overall productivity is average.
   As a direct supervisor of this individual, your BEST course of action would be to
   A. attempt to develop the investigator's capacity to execute the problematical facets of his assignments
   B. diversify the investigator's work assignments in order to build up his confidence
   C. reassign the investigator to less difficult tasks
   D. request in a private conversation that the investigator improve his work output

8. A supervisor who uses persuasion as a means of supervising a unit would GENERALLY also use which of the following practices to supervise his unit?
   A. Supervises and control the staff with an authoritative attitude to indicate that he is a *take-charge* individual
   B. Make significant changes in the organizational operations so as to improve job efficiency
   C. Remove major communication barriers between himself, subordinates, and management
   D. Supervise everyday operations while being mindful of the problems of his subordinates

9. Whenever a supervisor in charge of a unit delegates a routine task to a capable subordinate, he tells him exactly how to do it.
   This practice is GENERALLY
   A. *desirable*, chiefly because good supervisors should be aware of the traits of their subordinates and delegate responsibilities to them accordingly
   B. *undesirable*, chiefly because only non-routine tasks should be delegated
   C. *desirable*, chiefly because a supervisor should frequently test the willingness of his subordinates to perform ordinary tasks
   D. *undesirable*, chiefly because a capable subordinate should usually be allowed to exercise his own discretion in doing a routine job

10. The one of the following activities through which a supervisor BEST demonstrates leadership ability is by
    A. arranging periodic staff meetings in order to keep his subordinates informed about professional developments in the field of investigation
    B. frequently issuing definite orders and directives which will lessen the need for subordinates to make decisions in handling any investigations assigned to them
    C. devoting the major part of his time to supervising subordinates so as to stimulate continuous improvement
    D. setting aside time for self-development and research so as to improve the investigative techniques and procedures of his unit

11. The following three statements relate to supervision of employees:
    I. The assignment of difficult tasks that offer a challenge is more conducive to good morale than the assignment of easy tasks.
    II. The same general principles of supervision that apply to men are equally applicable to women.
    III. The best restraining program should cover all phases of an employee's work in a general manner.
    Which of the following choices lists ALL of the above statements that are generally CORRECT?
    A. II, III   B. I   C. I, II   D. I, II, III

12. Which of the following examples BEST illustrates the application of the *exception principle* as a supervisory technique? A(n)
    A. complex job is divided among several employees who work simultaneously to complete the whole job in a shorter time
    B. employee is required to complete any task delegated to him to such an extent that nothing is left for the superior who delegated the task except to approve it
    C. superior delegates responsibility to a subordinate but retains authority to make the final decisions
    D. superior delegates all work possible to his subordinates and retains that which requires his personal attention or performance

13. Assume that you are a supervisor. Your immediate superior frequently gives orders to your subordinates without your knowledge.
    Of the following, the MOST direct and effective way for you to handle this problem is to
    A. tell your subordinates to take orders only from you
    B. submit a report to higher authority in which you cite specific instances
    C. discuss it with your immediate superior
    D. find out to what extent you authority and prestige as a supervisor have been affected

14. In an agency which has as its primary purpose the protection of the public against fraudulent business practices, which of the following would GENERALLY be considered an auxiliary or staff rather than a line function?

A. Interviewing victims of frauds and advising them about their legal remedies
B. Daily activities directed toward prevention of fraudulent business practices
C. Keeping records and statistics about business violations reported and corrected
D. Follow-up inspections by investigators after corrective action has been taken

15. A supervisor can MOST effectively reduce the spread of false rumors through the *grapevine* by
    A. identifying and disciplining any subordinate responsible for initiating such rumors
    B. keeping his subordinates informed as much as possible about matters affecting them
    C. denying false rumors which might tend to lower staff morale and productivity
    D. making sure confidential matters are kept secure from access by unauthorized employees

16. A supervisor has tried to learn about the background, education, and family relationships of his subordinates through observation, personal contact, and inspection of their personnel records.
    These supervisory actions are GENERALLY
    A. *inadvisable*, chiefly because they may lead to charges of favoritism
    B. *advisable*, chiefly because they may make him more popular with his subordinates
    C. *inadvisable*, chiefly because his efforts may be regarded as an invasion of privacy
    D. *advisable*, chiefly because the information may enable him to develop better understanding of each of his subordinates

17. In an emergency situation, when action must be taken immediately, it is BEST for the supervisor to give orders in the form of
    A. direct commands, which are brief and precise
    B. requests, so that his subordinate will not become alarmed
    C. suggestions, which offer alternative courses of action
    D. implied directive, so that his subordinates may use their judgment in carrying them out

18. When demonstrating a new and complex procedure to a group of subordinates, it is ESSENTIAL that a supervisor
    A. go slowly and repeat the steps involved at least once
    B. show the employees common errors and the consequences of such errors
    C. go through the process at the usual speed so that the employees can see the rate at which they should work
    D. distribute summaries of the procedure during the demonstration and instruct his subordinates to refer to them afterwards

19. The PRIMARY value of office reports and procedures is to
    A. assist top management in controlling key agency functions
    B. measure job performance
    C. save time and labor
    D. control the activities and use of time of all staff members

19.____

20. Of the following, which is considered to be the GREATEST advantage of the oral report? It
    A. allows for accurate transmission of information from one individual to another
    B. presents an opportunity to discuss or clarify any immediate questions raised by the receiver of the report
    C. requires less office work to maintain records on actions taken when an oral report is involved
    D. takes only a short amount of time to plan and prepare material for an oral report

20.____

21. A supervisor who is to make a report about a job he has done can make an oral report of a written report.
    Of the following, which is the BEST time to make an oral report? When
    A. the work covers an emergency situation
    B. a record is needed for the files
    C. the report is channeled to other departments
    D. the report covers additional work he will do

21.____

22. Suppose that a new employee has been assigned to you. It is your responsibility to see to it that he understands how to fill out properly the forms he is required to use.
    What would be the BEST way to do this?
    A. Explain the use of each form to the new technician and show him how to fill them out
    B. Give the new employee a copy of each form he must use so that he can learn by studying them
    C. Ask an experienced worker to explain clearly to him how the forms should be filled out
    D. Tell the new employee that filling out forms is simple and he should follow the instructions on each form

22.____

23. As a supervisor, you want to have your staff take part in improving work methods.
    Of the following, the BEST way to do this is to
    A. make critical appraisals of their work frequently
    B. encourage them to make suggestions
    C. make no change without their approval
    D. hold regular staff meetings

23.____

24. A good relationship with other supervisors is important to a senior supervisor. Close cooperation among supervisory personnel is MOST likely to result in
    A. increasing the probability for support of supervisory actions and decisions
    B. stimulating supervisors to achieve higher status in the organization
    C. helping to control the flow of work within a unit
    D. a clearer definition of the responsibilities of individual supervisors

25. Which of the following is MOST likely to gain a supervisor the respect and cooperation of his staff?
    A. Assigning the most difficult jobs to the experienced staff members
    B. Giving each staff member the same number of assignments
    C. Assigning jobs according to each staff member's ability
    D. Giving each staff member the same types of assignments

KEY (CORRECT ANSWERS)

1.	D	11.	C
2.	A	12.	D
3.	D	13.	C
4.	B	14.	C
5.	D	15.	B
6.	B	16.	D
7.	A	17.	A
8.	D	18.	A
9.	D	19.	A
10.	C	20.	B

21.	A
22.	A
23.	B
24.	A
25.	C

PHILOSOPHY, PRINCIPLES, PRACTICES, AND TECHNICS OF SUPERVISION, ADMINISTRATION, MANAGEMENT, AND ORGANIZATION

TABLE OF CONTENTS

	Page
MEANING OF SUPERVISION	1
THE OLD AND THE NEW SUPERVISION	1
THE EIGHT (8) BASIC PRINCIPLES OF THE NEW SUPERVISION	1
I. Principle of Responsibility	1
II. Principle of Authority	2
III. Principle of Self-Growth	2
IV. Principle of Individual Worth	2
V. Principle of Creative Leadership	2
VI. Principle of Success and Failure	2
VII. Principle of Science	3
VIII. Principle of Cooperation	3
WHAT IS ADMINISTRATION?	3
I. Practices Commonly Classed as "Supervisory"	3
II. Practices Commonly Classed as "Administrative"	3
III. Practices Commonly Classed as Both "Supervisory" and "Administrative"	4
RESPONSIBILITIES OF THE SUPERVISOR	4
COMPETENCIES OF THE SUPERVISOR	4
THE PROFESSIONAL SUPERVISOR-EMPLOYEE RELATIONSHIP	4
MINI-TEXT IN SUPERVISION, ADMINISTRATION, MANAGEMENT, AND ORGANIZATION	5
I. Brief Highlights	5
A. Levels of Management	6
B. What the Supervisor Must Learn	6
C. A Definition of Supervision	6
D. Elements of the Team Concept	6
E. Principles of Organization	6
F. The Four Important Parts of Every Job	7
G. Principles of Delegation	7
H. Principles of Effective Communications	7
I. Principles of Work Improvement	7
J. Areas of Job Improvement	7
K. Seven Key Points in Making Improvements	8

	L.	Corrective Techniques for Job Improvement	8
	M.	A Planning Checklist	8
	N.	Five Characteristics of Good Directions	9
	O.	Types of Directions	9
	P.	Controls	9
	Q.	Orienting the New Employee	9
	R.	Checklist for Orienting New Employees	9
	S.	Principles of Learning	10
	T.	Causes of Poor Performance	10
	U.	Four Major Steps in On-the-Job Instructions	10
	V.	Employees Want Five Things	10
	W.	Some Don'ts in Regard to Praise	11
	X.	How to Gain Your Workers' Confidence	11
	Y.	Sources of Employee Problems	11
	Z.	The Supervisor's Key to Discipline	11
	AA.	Five Important Processes of Management	12
	BB.	When the Supervisor Fails to Plan	12
	CC.	Fourteen General Principles of Management	12
	DD.	Change	12

II. Brief Topical Summaries — 13
- A. Who/What is the Supervisor? — 13
- B. The Sociology of Work — 13
- C. Principles and Practices of Supervision — 14
- D. Dynamic Leadership — 14
- E. Processes for Solving Problems — 15
- F. Training for Results — 15
- G. Health, Safety, and Accident Prevention — 16
- H. Equal Employment Opportunity — 16
- I. Improving Communications — 16
- J. Self-Development — 17
- K. Teaching and Training — 17
  1. The Teaching Process — 17
     a. Preparation — 17
     b. Presentation — 18
     c. Summary — 18
     d. Application — 18
     e. Evaluation — 18
  2. Teaching Methods — 18
     a. Lecture — 18
     b. Discussion — 18
     c. Demonstration — 19
     d. Performance — 19
     e. Which Method to Use — 19

PHILOSOPHY, PRINCIPLES, PRACTICES, AND TECHNICS OF SUPERVISION, ADMINISTRATION, MANAGEMENT, AND ORGANIZATION

MEANING OF SUPERVISION

The extension of the democratic philosophy has been accompanied by an extension in the scope of supervision. Modern leaders and supervisors no longer think of supervision in the narrow sense of being confined chiefly to visiting employees, supplying materials, or rating the staff. They regard supervision as being intimately related to all the concerned agencies of society, they speak of the supervisor's function in terms of "growth," rather than the "improvement" of employees.

This modern concept of supervision may be defined as follows: Supervision is leadership and the development of leadership within groups which are cooperatively engaged in inspection, research, training, guidance, and evaluation.

THE OLD AND THE NEW SUPERVISION

TRADITIONAL
1. Inspection
2. Focused on the employee
3. Visitation
4. Random and haphazard
5. Imposed and authoritarian
6. One person usually

MODERN
1. Study and analysis
2. Focused on aims, materials, methods, supervisors, employees, environment
3. Demonstrations, intervisitation, workshops, directed reading, bulletins, etc.
4. Definitely organized and planned (scientific)
5. Cooperative and democratic
6. Many persons involved (creative)

THE EIGHT (8) BASIC PRINCIPLES OF THE NEW SUPERVISION

I. Principle of Responsibility
   Authority to act and responsibility for acting must be joined.
   A. If you give responsibility, give authority.
   B. Define employee duties clearly.
   C. Protect employees from criticism by others.
   D. Recognize the rights as well as obligations of employees.
   E. Achieve the aims of a democratic society insofar as it is possible within the area of your work.
   F. Establish a situation favorable to training and learning.
   G. Accept ultimate responsibility for everything done in your section, unit, office, division, department.
   H. Good administration and good supervision are inseparable.

II. Principle of Authority
The success of the supervisor is measured by the extent to which the power of authority is not used.
  A. Exercise simplicity and informality in supervision
  B. Use the simplest machinery of supervision
  C. If it is good for the organization as a whole, it is probably justified.
  D. Seldom be arbitrary or authoritative.
  E. Do not base your work on the power of position or of personality.
  F. Permit and encourage the free expression of opinions.

III. Principle of Self-Growth
The success of the supervisor is measured by the extent to which, and the speed with which, he is no longer needed.
  A. Base criticism on principles, not on specifics.
  B. Point out higher activities to employees.
  C. Train for self-thinking by employees to meet new situations.
  D. Stimulate initiative, self-reliance, and individual responsibility
  E. Concentrate on stimulating the growth of employees rather than on removing defects.

IV. Principle of Individual Worth
Respect for the individual is a paramount consideration in supervision.
  A. Be human and sympathetic in dealing with employees.
  B. Don't nag about things to be done.
  C. Recognize the individual differences among employees and seek opportunities to permit best expression of each personality.

V. Principle of Creative Leadership
The best supervision is that which is not apparent to the employee.
  A. Stimulate, don't drive employees to creative action.
  B. Emphasize doing good things.
  C. Encourage employees to do what they do best.
  D. Do not be too greatly concerned with details of subject or method.
  E. Do not be concerned exclusively with immediate problems and activities.
  F. Reveal higher activities and make them both desired and maximally possible.
  G. Determine procedures in the light of each situation but see that these are derived from a sound basic philosophy.
  H. Aid, inspire, and lead so as to liberate the creative spirit latent in all good employees.

VI. Principle of Success and Failure
There are no unsuccessful employees, only unsuccessful supervisors who have failed to give proper leadership.
  A. Adapt suggestions to the capacities, attitudes, and prejudices of employees.
  B. Be gradual, be progressive, be persistent.
  C. Help the employee find the general principle; have the employee apply his own problem to the general principle.
  D. Give adequate appreciation for good work and honest effort.
  E. Anticipate employee difficulties and help to prevent them.
  F. Encourage employees to do the desirable things they will do anyway.
  G. Judge your supervision by the results it secures.

VII. Principle of Science
Successful supervision is scientific, objective, and experimental. It is based on facts, not on prejudices.
   A. Be cumulative in results.
   B. Never divorce your suggestions from the goals of training.
   C. Don't be impatient of results.
   D. Keep all matters on a professional, not a personal, level.
   E. Do not be concerned exclusively with immediate problems and activities.
   F. Use objective means of determining achievement and rating where possible.

VIII. Principle of Cooperation
Supervision is a cooperative enterprise between supervisor and employee.
   A. Begin with conditions as they are.
   B. Ask opinions of all involved when formulating policies.
   C. Organization is as good as its weakest link.
   D. Let employees help to determine policies and department programs.
   E. Be approachable and accessible—physically and mentally.
   F. Develop pleasant social relationships.

WHAT IS ADMINISTRATION

Administration is concerned with providing the environment, the material facilities, and the operational procedures that will promote the maximum growth and development of supervisors and employees. (Organization is an aspect and a concomitant of administration.)

There is no sharp line of demarcation between supervision and administration; these functions are intimately interrelated and, often, overlapping. They are complementary activities.

I. Practices Commonly Classed as "Supervisory"
   A. Conducting employees' conferences
   B. Visiting sections, units, offices, divisions, departments
   C. Arranging for demonstrations
   D. Examining plans
   E. Suggesting professional reading
   F. Interpreting bulletins
   G. Recommending in-service training courses
   H. Encouraging experimentation
   I. Appraising employee morale
   J. Providing for intervisitation

II. Practices Commonly Classified as "Administrative"
   A. Management of the office
   B. Arrangement of schedules for extra duties
   C. Assignment of rooms or areas
   D. Distribution of supplies
   E. Keeping records and reports
   F. Care of audio-visual materials
   G. Keeping inventory records
   H. Checking record cards and books

      I. Programming special activities
      J. Checking on the attendance and punctuality of employees

III. Practices Commonly Classified as Both "Supervisory" and "Administrative"
    A. Program construction
    B. Testing or evaluating outcomes
    C. Personnel accounting
    D. Ordering instructional materials

RESPONSIBILITIES OF THE SUPERVISOR

A person employed in a supervisory capacity must constantly be able to improve his own efficiency and ability. He represent the employer to the employees and only continuous self-examination can make him a capable supervisor.

Leadership and training are the supervisor's responsibility. An efficient working unit is one in which the employees work with the supervisor. It is his job to bring out the best in his employees. He must always be relaxed, courteous, and calm in his association with his employees. Their feelings are important, and a harsh attitude does not develop the most efficient employees.

COMPETENCES OF THE SUPERVISOR

    I. Complete knowledge of the duties and responsibilities of his position.
    II. To be able to organize a job, plan ahead, and carry through.
    III. To have self-confidence and initiative.
    IV. To be able to handle the unexpected situation and make quick decisions.
    V. To be able to properly train subordinates in the positions they are best suited for.
    VI. To be able to keep good human relations among his subordinates.
    VII. To be able to keep good human relations between his subordinates and himself and to earn their respect and trust.

THE PROFESSIONAL SUPERVISOR-EMPLOYEE RELATIONSHIP

There are two kinds of efficiency: one kind is only apparent and is produced in organizations through the exercise of mere discipline; this is but a simulation of the second, or true, efficiency which springs from spontaneous cooperation. If you are a manager, no matter how great or small your responsibility, it is your job, in the final analysis, to create and develop this involuntary cooperation among the people whom you supervise. For, no matter how powerful a combination of money, machines, and materials a company may have, this is a dead and sterile thing without a team of willing, thinking, and articulate people to guide it.

The following 21 points are presented as indicative of the exemplary basic relationship that should exist between supervisor and employee:

1. Each person wants to be liked and respected by his fellow employee and wants to be treated with consideration and respect by his superior.
2. The most competent employee will make an error. However, in a unit where good relations exist between the supervisor and his employees, tenseness and fear do not exist. Thus, errors are not hidden or covered up, and the efficiency of a unit is not impaired.

3. Subordinates resent rules, regulations, or orders that are unreasonable or unexplained.
4. Subordinates are quick to resent unfairness, harshness, injustices, and favoritism.
5. An employee will accept responsibility if he knows that he will be complimented for a job well done, and not too harshly chastised for failure; that his supervisor will check the cause of the failure, and, if it was the supervisor's fault, he will assume the blame therefore. If it was the employee's fault, his supervisor will explain the correct method or means of handling the responsibility.
6. An employee wants to receive credit for a suggestion he has made, that is used. If a suggestion cannot be used, the employee is entitled to an explanation. The supervisor should not say "no" and close the subject.
7. Fear and worry slow up a worker's ability. Poor working environment can impair his physical and mental health. A good supervisor avoids forceful methods, threats, and arguments to get a job done.
8. A forceful supervisor is able to train his employees individually and as a team, and is able to motivate them in the proper channels.
9. A mature supervisor is able to properly evaluate his subordinates and to keep them happy and satisfied.
10. A sensitive supervisor will never patronize his subordinates.
11. A worthy supervisor will respect his employees' confidences.
12. Definite and clear-cut responsibilities should be assigned to each executive.
13. Responsibility should always be coupled with corresponding authority.
14. No change should be made in the scope or responsibilities of a position without a definite understanding to that effect on the part of all persons concerned.
15. No executive or employee, occupying a single position in the organization, should be subject to definite orders from more than one source.
16. Orders should never be given to subordinates over the head of a responsible executive. Rather than do this, the officer in question should be supplanted.
17. Criticisms of subordinates should, whoever possible, be made privately, and in no case should a subordinate be criticized in the presence of executives or employees of equal or lower rank.
18. No dispute or difference between executives or employees as to authority or responsibilities should be considered too trivial for prompt and careful adjudication.
19. Promotions, wage changes, and disciplinary action should always be approved by the executive immediately superior to the one directly responsible.
20. No executive or employee should ever be required, or expected, to be at the same time an assistant to, and critic of, another.
21. Any executive whose work is subject to regular inspection should, wherever practicable, be given the assistance and facilities necessary to enable him to maintain an independent check of the quality of his work.

MINI-TEXT IN SUPERVISION, ADMINISTRATION, MANAGEMENT, AND ORGANIZATION

I. Brief Highlights

Listed concisely and sequentially are major headings and important data in the field for quick recall and review.

A. Levels of Management
Any organization of some size has several levels of management. In terms of a ladder, the levels are:

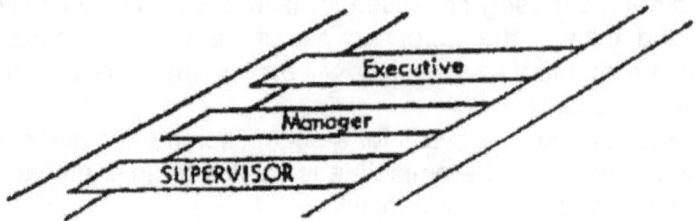

The first level is very important because it is the beginning point of management leadership.

B. What the Supervisor Must Learn
A supervisor must learn to:
1. Deal with people and their differences
2. Get the job done through people
3. Recognize the problems when they exist
4. Overcome obstacles to good performance
5. Evaluate the performance of people
6. Check his own performance in terms of accomplishment

C. A Definition of Supervisor
The term supervisor means any individual having authority, in the interests of the employer, to hire, transfer, suspend, lay-off, recall, promote, discharge, assign, reward, or discipline other employees or responsibility to direct them, or to adjust their grievances, or effectively to recommend such action, if, in connection with the foregoing, exercise of such authority is not of a merely routine or clerical nature but requires the use of independent judgment.

D. Elements of the Team Concept
What is involved in teamwork? The component parts are:
1. Members
2. A leader
3. Goals
4. Plans
5. Cooperation
6. Spirit

E. Principles of Organization
1. A team member must know what his job is.
2. Be sure that the nature and scope of a job are understood.
3. Authority and responsibility should be carefully spelled out.
4. A supervisor should be permitted to make the maximum number of decisions affecting his employees.
5. Employees should report to only one supervisor.
6. A supervisor should direct only as many employees as he can handle effectively.
7. An organization plan should be flexible.

8. Inspection and performance of work should be separate.
9. Organizational problems should receive immediate attention.
10. Assign work in line with ability and experience.

F. The Four Important Parts of Every Job
1. Inherent in every job is the *accountability* for results.
2. A second set of factors in every job is *responsibilities*.
3. Along with duties and responsibilities one must have the *authority* to act within certain limits without obtaining permission to proceed.
4. No job exists in a vacuum. The supervisor is surrounded by key *relationships*.

G. Principles of Delegation
Where work is delegated for the first time, the supervisor should think in terms of these questions:
1. Who is best qualified to do this?
2. Can an employee improve his abilities by doing this?
3. How long should an employee spend on this?
4. Are there any special problems for which he will need guidance?
5. How broad a delegation can I make?

H. Principles of Effective Communications
1. Determine the media.
2. To whom directed?
3. Identification and source authority.
4. Is communication understood?

I. Principles of Work Improvement
1. Most people usually do only the work which is assigned to them.
2. Workers are likely to fit assigned work into the time available to perform it.
3. A good workload usually stimulates output.
4. People usually do their best work when they know that results will be reviewed or inspected.
5. Employees usually feel that someone else is responsible for conditions of work, workplace layout, job methods, type of tools/equipment, and other such factors.
6. Employees are usually defensive about their job security.
7. Employees have natural resistance to change.
8. Employees can support or destroy a supervisor.
9. A supervisor usually earns the respect of his people through his personal example of diligence and efficiency.

J. Areas of Job Improvement
The areas of job improvement are quite numerous, but the most common ones which a supervisor can identify and utilize are:
1. Departmental layout
2. Flow of work
3. Workplace layout
4. Utilization of manpower
5. Work methods
6. Materials handling

7. Utilization
8. Motion economy

K. Seven Key Points in Making Improvements
1. Select the job to be improved
2. Study how it is being done now
3. Question the present method
4. Determine actions to be taken
5. Chart proposed method
6. Get approval and apply
7. Solicit worker participation

l. Corrective Techniques of Job Improvement
Specific Problems
1. Size of workload
2. Inability to meet schedules
3. Strain and fatigue
4. Improper use of men and skills
5. Waste, poor quality, unsafe conditions
6. Bottleneck conditions that hinder output
7. Poor utilization of equipment and machine
8. Efficiency and productivity of labor

General Improvement
1. Departmental layout
2. Flow of work
3. Work plan layout
4. Utilization of manpower
5. Work methods
6. Materials handling
7. Utilization of equipment
8. Motion economy

Corrective Techniques
1. Study with scale model
2. Flow chart study
3. Motion analysis
4. Comparison of units produced to standard allowance
5. Methods analysis
6. Flow chart and equipment study
7. Down time vs. running time
8. Motion analysis

M. A Planning Checklist
1. Objectives
2. Controls
3. Delegations
4. Communications
5. Resources
6. Manpower

7. Equipment
8. Supplies and materials
9. Utilization of time
10. Safety
11. Money
12. Work
13. Timing of improvements

N. Five Characteristics of Good Directions
In order to get results, directions must be:
1. Possible of accomplishment
2. Agreeable with worker interests
3. Related to mission
4. Planned and complete
5. Unmistakably clear

O. Types of Directions
1. Demands or direct orders
2. Requests
3. Suggestion or implication
4. volunteering

P. Controls
A typical listing of the overall areas in which the supervisor should establish controls might be:
1. Manpower
2. Materials
3. Quality of work
4. Quantity of work
5. Time
6. Space
7. Money
8. Methods

Q. Orienting the New Employee
1. Prepare for him
2. Welcome the new employee
3. Orientation for the job
4. Follow-up

R. Checklist for Orienting New Employees   Yes   No
1. Do you appreciate the feelings of new employees
   when they first report for work?   ___   ___
2. Are you aware of the fact that the new employee must
   make a big adjustment to his job?   ___   ___
3. Have you given him good reasons for liking the job and
   the organization?   ___   ___
4. Have you prepared for his first day on the job?   ___   ___
5. Did you welcome him cordially and make him feel needed?   ___   ___

	Yes	No

6. Did you establish rapport with him so that he feels free to talk and discuss matters with you? ___ ___
7. Did you explain his job to him and his relationship to you? ___ ___
8. Does he know that his work will be evaluated periodically on a basis that is fair and objective? ___ ___
9. Did you introduce him to his fellow workers in such a way that they are likely to accept him? ___ ___
10. Does he know what employee benefits he will receive? ___ ___
11. Does he understand the importance of being on the job and what to do if he must leave his duty station? ___ ___
12. Has he been impressed with the importance of accident prevention and safe practice? ___ ___
13. Does he generally know his way around the department? ___ ___
14. Is he under the guidance of a sponsor who will teach the right way of doing things? ___ ___
15. Do you plan to follow-up so that he will continue to adjust successfully to his job? ___ ___

S. Principles of Learning
   1. Motivation
   2. Demonstration or explanation
   3. Practice

T. Causes of Poor Performance
   1. Improper training for job
   2. Wrong tools
   3. Inadequate directions
   4. Lack of supervisory follow-up
   5. Poor communications
   6. Lack of standards of performance
   7. Wrong work habits
   8. Low morale
   9. Other

U. Four Major Steps in On-The-Job Instruction
   1. Prepare the worker
   2. Present the operation
   3. Tryout performance
   4. Follow-up

V. Employees Want Five Things
   1. Security
   2. Opportunity
   3. Recognition
   4. Inclusion
   5. Expression

11

W. Some Don'ts in Regard to Praise
1. Don't praise a person for something he hasn't done.
2. Don't praise a person unless you can be sincere.
3. Don't be sparing in praise just because your superior withholds it from you.
4. Don't let too much time elapse between good performance and recognition of it

X. How to Gain Your Workers' Confidence
Methods of developing confidence include such things as:
1. Knowing the interests, habits, hobbies of employees
2. Admitting your own inadequacies
3. Sharing and telling of confidence in others
4. Supporting people when they are in trouble
5. Delegating matters that can be well handled
6. Being frank and straightforward about problems and working conditions
7. Encouraging others to bring their problems to you
8. Taking action on problems which impede worker progress

Y. Sources of Employee Problems
On-the-job causes might be such things as:
1. A feeling that favoritism is exercised in assignments
2. Assignment of overtime
3. An undue amount of supervision
4. Changing methods or systems
5. Stealing of ideas or trade secrets
6. Lack of interest in job
7. Threat of reduction in force
8. Ignorance or lack of communications
9. Poor equipment
10. Lack of knowing how supervisor feels toward employee
11. Shift assignments

Off-the-job problems might have to do with:
1. Health
2. Finances
3. Housing
4. Family

Z. The Supervisor's Key to Discipline
There are several key points about discipline which the supervisor should keep in mind:
1. Job discipline is one of the disciplines of life and is directed by the supervisor.
2. It is more important to correct an employee fault than to fix blame for it.
3. Employee performance is affected by problems both on the job and off.
4. Sudden or abrupt changes in behavior can be indications of important employee problems.
5. Problems should be dealt with as soon as possible after they are identified.
6. The attitude of the supervisor may have more to do with solving problems than the techniques of problem solving.
7. Correction of employee behavior should be resorted to only after the supervisor is sure that training or counseling will not be helpful.

8. Be sure to document your disciplinary actions.
9. Make sure that you are disciplining on the basis of facts rather than personal feelings.
10. Take each disciplinary step in order, being careful not to make snap judgments, or decisions based on impatience.

AA. Five Important Processes of Management
1. Planning
2. Organizing
3. Scheduling
4. Controlling
5. Motivating

BB. When the Supervisor Fails to Plan
1. Supervisor creates impression of not knowing his job
2. May lead to excessive overtime
3. Job runs itself—supervisor lacks control
4. Deadlines and appointments missed
5. Parts of the work go undone
6. Work interrupted by emergencies
7. Sets a bad example
8. Uneven workload creates peaks and valleys
9. Too much time on minor details at expense of more important tasks

CC. Fourteen General Principles of Management
1. Division of work
2. Authority and responsibility
3. Discipline
4. Unity of command
5. Unity of direction
6. Subordination of individual interest to general interest
7. Remuneration of personnel
8. Centralization
9. Scalar chain
10. Order
11. Equity
12. Stability of tenure of personnel
13. Initiative
14. Esprit de corps

DD. Change

Bringing about change is perhaps attempted more often, and yet less well understood, than anything else the supervisor does. How do people generally react to change? (People tend to resist change that is imposed upon them by other individuals or circumstances.

Change is characteristic of every situation. It is a part of every real endeavor where the efforts of people are concerned.

1. Why do people resist change?
   People may resist change because of:
   a. Fear of the unknown
   b. Implied criticism
   c. Unpleasant experiences in the past
   d. Fear of loss of status
   e. Threat to the ego
   f. Fear of loss of economic stability

2. How can we best overcome the resistance to change?
   In initiating change, take these steps:
   a. Get ready to sell
   b. Identify sources of help
   c. Anticipate objections
   d. Sell benefits
   e. Listen in depth
   f. Follow up

II. Brief Topical Summaries

   A. Who/What is the Supervisor?
      1. The supervisor is often called the "highest level employee and the lowest level manager."
      2. A supervisor is a member of both management and the work group. He acts as a bridge between the two.
      3. Most problems in supervision are in the area of human relations, or people problems.
      4. Employees expect: Respect, opportunity to learn and to advance, and a sense of belonging, and so forth.
      5. Supervisors are responsible for directing people and organizing work. Planning is of paramount importance.
      6. A position description is a set of duties and responsibilities inherent to a given position.
      7. It is important to keep the position description up-to-date and to provide each employee with his own copy.

   B. The Sociology of Work
      1. People are alike in many ways; however, each individual is unique.
      2. The supervisor is challenged in getting to know employee differences. Acquiring skills in evaluating individuals is an asset.
      3. Maintaining meaningful working relationships in the organization is of great importance.
      4. The supervisor has an obligation to help individuals to develop to their fullest potential.
      5. Job rotation on a planned basis helps to build versatility and to maintain interest and enthusiasm in work groups.
      6. Cross training (job rotation) provides backup skills.

7. The supervisor can help reduce tension by maintaining a sense of humor, providing guidance to employees, and by making reasonable and timely decisions. Employees respond favorably to working under reasonably predictable circumstances.
8. Change is characteristic of all managerial behavior. The supervisor must adjust to changes in procedures, new methods, technological changes, and to a number of new and sometimes challenging situations.
9. To overcome the natural tendency for people to resist change, the supervisor should become more skillful in initiating change.

C. Principles and Practices of Supervision
1. Employees should be required to answer to only one superior.
2. A supervisor can effectively direct only a limited number of employees, depending upon the complexity, variety, and proximity of the jobs involved.
3. The organizational chart presents the organization in graphic form. It reflects lines of authority and responsibility as well as interrelationships of units within the organization.
4. Distribution of work can be improved through an analysis using the "Work Distribution Chart."
5. The "Work Distribution Chart" reflects the division of work within a unit in understandable form.
6. When related tasks are given to an employee, he has a better chance of increasing his skills through training.
7. The individual who is given the responsibility for tasks must also be given the appropriate authority to insure adequate results.
8. The supervisor should delegate repetitive, routine work. Preparation of recurring reports, maintaining leave and attendance records are some examples.
9. Good discipline is essential to good task performance. Discipline is reflected in the actions of employees on the job in the absence of supervision.
10. Disciplinary action may have to be taken when the positive aspects of discipline have failed. Reprimand, warning, and suspension are examples of disciplinary action.
11. If a situation calls for a reprimand, be sure it is deserved and remember it is to be done in private.

D. Dynamic Leadership
1. A style is a personal method or manner of exerting influence.
2. Authoritarian leaders often see themselves as the source of power and authority.
3. The democratic leader often perceives the group as the source of authority and power.
4. Supervisors tend to do better when using the pattern of leadership that is most natural for them.
5. Social scientists suggest that the effective supervisor use the leadership style that best fits the problem or circumstances involved.
6. All four styles—telling, selling, consulting, joining—have their place. Using one does not preclude using the other at another time.

7. The theory X point of view assumes that the average person dislikes work, will avoid it whenever possible, and must be coerced to achieve organizational objectives.
8. The theory Y point of view assumes that the average person considers work to be a natural as play, and, when the individual is committed, he requires little supervision or direction to accomplish desired objectives.
9. The leader's basic assumptions concerning human behavior and human nature affect his actions, decisions, and other managerial practices.
10. Dissatisfaction among employees is often present, but difficult to isolate. The supervisor should seek to weaken dissatisfaction by keeping promises, being sincere and considerate, keeping employees informed, and so forth.
11. Constructive suggestions should be encouraged during the natural progress of the work.

E. Processes for Solving Problems
1. People find their daily tasks more meaningful and satisfying when they can improve them.
2. The causes of problems, or the key factors, are often hidden in the background. Ability to solve problems often involves the ability to isolate them from their backgrounds. There is some substance to the cliché that some persons "can't see the forest for the trees."
3. New procedures are often developed from old ones. Problems should be broken down into manageable parts. New ideas can be adapted from old one.
4. People think differently in problem-solving situations. Using a logical, patterned approach is often useful. One approach found to be useful includes these steps:
   a. Define the problem
   b. Establish objectives
   c. Get the facts
   d. Weigh and decide
   e. Take action
   f. Evaluate action

F. Training for Results
1. Participants respond best when they feel training is important to them.
2. The supervisor has responsibility for the training and development of those who report to him.
3. When training is delegated to others, great care must be exercised to insure the trainer has knowledge, aptitude, and interest for his work as a trainer.
4. Training (learning) of some type goes on continually. The most successful supervisor makes certain the learning contributes in a productive manner to operational goals.
5. New employees are particularly susceptible to training. Older employees facing new job situations require specific training, as well as having need for development and growth opportunities.
6. Training needs require continuous monitoring.
7. The training officer of an agency is a professional with a responsibility to assist supervisors in solving training problems.

8. Many of the self-development steps important to the supervisor's own growth are equally important to the development of peers and subordinates. Knowledge of these is important when the supervisor consults with others on development and growth opportunities.

G. Health, Safety, and Accident Prevention
1. Management-minded supervisors take appropriate measures to assist employees in maintaining health and in assuring safe practices in the work environment.
2. Effective safety training and practices help to avoid injury and accidents.
3. Safety should be a management goal. All infractions of safety which are observed should be corrected without exception.
4. Employees' safety attitude, training and instruction, provision of safe tools and equipment, supervision, and leadership are considered highly important factors which contribute to safety and which can be influenced directly by supervisors.
5. When accidents do occur, they should be investigated promptly for very important reasons, including the fact that information which is gained can be used to prevent accidents in the future.

H. Equal Employment Opportunity
1. The supervisor should endeavor to treat all employees fairly, without regard to religion, race, sex, or national origin.
2. Groups tend to reflect the attitude of the leader. Prejudice can be detected even in very subtle form. Supervisors must strive to create a feeling of mutual respect and confidence in every employee.
3. Complete utilization of all human resources is a national goal. Equitable consideration should be accorded women in the work force, minority-group members, the physically and mentally handicapped, and the older employee. The important question is: "Who can do the job?"
4. Training opportunities, recognition for performance, overtime assignments, promotional opportunities, and all other personnel actions are to be handled on an equitable basis.

I. Improving Communications
1. Communications is achieving understanding between the sender and the receiver of a message. It also means sharing information—the creation of understanding.
2. Communication is basic to all human activity. Words are means of conveying meanings; however, real meanings are in people.
3. There are very practical differences in the effectiveness of one-way, impersonal, and two-way communications. Words spoken face-to-face are better understood. Telephone conversations are effective, but lack the rapport of person-to-person exchanges. The whole person communicates.
4. Cooperation and communication in an organization go hand in hand. When there is a mutual respect between people, spelling out rules and procedures for communicating is unnecessary.
5. There are several barriers to effective communications. These include failure to listen with respect and understanding, lack of skill in feedback, and misinterpreting the meanings of words used by the speaker. It is also common

practice to listen to what we want to hear, and tune out things we do not want to hear.
6. Communication is management's chief problem. The supervisor should accept the challenge to communicate more effectively and to improve interagency and intra-agency communications.
7. The supervisor may often plan for and conduct meetings. The planning phase is critical and may determine the success or the failure of a meeting.
8. Speaking before groups usually requires extra effort. Stage fright may never disappear completely, but it can be controlled.

J. Self-Development
1. Every employee is responsible for his own self-development.
2. Toastmaster and toastmistress clubs offer opportunities to improve skills in oral communications.
3. Planning for one's own self-development is of vital importance. Supervisors know their own strengths and limitations better than anyone else.
4. Many opportunities are open to aid the supervisor in his developmental efforts, including job assignments; training opportunities, both governmental and non-governmental—to include universities and professional conferences and seminars.
5. Programmed instruction offers a means of studying at one's own rate.
6. Where difficulties may arise from a supervisor's being away from his work for training, he may participate in televised home study or correspondence courses to meet his self-development needs.

K. Teaching and Training
1. The Teaching Process
Teaching is encouraging and guiding the learning activities of students toward established goals. In most cases this process consists of five steps: preparation, presentation, summarization, evaluation, and application.

   a. Preparation
   Preparation is two-fold in nature; that of the supervisor and the employee. Preparation by the supervisor is absolutely essential to success. He must know what, when, where, how, and whom he will teach. Some of the factors that should be considered are:
   1) The objectives
   2) The materials needed
   3) The methods to be used
   4) Employee participation
   5) Employee interest
   6) Training aids
   7) Evaluation
   8) Summarization

   Employee preparation consists in preparing the employee to receive the material. Probably the most important single factor in the preparation of the employee is arousing and maintaining his interest. He must know the objectives of the training, why he is there, how the material can be used, and its importance to him.

b. Presentation
In presentation, have a carefully designed plan and follow it. The plan should be accurate and complete, yet flexible enough to meet situations as they arise. The method of presentation will be determined by the particular situation and objectives.

c. Summary
A summary should be made at the end of every training unit and program. In addition, there may be internal summaries depending on the nature of the material being taught. The important thing is that the trainee must always be able to understand how each part of the new material relates to the whole.

d. Application
The supervisor must arrange work so the employee will be given a chance to apply new knowledge or skills while the material is still clear in his mind and interest is high. The trainee does not really know whether he has learned the material until he has been given a chance to apply it. If the material is not applied, it loses most of its value.

e. Evaluation
The purpose of all training is to promote learning. To determine whether the training has been a success or failure, the supervisor must evaluate this learning.
In the broadest sense, evaluation includes all the devices, methods, skills, and techniques used by the supervisor to keep himself and the employees informed as to their progress toward the objectives they are pursuing. The extent to which the employee has mastered the knowledge, skills, and abilities, or changed his attitudes, as determined by the program objectives, is the extent to which instruction has succeeded or failed.
Evaluation should not be confined to the end of the lesson, day, or program but should be used continuously. We shall note later the way this relates to the rest of the teaching process.

2. Teaching Methods
A teaching method is a pattern of identifiable student and instructor activity used in presenting training material.
All supervisors are faced with the problem of deciding which method should be used at a given time.

a. Lecture
The lecture is direct oral presentation of material by the supervisor. The present trend is to place less emphasis on the trainer's activity and more on that of the trainee.

b. Discussion
Teaching by discussion or conference involves using questions and other techniques to arouse interest and focus attention upon certain areas, and by doing so creating a learning situation. This can be one of the most

valuable methods because it gives the employees an opportunity to express their ideas and pool their knowledge.

    c. Demonstration

The demonstration is used to teach how something works or how to do something. It can be used to show a principle or what the results of a series of actions will be. A well-staged demonstration is particularly effective because it shows proper methods of performance in a realistic manner.

    d. Performance

Performance is one of the most fundamental of all learning techniques or teaching methods. The trainee may be able to tell how a specific operation should be performed but he cannot be sure he knows how to perform the operation until he has done so.
As with all methods, there are certain advantages and disadvantages to each method.

    e. Which Method to Use

Moreover, there are other methods and techniques of teaching. It is difficult to use any method without other methods entering into it. In any learning situation, a combination of methods is usually more effective than any one method alone.

Finally, evaluation must be integrated into the other aspects of the teaching-learning process.

It must be used in the motivation of the trainees; it must be used to assist in developing understanding during the training; and it must be related to employee application of the results of training.

This is distinctly the role of the supervisor.

CONTROL AND MANAGEMENT OF PRISON INMATES
TABLE OF CONTENTS

FACTORS IN PRISONER UNREST 1
   External Factors 1
      Indifference 1
      Politics 1
      Unwise commitment and release procedures 2
      Overcrowding 2
      Emotional tone of the community 2
   Internal Factors 2
      The society of prisoners 2
      The society of personnel 3
      Social caste in institutions 4

PREVENTIVE MEASURES 4
   Personnel Administration 5
      Development of correctional careers 6
      Support of staff development programs 6
      Removal of job dissatisfactions 6
   Policies and Operating Procedures 7
      Prisoner rights and attention to complaints 7
      Communication 8
      Correspondence regulations 9
      Visiting regulations 10
      Prisoner discipline 11
   Improvement of Correctional Programs 13

HANDLING EMERGENCIES 14
   Escape Plans 14
      Prevention   15
      Sounding the alarm   15
      Mobilization of resources   15
      Establishing control   16
      Returning to normal 16

   Plans for Riots and Disturbances 17
      Containment 18
      Use of force and defensive equipment 18
      Post-riot procedures 19
   Plans for Civil Disorder 19
   Plans for Civil Disaster 20
   Fire Plans 20

CONCLUSION 20

CONTROL AND MANAGEMENT OF PRISON INMATES

FACTORS IN PRISONER UNREST

". . . and him safely keep," whether directly expressed or not, is the universal mandate that accompanies every order of commitment to a lock-up, jail, prison or other correctional facility. Ultimate responsibility for this rests upon the administrator of the facility, together with responsibilities for the training, use and performance of personnel. He also bears stewardship responsibilities for the proper care and use of government property and the wise expenditure of public funds. For these reasons, if no other, the institution administrator is very much concerned over the ever-present potentials of prisoner disorder.

The possible consequences of prisoner unrest, whether expressed in misconduct, escape or riot, can be serious. At the least, disorder of any significant magnitude can interfere with the efficient operation of the institution. For example, staff time and energies that are devoted to handling an excessive number of misconduct reports detracts from more productive pursuits of the personnel involved. Escapes not only can be disruptive of normal operations but require the deployment of personnel who have other primary duties to perform. In extreme degree, a major riot which results in extensive property damage can cripple an institution for months. Beyond this, disorder can produce negative reactions in officials and the general public by undermining confidence in the management of the institution and by reinforcing existing rejective attitudes toward offenders and employees as classes of people.

It is generally true that the potentials for disorder within an institution are in inverse ratio to the effectiveness of institutional management and control. But this explains nothing and any attempt either to apply preventive measures or to cope successfully with incidents as they occur can fall short unless there is, first, some understanding of the many factors which figure prominently in prisoner unrest. In the discussion that follows, an arbitrary distinction is made between "external" and "internal" factors. This distinction may not appear in real life. Likewise, the discussion deals with a number of separate items when, in reality, all may be interrelated.

EXTERNAL FACTORS

Indifference. It is entirely possible that what appears as indifference is actually a perfectly "natural" reaction of people who look upon irrational, irresponsible and, at times, unpredictable and threatening behavior with a mixture of fear, frustration and frank bewilderment. Rather than indifference, the reaction may be outright rejection. The term "offender," alone, expresses an attitude of rejection. Certainly imprisonment is a form of rejection or banishment, however brief.

Whatever the reasons for it, the most visible evidence of indifference is withholding support. The expenditure of public funds for the operation of prisons and jails is politically unpopular under ordinary circumstances. Hospitals, schools, highways, aid to needy children and other competing demands on the public treasury have far more appeal than the correctional needs of offenders. Hand-to-mouth budget practices and deficit financing can account heavily for the inadequacies of personnel, facilities and programs.

Politics. Typically, jail management is the responsibility of elected local officials. Unlike schools, hospitals and mental health programs, where the need for competent, trained and full-time leadership has long been recognized, the administration of local correctional facilities is more often than not one of the many responsibilities of the sheriff. He, in turn, must rely on subordinates who ordinarily have had no preparation for their jobs.

In any institution there can be less visible but more insidious kinds of politically-motivated activity which sap the vitality and undermine the integrity of operations. Some of these involve pressures to extend improper favors to certain prisoners, efforts to obtain early releases, favoritism in the assignment of personnel and misuse of institutional property and supplies.

Unwise commitment and release procedures. Prisoners, like other people, tend to excuse and rationalize their own behavior. Unfortunately, many of the excuses are easily found in the machinery of criminal justice where there are all-too-obvious inequities and injustices. Problems in this area are numerous.

The system which permits accused persons with money to be free awaiting trial while those without resources have to stay in jail is both a blot on our notions of equal justice and the cause of many people being in jail needlessly. The mystique of a "taste of jail" is still popular in the minds of police, prosecutors and judges with the resultant confinement of many people who otherwise might have been released on bond or their own recognizance, placed on probation or assessed a fine.

Disparity in sentencing practices is a prime source of prisoner discontent. All judges do not think alike about how the law should be administered. Legislatures may impose unwise limits on judicial discretion, as when laws are enacted that require long minimum sentences or which establish ineligibility for probation or parole. In addition, decisions to release from jail are often viewed by prisoners as having been based on prejudice, caprice, or the "right connections."

Overcrowding. Emotional tensions are developed by the irritations of people upon each other. The more congested the conditions under which they must live, the greater the risks of frustration, anger and open conflict. All too frequently institutions have to operate over capacity. Two beds being placed in cells built for one, mattresses spread on corridor floors, overtaxed facilities, overworked personnel and failure generally to meet the most elementary requirements of differentiating among prisoners and maintaining acceptable standards of decency.

Emotional tone of the community. Prisoners are not nearly so isolated from the free community as may be supposed. They are aware of the attitudes of employees and visitors who live in the outside world. They have access to newspapers, radio, television and other means of communication with the outside. It is widely believed by institution people that the emotional tone of the free community is reflected inside the walls as truly as upon other groups. In fact, there are many who believe that the tone is magnified because prisoners are held in confinement under duress and they tend to seek support for their own reactions to real or fancied wrongs.

INTERNAL FACTORS

Seeds of discontent abound in the very nature of life in a prison, jail or other correctional facility. An institution is a community of people set apart. It has its society of inmates, its society of personnel, and its own peculiar culture of many conflicts.

The society of prisoners. Of the hundreds of thousands of offenders who pass through correctional institutions in the course of a year, some are committed irrevocably to criminal careers while others subscribe to quite conventional values or are aimless and uncommitted to goals of any kind. Some are alcoholics, some narcotic addicts, some sexual deviates and so on through the catalog of human frailties and personal problems. Behind the visible few who are conspicuous by their offenses are nameless numbers of nondescript human beings, more characterized by imprudence and inability to cope with the demands of a complex society than by any pattern of malicious willfulness.

Many offenders are members of minority groups whose values and objectives may be quite different from the middle class standards to which members of the staff subscribe and upon which correctional goals are based. Poverty may be a common denominator among them. They may have a language barrier. A sense of low status may lie at the root of the frustration and hostility that often mark minority attitudes toward the dominant society. Almost all minority groups will have had some bad experiences with authority.

Confinement is a stressful experience under the best of circumstances. Under the worst, it can become intolerable. There are many sources of stress for the prisoner. The closing of the front gate behind him is a denial of his freedom, a frustration of his accustomed ways of life, a humiliation and a label of being an undesirable member of society. Isolation, inflexible routine and monotony are characteristic of most correctional institutions. Its most visible feature is enforced idleness which imposes a heavy burden on all concerned and may produce deterioration in once-able people who leave with neither the ability nor the will to earn an honest living.

The society of personnel. Not all institutional problems of management and control are generated by the society of prisoners. A second set of problems can be created by the staff.

Without question, the greatest single resource for correctional management and control is personnel. Prisons and jails are run by people. The quality of the operation depends directly upon the skills, experience, performance standards and morale of the staff. Well qualified and promising recruits can be attracted to correctional work only as they are offered appropriate salaries and conditions of service which encourage life-time rather than casual, periods of employment. Lack of a sufficient number of employees to provide adequate supervision for safety, to say nothing of correctional programs, is too often the rule rather than the exception. In many jurisdictions, the number of positions allowed is usually far below an acceptable level of efficient service and safe coverage.

Employees who are expected to promote the aims of the institution in keeping with philosophies and procedures laid down for them, and who are the first to bear the brunt of inmate pressures, are human beings too. To a great extent, their effectiveness is determined by what they and the administration perceive their roles to be.

There are many factors which may result in a curious combination of laxity, harshness and even brutality. One is insensitivity to the legitimate needs and rights of prisoners. Another is inattention to bona fide complaints and grievances. Laxity may result from the necessity of using prisoners to perform work which should be done by personnel. Compensation for these services may be in the form of unwarranted trust or special and unusual privileges. Laxity can be found where personnel are unqualified for the jobs they perform.

Staff failure to recognize the existence of cultural differences among offenders or to understand why people who are shaped by them fail to respond "like everybody else" can interfere seriously with working relationships between inmates and staff. When intolerance and lack of understanding foster beliefs among members of the staff that prisoners are possessed of traits that are unacceptable, inferior or repugnant, effective working relationships are impossible. Personnel are subject to emotional stress too and when this happens they are inclined to be less tolerant of beliefs which they consider to be different from their own. This may result in their unwillingness to accept policies and programs established by the administration, as well as the philosophies upon which they are based. They may become intolerant of anything that disturbs their own perceptions, their sense of knowing where they stand. They tend to resent challenges to the familiar signposts of values upon which they have counted.

Social caste in institutions. Life in a correctional institution is actually a caste system in which prisoners and personnel are divided into two distinctly separate groups. The prisoner caste is at the bottom of the ladder and even though some inmates may share some of the same values and ways of behaving as staff members, they cannot enjoy the same status and rewards. As a result, communication and collaboration between inmates and staff are hindered. The pressures upon inmates to adapt themselves to social relationships within their own caste may be greater than pressures for them to identify with the upper caste.

Traditional prisons and other correctional institutions are highly authoritarian communities. Mass handling, countless ways of making inmates subservient to rules and orders and special forms of "etiquette" have the effect of creating and maintaining social distance between keepers and prisoners. Frisking of inmates and regimented movement about the institution tend to depersonalize prisoners and make their stance toward authority increasingly obdurate. The admonition "do your own time" is a slogan which endorses alienation and indifference to the interests of both staff and other inmates.

PREVENTIVE MEASURES

Many of the factors in prisoner unrest—forces that influence the environment in which prisoner management and control takes place—cannot be changed immediately or directly. The institution manager by himself can do little about public indifference, overcrowding, political meddling or unwise commitments and releases. These are matters for which responsibility must be shared with others outside the institution. There are, however, many things that can be done to improve the climate within the institution.

Borrowing from military experience, it is too easy to think of the problems of prisoner management and control as being represented by good morale or poor morale among inmates and personnel. Not only is this a dangerous over-simplification of the problems involved but, like the military formula of command—organize, deputize, supervise, it is not particularly instructive. A short-sighted resolve to improve morale, alone, can result in misspent effort and a further complication of the underlying problems that contributed to poor morale in the first place. For example, an unwise institution manager may be tempted to accede to demands (real or anticipated) for more privileges. Unless the privileges sought will contribute directly to operational and program objectives, to grant them would risk strengthening the manager's own position at the expense of the total responsibilities he holds. Moreover, by pursuing such a course of action long enough he might discover one day that he had no more privileges to offer. The basic error in such an approach, however, is that the symptoms, rather than the causes, become the object of attention. It is not unlike taking aspirin for the temporary relief of a headache which may have serious unrelieved causes.

Obviously, the immediate purposes of prisoner management and control are security and the protection of persons and property. But there are additional concerns that are consistent with the broad objectives of imprisonment and that contain the clues to the manner in which management and control is achieved. These involve (a) reducing the damaging effects of confinement, (b) minimizing the offender's alienation from the rest of society, (c) maintaining human dignity and self-respect and (d) developing a sense of constructive purpose.

These concerns do not stem from maudlin sympathy toward offenders at all. They are based on facts. One fact is that there is nothing in the language or intent of existing statutes that says prisoners should be subjected to degradation, humiliation, privation or that confinement should be a debilitating, handicapping experience. On the contrary, there is a growing body of court decisions which state that, while prison and jail administrators must be accorded wide latitude in their actions, this shall not be disproportionate to the latitude accorded officials at every other point along the process of criminal justice. The thrust of these decisions is that prisoners do have rights, including rights to humane and equitable treatment, and that it is incumbent upon institution administrators to achieve essential security without imposing adverse restrictions. *

The other basic fact is that with few exceptions every person committed to a jail or prison is released sooner or later. A large percentage of awaiting trial prisoners are released on bail within days and many others do not return from court because they were acquitted or have been fined or their sentences were suspended. Most of the sentenced prisoners committed to jail are released in a matter of days, weeks or months. If released prisoners are bitter, hostile or further incapacitated by the experience of confinement, the institution has done nothing to contribute to the control of crime—to say the least.

The manner in which prisoner management and control is achieved is largely in the hands of the administrator and his staff. For the administrator this becomes a matter of applying philosophies and techniques to personnel management, the formulation of policies and operating procedures and the improvement of correctional programs.

PERSONNEL ADMINISTRATION

The preceding chapter identified a number of personnel problems. There is another that should be mentioned here. According to a recent survey conducted for the Joint Commission on Correctional Manpower and Training, correctional workers feel that their programs must be improved. Their concern over existing program results causes frustration and can lead to apathy or cynicism. Competent personnel faced with system shortcomings they cannot overcome will resign rather than continue their association with an organization which appears to them to be prone to failure. While dissatisfaction with the ineffectiveness of programs is general among correctional personnel, the higher the educational achievement of employees, the greater is their dissatisfaction. The field of corrections, which has always found it difficult to recruit highly trained personnel, can ill afford to suffer steady loss of those it succeeds in hiring. Moreover, when a sizable group of workers in an institution or agency holds views opposed to those of the administration, disruptions in correctional operations can be expected.

Development of correctional careers. It is an established fact that careers in correctional work are not well defined. The manner and conditions of entry into this work differ widely from one jurisdiction to another and between correctional agencies. The circumstances also differ considerably from entry into education, social welfare and other government programs or private industry. Job dissatisfaction soon arises from awareness that promotions are slow in coming and may bear little apparent relationship to experience and ability.

The need to provide real career opportunities in correctional work is obvious. Correctional managers must begin the development of such careers by taking the initiative in aggressive recruitment of qualified people, as industry, education and other public services have done for a long time. Correctional agencies must begin to compete seriously for qualified or trainable people if they are not to continue to be second and third career choices for applicants years after graduation from school and probably on the heels of dissatisfactions in other jobs.

But even the most aggressive recruitment will fail unless program managers are given more freedom in offering jobs. Age and residence requirements, which are now imposed formally or informally, should be eliminated. Some requirements of previous experience should be reconsidered if young people are to be attracted to available jobs.

Education and training must be recognized in the corrections career ladder. Management trainee posts should be established. Young people today are attracted to jobs which offer challenge and some potential for personal success. Once a person starts in correctional work, he should be able to look upon his choice as a career matching others in prestige, salary and opportunity for advancement.

Support of staff development programs. In today's world, knowledge increases so rapidly that the need for continuing education and training for most occupations is generally acknowledged. There is no reason to dispute this need in corrections. While few correctional systems now offer well-developed training programs, many have the capability for this, either by utilizing their own resources or in collaboration with nearby industries and institutions of higher learning. These programs should include training in principles of management and supervision, as well as in the dynamics of human behavior, community relations, law and correctional methods.

If staff development is to be improved in both quality and quantity, correctional leaders will need to provide the necessary funds and other forms of support required. Legislators and government officials must be impressed with the urgency of the need for staff development. This is a broader need than training alone. It includes exchange of personnel, tuition support for employees who wish to take academic courses, opportunities to conduct research, visits to other agencies and involvement in professional organizations.

Removal of job dissatisfactions. Since administrators are responsible for the establishment of policy, they must be continually alert to employees' dissatisfactions with this work. Aggressive efforts should be made to obtain higher salaries and to provide opportunities for upward mobility. Other sources of dissatisfaction are no less important. Understaffing is more than a matter of overwork for the employees on duty. The necessity of dealing with excessive numbers of offenders may result in less than adequate supervision and control, gross inefficiency and inability to help any of them. There is need to reexamine traditional utilization of personnel in the light of techniques which will improve program effectiveness. Even the nature of the services themselves should be studied carefully.

Much more than this needs to be said about personnel. But personnel administration is not the only area which can contribute to reduction of management and control problems.

POLICIES AND OPERATING PROCEDURES

There is an old prison saying to the effect that an institution is but the lengthened shadow of the warden. In a literal sense, this is only a part truth since the shadow is actually a composite of many. However, it is meant to imply that institutional programs and policies and the operating procedures which dictate the ways in which things are done reflect an underlying administrative philosophy of correctional treatment and control. There is also the accurate inference that this philosophy pervades all activities throughout the entire institution, as well as the relationships which exist between the institution and other agencies, organizations and the public. Broadly, the physical appearance of the institution and every regulation, activity and personal contact has a bearing on prisoner management and control. Four representative situations have been singled out for attention here.

Prisoner rights and attention to complaints. It has long been established that lawful imprisonment necessarily causes the withdrawal or limitation of many rights to which the average citizen is fully entitled. This does not mean that the institution manager can do as he wishes without fear of criticism, censure or judicial intervention. Neither does it mean that a prisoner is without rights. One of the great problems for the administrator is determination of what restrictions and conditions may appropriately be imposed upon prisoners when the guidelines seem to be ever-changing. Yesterday's preposterous expectations can well be today's privileges and tomorrow's rights. It is nearly impossible to predict which administrative decisions will become the subject of judicial disapproval or new legislation, but there are many indications to be found. The earlier reference to a particular issue of The Prison Journal is only one of many sources of information. The trick is to utilize these indications to insure that reasonable rules are established which will insure fair treatment of prisoners and, at the same time, allow the administrator to do his job without undue hindrance. Prisoner rights comprise only one point of view from which the new administrator should carefully study the rules and policy decisions which he inherits. This is only one reason why all regulations and procedures should be reexamined frequently.

Food service is an example of the importance of other reasons. It is assumed that every prisoner has the legal right to be adequately nourished throughout his confinement. Presumably, this means that his food intake for an average day will be in ample quantity and nutritive value to sustain him. From a nutritional point of view this amounts simply to meeting needs based on such factors as age, weight, size, sex, physical activity and conditions of health. But in jails and prisons, as elsewhere, adequate food service depends upon budgetary allowance, procurement, storage, preparation, the manner in which meals are served, sanitation, appearance and many other considerations. Not the least of them is menu planning. Menus can be effective substitutes for calendars in determining the day of the week, or they can provide variety and reflect the particular tastes of the people being fed.

Numerous similar examples can be found in the day-to-day operation of any institution. Take clothing. A prisoner's right to human dignity demands that his nakedness be covered. His right to humane treatment requires that this covering be appropriate to the climate and circumstances in which he finds himself. Health standards dictate that clothing shall be free from vermin and reasonably clean. But these are not the only considerations. If an institution is to furnish clothing, it should also be reasonably well-fitting and in an acceptable state of repair.

Beyond the issue of rights, the problems underlying the examples given are less a matter of what policies and rules may require than of how they are carried out. Thus, the administrator should be concerned both with the substance or content of programs, policies and rules and with the ways of implementing them. In part, this becomes a matter of sensitizing personnel to the fact that they deal with fellow human beings, even though they be prisoners. To illustrate further: every correctional institution conducts a "count" several times a day. This can be done promptly, accurately and with a minimum of confusion, or it can be a recurring aggravation and unnecessarily harassing inconvenience to the inmates. A strip search for contraband can be conducted efficiently, privately and with as much dignity as circumstances permit, or it can be a disgusting, humiliating spectacle. A cell "shake-down" can accomplish its purpose and leave authorized personal belongings in good order, or it can make a shambles of the cell with ruthless destruction of "junk" items which the prisoner happens to value highly.

The kinds of sensitivity and good judgment that apply to operating procedures and daily activities are equally applicable to the attention given prisoner complaints. Inattention to prisoner complaints can lead from uncertainty and dismay to distrust and rebellion that may produce an incident to attract attention. This is particularly likely to happen if the prisoner believes that his problem would be solved if it reached the proper officials. Areas in which complaints and grievances are most often expressed are: food, handling of mail and visits, disciplinary procedures and punishments, and work or quarters assignments which are thought to be inappropriate for some reason.

It goes without saying that legitimate complaints should be heard and the condition corrected as soon as possible. Not all situations can be corrected. In this event, the matter should be discussed with the complaining prisoner and dealt with openly. A number of jurisdictions have adopted a technique having at least psychological value. A special mailbox is installed in a prominent place within the institution. Any prisoner, at any time, may deposit a letter for prompt mailing without inspection or censorship to listed government officials whose office has some responsibility for the handling of prisoners' cases or for the operation of the institution.

Communications. It is probable that maintaining effective communications in a prison or jail is more of a problem than in other organizations. In addition to communications between management and staff, there must be communication between prisoners, staff and management.

There are many ways in which communication occurs. The choice of method may well depend upon circumstances, but it should also be considered in terms of why communication is necessary. Obviously one purpose is to instruct personnel. This can be accomplished by staff training, whether formal or informal, the issuance of policies and rules, written post orders which contain a detailed listing of duties, staff meetings, roll-call announcements and conversations with supervisors. Another purpose is to keep management informed of what is going on. There is no good substitute for day-to-day personal observations of management personnel, but these can be augmented by personal interviews, whether scheduled or casual, staff meetings, reports and reviews of records. Communication is an inevitable part of effective planning. Various techniques of utilizing subordinate personnel in planning assignments claim the advantages of employing staff knowledge and skills and, at the same time, insuring a sense of involvement on the part of staff in the solution of problems, program development or other planning purpose.

Adaptations of these methods are equally applicable to communications between prisoners and staff. It is just as important that prisoners know from official sources, rather than from rumors, what is expected of them and what management is doing or planning that affects their welfare. Similarly, management needs to know what the prisoners are thinking and how they feel about things in general. Beyond this, is only by increasing communications between staff and inmates that correctional programs, such as counseling, can be introduced or improved. Additional benefits are that loosening of inmate-to-staff and inmate-to-inmate communication tends to reduce the inmate politicians' power and to minimize the traditional stigma and physical danger of cooperating with the staff.

Correspondence regulations. Correspondence with members of the family and with close friends and associates is essential to the morale of all confined persons and may form the basis for both present and future good adjustment.

Traditionally, inmate correspondence has been surrounded by restrictions designed to limit the number of letters which could be posted or received, including elaborate record-keeping systems to assure that quotas were not violated. Close scrutiny of both outgoing and incoming mail was considered essential to the security of the institution and for the maintenance of prisoner discipline and control. Censorship was thought to be necessary to prevent the introduction of contraband, to minimize involvement in criminal activities and to prevent correspondence becoming a tool for planning escapes or plots of violence. Experience in a number of jurisdictions has demonstrated that some of these restrictions can be eliminated with safety in certain institutions and substantially revised in others, without loss of essential control and with important savings in time, expense and inconvenience.

The size and complexity of each institution, the status and degree of sophistication of the inmates confined, along with other variables, will determine the extent of regulations required. Generally, they should include the following:

Ordinarily there should be no question about the propriety of correspondence with members of the immediate family. Friends, former business associates and others may be considered whenever it appears that the proposed correspondence will not be detrimental to the inmate or the correspondent. Inmates should be permitted correspondence with attorneys of record or attorneys under contract without limitation. Such correspondence should be regarded as privileged in that it should be subjected to inspection only to prevent the introduction of contraband or other threat to the good order and security of the institution.

A number of institutions have demonstrated that it may not be necessary to limit the number of persons on the approved correspondence list.

Similarly, to the extent that administrative considerations permit, no limit need be placed on the number of outgoing letters authorized for mailing. (Experience has shown that the volume of correspondence remains fairly constant whether or not limitations are imposed). Recognizing the importance of maintaining family and community contacts, the institution should expect to pay postage on a "reasonable" number of letters if the inmate is substantially lacking funds.

At time of commitment, each prisoner should be expected to sign an authorization for the head of the institution or his representative to open, read and inspect all mail. Failure to sign this authorization may result in withholding of all correspondence privileges.

While all mail of a particular inmate may need to be subjected to close scrutiny, more flexible procedures for reading, scanning or otherwise spot-checking incoming and outgoing mail will suffice for most prisoners. This should be done frequently enough to maintain security, to learn about any particular problem confronting the inmate or to alert other members of the staff to any matter that may help in evaluating the inmate. "Censorship" of mail for any purpose is indefensible. That which violates postal regulations can be referred for possible prosecution. The institution cannot assume responsibility for the content of incoming or outgoing letters.

Prisoners should be informed of the reasons for which incoming and outgoing mail will be rejected and they should understand that they and their correspondents are responsible for the contents of their letters.

Petitions, motions, appeals and other legal papers related to a prisoner's commitment or sentence, or touching upon some legal question affecting his status in the institution, should be forwarded promptly to the appropriate court.

Visiting regulations. The formulation and administration of visiting regulations should encourage as much visiting as personnel and facilities will permit. The setting in which visits take place should also be as informal and attractive as facilities will permit with due regard for necessary controls. Visits should be conducted and supervised in such manner that an atmosphere of friendliness and lack of tension is achieved.

The following general principles underly the reasons for granting visit:

Like correspondence, visits are a means of maintaining family ties and wholesome personal relationships with relatives and friends.

These ties and relationships are important factors in prisoner morale and future adjustment.

Visits by family and friends provide an opportunity for closer relationships with staff members for the purpose of more effective program planning.

Properly handled, visits can contribute to good public relations and a better understanding of the institution's objectives.

The practical considerations which impose limits on visits include the size of visiting facilities, the time and expense of supervision and the need for maintaining other important institutional activities without unnecessary or extended interference.

Generally, persons who can be approved as correspondents are suitable as visitors. While it is reasonable to expect that most of the essential legal work which a recognized attorney performs for an inmate will be handled on the basis of correspondence between the attorney and his client, personal visits will be necessary when pending legal problems require, especially with persons awaiting trial and sentence. Such visits should be supervised by observation only for the purpose of contraband control and good order. The attorney and his client should be permitted to converse privately.

As with correspondence, both the prisoners and their visitors should clearly understand what the visiting regulations are.

Prisoner discipline. There probably is no aspect of correctional institution management more filled with emotion and less open to calm appraisal than that of discipline. Yet, there is no activity more in need of objective study and complete overhauling than the traditional ways of handling prisoners who misbehave and violate institution rules. Not only does tradition exact a double standard of behavior but frequently it may ignore guarantees of civil rights and due process.

The objectives of prisoner discipline and control should be fully consistent with the correctional objectives of the institution, the focus being on (a) individual adjustment to the programs, behavior standards and limitations imposed by the administration and (b) the general welfare of the institution community. Disciplinary policy and methods should reflect this statement of purpose and recognize that disciplinary sanction is but one factor in correctional treatment and control. As applied to a prisoner who has misbehaved, this means that the sole objective is his future voluntary acceptance of certain limitations which are being imposed upon him.

Following are essential principles in acceptable and effective disciplinary policy and procedures.

1. Disciplinary action shall be taken only at such times and in such measures and degree as is necessary to regulate a prisoner's behavior within acceptable limits.
2. Prisoner behavior must be controlled in a completely impersonal, impartial and consistent manner.
3. Disciplinary action shall not be capricious nor in the nature of retaliation or revenge.
4. Program assignments and changes are made to achieve treatment goals, not as punishment or reward.
5. Corporal punishment of any kind is strictly prohibited.
6. The initiation of disciplinary measures against any prisoner is the responsibility only of staff members (preferably a committee) to whom this authority has been defined and delegated.
7. Disciplinary action should be taken as soon after the occurrence of misconduct as circumstances permit.
8. Case records should include misconduct reports, their dispositions and should also include evaluative staff statements regarding them.

Delegation of disciplinary authority: Basic authority for the administration of prisoner discipline should be delegated by the chief executive officer of the institution. Where circumstances permit, this delegation should be to a committee of at least three staff members who are competent and who broadly represent the primary areas of correctional treatment. Such delegation should be accompanied by a specific charge which outlines duties and responsibilities.

In addition to receiving reports of misconduct, conducting hearings, making findings and imposing disciplinary actions, the adjustment committee should make referrals for diagnosis and special handling, make program changes indicated and otherwise have authoritative concern policies and operating procedures which affect discipline. The committee should also be concerned with evaluating the effectiveness of its decisions and other factors which have a bearing upon prisoner discipline and morale.

The adjustment committee should be given a broad range of dispositional alternatives. Its choice of alternatives in the disposition of each case should be consistent with the objectives of disciplinary policy. Committee action should be a composite group judgment which takes cognizance of the reasons for the adverse behavior, the setting and circumstances in which it occurred, the involved prisoner's accountability and the correctional program goals set for him. The choice of disposition goes far beyond mere compliance with regulations. To be fully effective, the prisoner must understand and accept the reasonableness of the limitations being imposed upon him. A system should be devised to provide follow-up of at least the more serious and persistent behavior problems dealt with.

Use of segregation: In most institutions there is a separate housing unit for prisoners who, at times, need to be segregated from the regular population. In keeping with the statement of disciplinary policy, above, this unit should be operated in accordance with the following basic requirements of control and supervision.

1. Segregation conditions. The quarters used for segregation should be well ventilated, adequately lighted, appropriately heated and maintained in a sanitary condition at all times.
2. Cell occupancy. Except in emergencies, the number of prisoners confined to each cell or room should not exceed the number for which the space was designed. Whenever an emergency arises which indicates that excess occupancy may be needed temporarily, an immediate report should be made to the head of the institution and his approval obtained.
3. Clothing and bedding. All prisoners should be admitted to segregation (after thorough search for contraband) dressed in normal institution clothing and should be furnished a mattress and bedding. In no circumstance should a prisoner be segregated without clothing except when prescribed by the institution physician for medical or psychiatric reasons. If a prisoner is so seriously disturbed that he is likely to destroy his clothing or bedding, the institution physician should be notified immediately and a regimen of treatment and control instituted with his concurrence.
4. Food. Segregated prisoners should be fed three times a day on the standard ration and menu of the day for the institution.
5. Personal hygiene. Segregated prisoners should have the same opportunities to maintain the level of personal hygiene available to all other prisoners. This should include the availability of toilet tissue, wash basin, drinking water, comb, eye glasses, dentures and opportunities for shaving and brushing teeth.
6. Duration of segregation. Consistent with the need for segregation, no prisoner should be held in this status longer than necessary. Special care should be taken that segregation does not become a haven for those who persistently fail to face their problems. The adjustment committee should be responsible for the program needs of prisoners who require or demand long-term segregation. The committee should conduct a formal review of such cases at least once each month and make recommendations to the head of the institution.

7. Supervision. In addition to the direct supervision afforded by the unit officer, each segregated prisoner should be seen daily by the institution physician or medical technician and one or more other responsible officers designated by the head of the institution.
8. Correspondence and visits. In the absence of direct and compelling reasons to the contrary, prisoners in segregation should not be required to forfeit correspondence and visiting privileges.
9. Records. A permanent log should be maintained in the segregation unit. All admissions should be recorded indicating date, reason for admission and the authorizing official. All releases from the unit should be similarly recorded. Officials required to visit the unit should sign the log, indicating time, date and purpose of visit. Unusual activity or behavior of individual prisoners should be recorded in the log with a follow-up memorandum to the head of the institution.

IMPROVEMENT OF CORRECTIONAL PROGRAMS

The third general area in which the administrator can effect improvements in prisoner management and control is program. While this is not the place to attempt a blueprint of program design, it is appropriate to examine the philosophy of correctional treatment and certain program premises.

To a great extent, many of the problems of correctional institution management are based on philosophical conflicts and controversies. Foremost among them, of course, is the argument of punishment versus treatment. Most administrators today tend to believe that correctional institutions serve to protect the public by keeping offenders locked up, as ordered by the courts, and by making an effort to at least reduce the future threat of offenders through correctional treatment. This is not a universal point of view. Thus some of the problems of management relate to false ideas that punishment and treatment are *inconsistent objectives. This may help account for the fact that, despite the belief of* administrators, the vast majority of correctional institutions still operate in traditional ways, in which the motive force is punishment, vengeful in character and expression.

Thoughtful observation has produced another point of view. While the philosophy of individualism has done much to advance correctional treatment, it has also produced a number of distortions. For example, both the law and operation of the criminal justice system tend to focus responsibility for crime and guilt on the individual offender. Thus the courts and correctional agencies become preoccupied with reforming the individual offender as an isolated problem. By channeling resources exclusively on the reformation of the offender, attention is diverted from correcting conditions in the community which encourage development of criminal behavior. Moreover, the treatment preoccupation with individual offenders has tended to obscure the fact that they do not function as unrelated individuals. As prisoners they are members of a social system, as they were in the community, and they are subject to the heavy impact of the total confinement experience.

The framework within which program planning and development are beginning to occur consists of a number of assumptions, because the state of the art of correctional treatment is still not very far advanced. Other than the theories that have been advanced, very little is known about the direct causes of criminal behavior. More discriminating selection factors with which to classify offenders are needed. Much more must be learned about the character types which can make the most and least effective use of correctional programs and services. There is a basic need for knowledge with which to train staff and prisoners in the specific behaviors which are required to master the specific tasks for successful adjustment in the community. In the meantime, primary program assumptions are:

1. The focus of corrections is intervention in delinquent and criminal careers, through management and control of crises and programs and services designed to overcome handicapping deficiencies.
2. The deeper an offender has to be plunged into correctional processes and the longer he has to be locked up, however humanely, the greater the cost and the more difficult the road back to the point of socialization that will permit successful reentry in the community
3. A person's needs for control or for help are not necessarily related to his legal status.

These assumptions have lead to a number of alternatives to confinement that are being tried in a number of jurisdictions and they suggest new functions and new program directions which open the possibility of more efficient and constructive uses of correctional institutions. As realistic programs are developed, the majority of prisoners will be eager to participate in them, both because of the opportunities they afford and because their mere existence is evidence that somebody cares.

HANDLING EMERGENCIES

In the first chapter a number of factors in prisoner unrest were discussed. Whether any of these, singly or in combination, can be identified as causing a particular problem or incident is another matter. Similarly, inattention to the control of locks and keys, arms and ammunition, tools, items of contraband and security inspections may well contribute to problems of management and control or, in a particular situation, become the cause of a particular emergency. The preceding chapter dealt with a number of preventive measures. Not all problems and incidents can be prevented and not all of them occur as emergencies. Being prepared is both a form of prevention, among others, and a means of minimizing the magnitude of disorder when it occurs.

The kinds of emergencies with which correctional institutions are most likely to deal are escapes and riots or disturbances. This chapter will be devoted mainly to the handling of these problems. But in these days of mass social protest and challenge of authority, local jails and correctional institutions, especially, are likely to be involved in the control of civil disorder in the community. For this reason, attention will be given the problem of emergency detention occasioned by mass arrests. Fire and civil disaster are emergency situations which will be mentioned.

ESCAPE PLANS

Although escapes or attempted escapes are comparatively rare in well-managed institutions, the entire staff must be constantly alert to prevent them. It is possible to reduce successful escapes to a minimum only through cooperative and coordinated planning. While the methods and circumstances of an escape will vary, certain basic policies and procedures are applicable to all of them. Every correctional institution should maintain a carefully developed and detailed plan for the prevention and apprehension of escapes. It is important that the plan be reviewed frequently and kept up to date. A copy should be furnished each employee with the requirement that all become thoroughly familiar with its contents.

In developing a comprehensive plan, an escape should be viewed as an incident which must be assessed in phases or series of action steps.
1. The alert—a period of time in which it may be possible to prevent the incident or to prepare for it.
2. Sounding the alarm—a brief interval for decision that an incident has occurred and for notifying others.
3. Mobilizing resources—final preparation for command and action.
4. Establishing control—thwarting the attempt or apprehending the escapee and assuring security of the institution.
5. Returning to normal operations—including investigations, reports and necessary repairs.

The elements of a comprehensive escape plan will establish policy, define responsibility and outline procedures to be followed in each of these phases. The plan itself should be developed around the following action steps.

Prevention. The plan statement should indicate the most common and immediate ways of preventing escapes. This should include reference to such items as: alertness to detect and report signs of unrest or tension; observation of anything unusual about participation in programs and activities; expression of complaints and requests for change; prompt and decisive action when the occasion demands; thorough security inspections and counts; and effective methods of selecting prisoners for work and quarters assignments.

Sounding the alarm. The plan should provide that any unauthorized absence from a work detail, living quarters or other location will be reported immediately to the supervisor in charge. When it is determined from the information at hand that an escape has occurred, prearranged signals should be sounded to notify all employees. The plan should distinguish the kinds of signals and the circumstances of their use as the sounding of a general alarm can create unnecessary tension and excitement.

Mobilization of resources of resources. A list of all employees with addresses and telephone numbers should be maintained and arranged so that a maximum number of employees may be contacted with a minimum number of calls. As soon as an escape occurs, an employee should be designated to contact the off-duty employees required and have them report for duty immediately.

The security posts and maintenance operations essential to continued functioning of the institution during an escape emergency should be identified. All other posts should be vacated and non-essential activities shut down so that all available personnel can report promptly to a central place for special duty assignments. Personnel in charge of non-essential activities should place all tools in a convenient, safe place, secure the area and check their prisoners in. The officer assigned to the armory, with whatever additional help may be needed, should prepare immediately to issue arms, ammunition and other equipment that may be requisitioned. The record clerk should be to issue escape notices, including identification pictures, for prompt distribution and mailing.

Concurrent with the initial assignment of personnel to escape posts and duties, one employee should be designated to notify all law enforcement agencies in the surrounding area by telephone or radio. Addresses and telephone numbers of the agencies to be notified should be part of the escape and apprehension plan. (In the development of the plan it will be helpful to determine with local law enforcement officials exactly what involvement each agency will have. A confidential copy of the plan might well be furnished each law enforcement agency for reference.) The possibility of asking nearby radio and television stations to assist by spot announcements of escape essentials should not be overlooked.

Establishing control. A complete list of all posts to be covered during a search should be maintained. These may be divided into various categories. The posts to be manned will depend on the information available as to the time the escape occurred, means of departure, direction of travel and other factors that will help insure that the search effort can be pinpointed as closely as possible. An instruction kit should be prepared for each post and handed to the officer at the time he is assigned. For posts located beyond the immediate vicinity of the institution, the instruction kit should include a map of the area, directions for transportation, the duties to be performed and other information, such as location of the nearest telephone, and anticipated relief schedule, that will be helpful to the officer assigned to the post.

The establishment of a special communications center, apart from the command post, can be most useful in conducting an orderly, efficient search. The person in charge of this center is usually authorized to issue press releases, answer numerous inquiries, receive and place telephone or radio calls and otherwise process and record messages and information incidental to the search.

While task forces are being deployed, the plan should establish procedures for starting the investigation. This may include the assignment of an employee to search the personal locker and effects of the escapee for evidence that may provide clues for the hunt. At this time, too, the preliminary investigation should be organized, starting with interviews with both staff members and prisoners who were in a position to know the escapee well and who might be able to shed some light on the escape.

It should be clearly established in policy that if a hostage is taken in an attempt to escape, all personnel should have clear instructions that orders given by any person under duress, including executive officers, are not valid and under no circumstances should the prisoner be permitted to escape from the institution.

The plan should make clear what authority is granted for the use of firearms and in what circumstances these should be used. Generally, firearms should be used as a last resort to prevent escape, prevent injury or loss of life to personnel or prisoners not involved and to protect property. Orders to halt or desist should be given first and, if ignored, a warning shot should be fired. Should this be ignored, subsequent shots should be aimed to disable rather than kill.

Also, the plan should include instructions to all personnel on all posts regarding the importance of tact and good judgment in contacts with other people, the authority granted for stop and search and the tasks that are to be performed in collaboration with representatives of other law enforcement agencies.

Returning to normal. As soon as the decision is made to discontinue the initial search effort, all law enforcement agencies, news media and other persons who were notified of the escape should be informed.

When an escape involves cutting of bars, window sash or other property damage, a careful record, both photographic and written, should be made and arrangements made for repairs. Attention should be given the gathering and safekeeping of other evidence that may be important to prosecution. Particular care must be taken in interviewing the apprehended escapee and other suspects. It is best that this be done only with the advice of the prosecuting attorney.

One of the important concluding steps in handling an escape incident is assessment and report of the experience. The adoption of a general reporting format will facilitate the process involved and provide clues to the lessons that can be learned from the incident.

PLANS FOR RIOTS AND DISTURBANCES

Prisoner disturbances are of two basic types: (a) a disturbance of a riotous nature between two or more prisoner factions which is related to animosities between prisoner groups and may not be well organized; and (b) a more general disturbance directed against the institution because of some real or fancied grievance or other objective, such as mass escape. Whenever prisoners or personnel are under great stress "spontaneous" disturbances can erupt for any reason. Once a disturbance starts, the measures taken to regain control may be the same, regardless of its type or precipitating causes. Yet, it is important that distinctions be made among them because of the few moments of decision as to how to proceed and because of the critical importance of keeping the disorder as isolated and as small as possible.

While it is impossible to detail the procedures that should be followed for the effective handling of all kinds of disturbances in all institutions, experience has shown that the following guidelines are generally applicable.

That each correctional institution should maintain a carefully developed plan for handling group disturbances of all kinds, that the plan be kept up to date and that all employees be familiar with its contents is evident enough. The steps involved in handling a riot or disturbance, as with an escape, must be thought through. These are: the interval of alert, sounding the alarm, mobilizing resources, establishing control and returning to normal. The same basic policies and principles expressed in the preceding discussion of an escape plan are applicable to plans for riots and disturbances.

As with escapes, there usually are signs of tensions among prisoners which portend a group disturbance. It is known that precipitating factors may be unresolved racial problems, complaints over food, dissatisfaction with the performance or attitudes of personnel, complaints over recreation, visiting or formation. With this knowledge, promptness in detecting and reporting unusual mail privileges, complaints over medical treatment, gang problems and misinformation. With this knowledge, promptness in detecting and reporting unusual activity or bad "climate" may enable getting at the root of the trouble and possibly forestalling incidents that could result in a riot.

An action plan should be developed from the primary responsibilities of institution management and in this order: public safety; safety and welfare of hostages; prevention of loss of life or injury to other personnel; prisoner welfare; protection of property.

When, despite all efforts to prevent them, riots or disturbances do occur, they begin with startling suddenness, spread rapidly and can cause major damage. Prompt activation of the riot plan, in which the following elements are incorporated, is absolutely necessary.

Containment. Immediate steps to close any possible avenues of escape are mandatory. The trouble should be localized and access to other areas cut off to prevent the disorder from spreading. Careful appraisal of the situation should be made before rushing in or committing personnel to a situation that might result in their being taken hostage. The immediate objective should be determined, the necessary reinforcements called and equipment required assembled. The safety of employees and prisoners must be considered if it becomes apparent that force and the use of defensive equipment will be necessary. Force and the use of defensive equipment should be used only when ordered by the head of the institution or his representative. Any person held hostage has no authority while under duress, regardless of rank.

It is noteworthy that even in the worst prison riots only a relatively small percentage of the total prisoner population has been actively involved. It is important that prisoners not wishing to participate be given an opportunity to withdraw from the area of disturbance. They should be provided safe conduct to secure quarters.

Employees should be instructed to observe the activity closely to identify ringleaders and subsequently report their participation. Recurring efforts should be made to determine the cause of the disturbance and participants should be urged to select one or more spokesmen to confer with the head of the institution or his representative. No promises should be made to demands other than assurance of fair hearing.

Use of force and defensive equipment. When the decision has been made to use force or defensive equipment, the kind and amount will be dictated by the situation but only for the purposes of control and protection.

Riot squads. As part of a basic riot control plan, it is assumed that a number of personnel will have been selected, organized and trained both in the proper use of special equipment and in the tactics to be used in various situations. When it is necessary to use riot squads, their members should be properly equipped. Injury should not be risked unnecessarily. Each squad should be instructed in the specific tasks it is to perform. Squads should enter the area of disturbance simultaneously from as many entrances as are available.

Water. A riot can often be brought under control by the effective use of water. The riot control plan should identify the location of hydrants and other water outlets, the availability of hose and other fire fighting equipment. Further, the plan should afford protection of hydrants, valves and exposed water pipes during a disturbance. Water may be used to disperse participants, to bring sporadic fires under control and to create dampness necessary to the most effective concentrations of gas should its use be required.

Gas. Gas of various types may be useful in situations where it would otherwise be hazardous to break up a rioting group. Sufficient gas should be used in the first attempt. (Minimum and maximum amounts that can be used safely under various circumstances should be computed in advance and this information should be incorporated in the riot plan). Provisions must be made for follow-up. Gas will break resistance, but participating prisoners may have to be removed forcibly. A squad equipped with gas masks should be assigned this task. The gas should be permitted to develop fully, but not to dissipate, before the squad enters the area. Sometimes a single gas shell or grenade will break up a large group so that smaller groups can be split off. When this tactic is used, the group will quickly re-form unless the follow-up is properly timed. Whenever gas is to be used in an enclosed area, it should be determined in advance that dispersed participants can exit easily.

Firearms. As with escapes, firearms should be used only as a last resort to prevent escapes, injury or loss of life of personnel or prisoners held hostage and to protect property. Orders to halt or desist should be given first and, if these are ignored, a warning shot should be fired. Subsequent shots should be aimed to disable rather than kill.

Post-riot procedures. Steps should be taken as soon as the disturbance is under control to insure that nobody has escaped and that the institution is physically secure. Initially, all participants in the disturbance should be confined and supervision augmented to insure that the disturbance will not break out anew. Extra help should also be assigned to all living quarters and other areas where it is necessary for groups of prisoners to congregate until it is certain that the disorder has completely subsided. If necessary, all non-essential activities can be suspended and feeding schedules rearranged to provide supervision over smaller groups and to meet supervision needs elsewhere.

The remaining steps are similar to those identified for escapes in the preceding section: photographic and written reports of damage, repair of damage, collection and preservation of evidence, notification of persons and agencies that had been informed of the disturbance and, finally, assessment and report of the experience.

PLANS FOR CIVIL DISORDER

The local jail or correctional institution is very likely to be involved in community efforts to control group protests and demonstrations. When mass arrests are made temporary detention facilities will be needed for large numbers of people, including women and juveniles. Obviously, correctional officials should participate in advance law enforcement planning for such emergency and the plans should include definitions of what specific services temporary detention facilities will be expected to provide for what numbers and kinds of arrested persons. It is possible that these services can be provided by existing jail and detention facilities under emergency conditions. In this event, operating problems will center around vast overcrowding, the processing of large numbers of people in and out of the institution and such accommodations as housing, feeding, telephone calls, visits and interviews with investigating officials and attorneys.

When it is known that existing facilities lack the capabilities required to meet anticipated needs, a much greater planning problem will involve the staffing and operation of an emergency detention center in some other setting, such as an armory, stadium or warehouse. Based on two such experiences of its own, the Bureau of Prisons has published an Emergency Detention Manual, copies of which are available upon request.

It is possible that situations may arise in which trained personnel of the local jail or correctional institution will be called upon to assist law enforcement agencies in controlling civil disturbances in the community. The riot squads referred to in the preceding section would be appropriate for this purpose under emergency conditions. Service of this kind should be based on important high-level policy decisions and careful planning.

PLANS FOR CIVIL DISASTER

The local institution may be a valuable resource for emergency services to the community in the face of disaster brought about by flood, fire, earthquake or other major happening involving extensive property damage, personal injury or large-scale displacement of people. The precise needs in such dire circumstances and the capabilities of local institutions to provide services vary so greatly that generalizations about them would be of little value. The institution manager should confer with local police, fire and civil defense officials about such matters. While it may not be possible to formulate definite plans in advance, at least general agreement can be reached as to the kinds of services the local institution might offer under given conditions.

FIRE PLANS

That the institution manager bears responsibility for the protection of lives and property goes without saying. It is equally evident that this responsibility cannot be borne without planning for fire prevention and fire fighting. Fire marshals and other officials can assist greatly in the development of such plans, in training personnel and prisoners in firefighting techniques and in making periodic inspections and investigations.

CONCLUSION

Disorder, including violent and destructive behavior of prisoners, is not unknown to jails, prisons and other correctional institutions. Mass demonstrations, organized social protest and natural disasters not only can cause institutions to operate under emergency conditions but they can contribute directly to emotional stress in prisoner populations.

The potential dangers inherent in these situations are sobering, indeed, especially when it is realized that so many of the basic causes, and even the triggering incidents, are beyond the immediate control of institution managers and personnel. Yet, there need be no feeling of alarm. On the contrary, institution managers and personnel can draw much self-assurance from the knowledge that they can acquire the capability of handling disorder and are prepared for it.

The preceding discussions have emphasized the importance of planning for emergency conditions. This is a difficult, time-consuming and continuing task. Yet, only in this way can the unnecessary handicaps of surprise, confusion and costly indecision be avoided.